Corresponding Motion

Corresponding Motion

Transcendental
Religion and the New America

Catherine L. Albanese

TEMPLE UNIVERSITY PRESS
Philadelphia

Temple University Press, Philadelphia 19122
© 1977 by Temple University. All rights reserved
Published 1977
Printed in the United States of America
International Standard Book Number: 0-87722-098-0
Library of Congress Catalog Card Number: 77-070329

TO PROFESSORS
MARTIN E. MARTY
and
CHARLES H. LONG

Contents

Acknowledgments

THE PRESENT STUDY has been a considerable time evolving. In germ, it began as long ago as the fall of 1968 in a class under the direction of Professor Martin E. Marty at the University of Chicago. Subsequent inquiry in classes with Professor Charles H. Long proved the beginning of its methodological concern, but it was only after several years involved in teaching an introductory course in religion at Wright State University in Dayton, Ohio, that the concern was clarified. Along the way, Professors Marty and Long directed me in a dissertation on the language of the members of the Transcendental Club, encouraged me in later efforts to rethink the material, and engaged me in fruitful conversations for its reconceptualization. Professor Arthur Mann, early in my efforts, raised important historical considerations, while Professor Jerald C. Brauer—with his timely call for history of religions method in interpreting American materials—influenced and ably criticized my work.

Professor Marty read and criticized a first draft of this manuscript and prompted me to invite my student, Patricia Carroll, to read and comment from her own perspective. Professors Sydney E. Ahlstrom of Yale University and Frank Reynolds of the University of Chicago also read the manuscript, offered helpful and insightful criticisms and bibliographic suggestions, and cheerfully submitted to rereading and recriticizing some portions. To all of these readers I am indebted for aid and assistance rendered.

I am indebted as well to Wright State University for a grant during the summer of 1974 which helped me in completing the study, and to Susan A. Mathes and Sue Dixon, who aided in the typing. Timothy J. Lockyer prepared the index. Portions of the work in earlier form have appeared in the *New England Quarterly*, the *Ohio Journal of Religious Studies,* and *Listening: Journal of Religion and Culture*. Finally, my parents, as always, have supported and encouraged my efforts along the way.

Introduction

THIS STUDY BEGAN with some questions about the sayings and doings of a group of Transcendentalists in nineteenth-century New England. Renowned for their role in the creation of a distinctively American literature and hailed for their contribution to American philosophical thought, the Transcendentalists have long been regarded in twentieth-century scholarship as a major movement in American culture. Their works have been celebrated, their words reprinted, their ideas and attitudes vaunted as the flowering of New England's golden day and America's as well. Recently, they have become heroes for a generation concerned with ecological problems and seeking new models for respect toward the land and the environment.

Amid the plethora of books and articles which the Transcendentalists have inspired, a number have noted the religious roots and manifestations of the movement. These nineteenth-century poet-philosophers, we have been told, were earnest seekers who took religion seriously. They were mystics and prophets. They were ministers or ex-ministers pushing to their farthest limits the boundaries of the Unitarian establishment.[1] Despite such interpretations, however, relatively little work has been done to explore the Transcendental interlude as an explicitly religious phenomenon. Relatively few have seen it as an appearance of religion in America providing an opportunity to address issues concerning religion in general and American religion in particular. Yet the

Transcendentalists were preeminently *religious* figures who understood their own enterprise in terms of the sacred. Their literary tropes and philosophical explanations, they conceived, should lead them and their followers to the comprehension of religious truth and the activation of a religious response to life.

With this Transcendental self-understanding in mind, the present essay addresses the movement as a specific instance of religion. It asks essentially three questions of its Transcendental subjects. First of all, if they were indeed religious, how were they religious? Where can the Transcendentalists be located religiously in the context of a comparative method suitable for the study of world religions? Secondly, how was the religiousness which the Transcendentalists manifested a case of *American* religion? What particularity set it off from religion in general and made it *this* cultural case, *this* idiosyncratic orientation toward life? Finally, since the Transcendentalists are usually considered as a group, how was their condition as a community related to their religiousness and their Americanness? What kinds of sharing and bonding occurred which both formed and expressed the movement as a collective American religious endeavor?

If we ask how the Transcendentalists were religious—our initial question—we must ask the question in terms of underlying ideas about what it means to be religious. It is here that the *Religionswissenschaft* school of the history of religions has been especially helpful. In this approach, being religious means having religious experience or, in the terse description of Joachim Wach, an "experience of the Holy."[2] While we can never have direct access to such experience in the case of another, we can recapture some sense of what the experience was about by means of the symbols in which it has been interpreted and recorded. These symbols provide a kind of code or shorthand which may be deciphered to reveal the religious impulse behind it. In forms as varied as theological dogmas and ecclesiastical structures, sacred places, times, and personages, holy objects and actions, language and music, these orientational signs disclose their content as religious meaning. They enable us to enter a world which might otherwise be closed to us, a world which may be different from our own but which inevitably turns out to be related to it in some manner, however slight. For, as history of religions encounters the sacred signs of other times and places, it begins to search for continuities. It views these forms with an eye to discovering a commonality in diverse manifestations. By placing religious structures on a spectrum which includes the cross-cultural dimension, history of religions offers a fresh perspective for observing the religiousness of long familiar forms. It makes them "other" and facilitates our ability to see them new. History of religions, therefore, can aid us in answering the question of what is religious about Transcendental religion.

As the study moves toward such an answer, it will be guided above all by the Transcendentalists themselves. In 1836, in a brief work entitled *Nature*, Ralph Waldo Emerson enunciated the key to the provocative new vision of the Transcendental movement. Here, Emerson spelled out for himself and his friends a view of the world in terms of the ancient doctrine of correspondence.[3] Different levels of the world expressed one another and reflected one another so that truth in one sphere told the tale of truth in another. The universe became a living book in which one could read the secrets of the soul; language, a cryptic system which mirrored the natural creation. The insights which Emerson and the others developed in the years which followed grew from this one. The Emersonian notion of compensation, as an example, was a subsidiary statement about correspondence. The Transcendental theory of history applied the worldview of correspondence to the events which formed the human drama. Transcendental literary theory offered an excursus into the domain of the word as again a corresponding sacred sphere.

The second question which the study asks—how this group of Transcendentalists was American in its religiousness—leads toward an inquiry which is served by the historical aspect of history of religions. Beyond looking for the forms of experience which shaped the continuity of the Transcendental circle with people in other cultures, the study takes up its differences. While Transcendental religion evoked ancient and universal forms of human religious experience, it was also new. And the newness bore the imprint of the America of the nineteenth century in which it was immersed. The harmony with the cosmos which was the core of Transcendental religious experience turned also upon harmony with a world which included American historical manifestations—the industrial and transportation revolutions, Jacksonian democracy, communes and protest movements, economic insecurities, and speed as a form of ecstasy. As the study progresses, it finds that, despite their cognitive disclaimers, at some level the Transcendentalists affirmed all of these. And finally, as they quietly displayed similar structures of consciousness to those of their rapidly changing culture, acting out their doctrine of correspondence in a way that they did not overtly anticipate, the Transcendentalists volunteered cultural prescriptions. Like the good Unitarian moralists from whom they had evolved, they tempered their correspondence with the fire of serious criticism.

Thus, addressing the question of Transcendentalism in historical terms, the essay is not so much seeking to discern how the Transcendentalists changed *through* time as how their movement became a specific cultural event *in* time. In this case, history of religions has been bound up more with questions about the particularity of one case of religious experience—a distinct departure from its immediate past—than with transformations in the experience itself as it passes along a temporal gradient. Moreover, the historical aspect of the study has had to take account of the fact that the Transcendentalists were filtering their religious experience not only through the lenses of the new America but also through the lenses of their own temperaments, with, in some notable cases, particular literary and artistic gifts. Hence, a rather complex picture of the religious life of the Transcendentalists emerges. And in explicating it, history of religions has had to make friends with "plain" history, with the sociology of knowledge, and even with some form of literary analysis. In this respect, the book has used the tools of a number of disciplines and is frankly an experiment.

The experiment has been tamed, however, by means of a heuristic framework developed again in a dialogue with Transcendental sources. From the point of view of this framework, the venerable doctrine of correspondence moved implicitly toward acausal and ahistorical understandings, for it posited a world eternally present and invited contemplation as its proper response. On the other hand, the Judaeo-Christian tradition which had nurtured these Transcendental dissidents had been more familiar with a world seen in terms of cause-and-effect relationships. Here, history in the human community had assumed a central position, while in the unraveling of this human story, past and future had nearly eclipsed the present, and action had become the proper mode of response to the world.

The two orientations were not mutually exclusive, as we shall see, nor did they exhaust the range of possibilities for imaging the nature of reality. As a matter of fact—without pretensions to their universality—they opened the door to both communal and individual forms of religious experience and interpretation which further qualified their initial outlooks. Thus, the theory of correspondence seemed related to the great communal traditions which looked toward harmony with the cosmos as central to their way of being religious. Correspondence also provided a basis for many, though not all, significant forms of mystical expression and at the same time grounded certain forms of myth and ritual which sought to return the human community to continuing harmony with nature. In turn, the worldview of causality identified an even more pronounced need for the religious expressions of myth and ritual because of the gap created by human history between the sacred and the profane. Meanwhile, it encouraged personal religious responses, in the modes of conversion and devotion, for those who had experienced the powerful and immediate presence of the holy.[4]

This conceptualization sheds a good deal of light on the "new religion" of the Transcendental group. Using the overall framework, the new religion involved a basic though not complete shift from the causal to the correspondential *Weltanschauung*. It involved this shift in ways directly applicable to a total community as well as in ways which focused more explicitly on individual religious expression within a group. It is the extent, the seriousness, and the subtleties of this shift which the book attempts to explore.

The reference to community leads to the third question of the essay, how existence as a community related both to Transcendental religiousness and Transcendental Americanness. Asking this question has meant a search for the sources and expressions of group life, for the collective manifestation of specifically Transcendental structures of consciousness.

Sociological and anthropological study have told us that a community, as a whole, is more than the sum of its individual parts. In the midst of the bonding process, the barriers which ordinarily separate persons from one another begin to break down. Instead of the one-to-one relationship which characterizes the interaction of individuals, a circular form of exchange develops in which each is related to all and all to each.[5] In certain stages of its existence, a community celebrates its union in an intrapersonal euphoria which signals the breakdown of structure and role differentiation in what Victor Turner has described as *communitas*.[6] In other stages, the members of the community are content with the expression of their oneness in structural and organizational terms.

Such descriptions are useful and illuminating for the sociologist and anthropologist who study the formation and function of groups in the present. But how do we go about recapturing the meaning of a religious community which, if it existed at all, lived and died well over a century ago? To try to recover its inner dynamic seems decidedly more difficult, and indeed, in some cases, impossible. For what we have to build upon in a study of a past community are, for the most part, written records, some public and official, and others, private and more personal. In the Transcendental case, we have at first glance little that suggests the dynamics of intrapersonal exchange among those identified with the movement.

Yet, in the Transcendental case, the written records are a fortunate legacy, for they contain abundant examples of a special language shared by members of the New School. We know that when people form a community united by the same religion, they also speak the same language to some extent. That is, there is a world of word and idea, shaped into definite and identifiable patterns, which the members of the community exhibit as a way of building and expressing their mutual identification with one another. Such language has the power to form and inform a world— a miracle of bonding which as human beings we all experience.[7] Hence, some part of the meaning of Transcendental community as an American religious group can be understood by studying the language which the members of the community spoke and wrote. The essay will try to undertake such a study in the belief that the common word of the Transcendentalists is significant as a vehicle for the mediation of their particular kind of American religion. This means that aesthetic qualities of the language will not figure prominently. It will be compelling for our purposes, not because it is beautiful or poetic or of considerable literary merit, but because it enables us to see the Transcendentalists as a community. The language of their community, we will discover, was intensely concerned with the perception of religious realities as moving and changing, transforming and being transformed, and this mode of perception, as we have also noted, complemented the world in which the Transcendentalists lived.

Six early Transcendentalists speak the new religious argot for us in the course of this essay. Ralph Waldo Emerson, Amos Bronson Alcott, George Ripley, James Freeman Clarke, Frederic Henry Hedge, and Convers Francis were all initial members of a small "organization" called the Transcendental Club. Rather loosely and casually gathered, the Club nonetheless hints at a focus for the development of community. Moreover, these six, who came together the night the Club was formed, were as nearly diverse a group of "like individuals" as one could hope to find for a study— good specimens, as it were, for an exploration of the transformations which community could bring about. There was Emerson, the acknowledged leader of the others, often the most articulate, and as a writer the most gifted. On the other hand, there was Francis, a relative unknown, who hardly created a ripple in the literary world of Boston. There were budding radicals (Emerson, Alcott, and Ripley), conservatives (Francis and Hedge), and a "liberal" (Clarke). There were future founders of communes (Ripley and Alcott) and solitaries (Emerson and Hedge). There were ministers (Clarke,

Francis, Hedge, Emerson, and Ripley) and eventual ex-ministers (Emerson and Ripley). There was even an outsider, one who did not share with the others a childhood and education in Brahmin Boston or its environs (Alcott).

In short, the six men, who were charter members of the Transcendental Club, provide a near-ideal mix for the study of religious community.[8] They are not important as the six most accomplished Transcendentalists, nor the six most clearly identifiable with the movement, nor the six who had contributed most effectively to the cultural heritage which Transcendentalism bequeathed to America. And this is all to the point. The book seeks to reflect not so much on their individual éclat, but rather on their membership—and the language which seems our surest entry into what that membership was about.

Still, it is important to add that Emerson dominates the study by the sheer volume of his linguistic expression as well as the deference which the others accorded him in making use of his idiom. With his penchant for exact word and precise phrase, Emerson often was able to express a religious sensibility which lay half-hidden for the others. Perhaps he told them what they already knew, but they were glad in his ability to name and order it. This he did in a seemingly endless flow of observations and analyses, frequently in a prose which verged on a kind of poetry religious to its core. But even as the essay turns to the prolific Emerson, it has been at pains to see him in the midst of his friends. To study communal religious experience exclusively through the perceptions of one of its participants seems incomplete at best.

Generally speaking, the time limits of the work are from 1836 to 1844. Eighteen hundred thirty-six, often called the *annus mirabilis* of Transcendentalism, was the year during which the Transcendental Club first met; the year when Emerson published *Nature* and Alcott published *Conversations with Children on the Gospels*; the year when Ripley first became embroiled in the controversy with Unitarian "pope" Andrews Norton on the validity of miracles as Christian evidence. Eighteen hundred forty-four marked the end of *The Dial*, which had been the most important group project of the Transcendental Club. The most celebrated years of the Transcendental movement ended with it, and, although the Transcendental Club did not die but gradually faded away, the demise of the periodical seemed a good place to stop. When there is a developmental relationship to the time of the study, however, the essay analyzes the Transcendentalists prior to 1836, and at times it also includes references to later expression when it is consistent with that during the period of the study.

Chapter I introduces the Transcendental religious consciousness by setting it in the context of world religions. It scrutinizes the Emersonian articulation of religious meaning for clues as to structure and theme, and establishes the family relationships of Emerson's religious sense to a long tradition in both the East and the West. In addition, the chapter sorts out some of the differences between the ancient tradition and its Emersonian transmutation, seeking to discern the connections between these differences, the more normative outlook of Emerson's Boston Christian background, and that of the new America beyond the gates of the city.

In Chapter II, the hints concerning a Boston Christian background are taken up and explored more fully. We catch the Transcendentalists in the midst of their formative meeting for their Club and discover them in the midst also of a profound sense of alienation from their immediate forebears. Federalist-turned-Whig, Unitarian, and Harvard-educated, Boston seemed to its newborn sons of the revolution to be suffering from acute symptoms of rigor mortis. We learn the background of each of the would-be innovators and follow each in the life trajectory which led to the moment when all could come together with hearts and spirits mutually set against the Boston which looked to the past.

After the biographical excursion through the lives and neighborhoods of the six, the third chapter focuses on the language in which they named, expressed, and communicated their fresh vision of the world. Recognized and sometimes condemned by others in its distinctiveness, this language repeated certain themes regularly so that its community was a community of content. But beyond such obvious enunciation of similar substance, the language ordered its message into certain patterns of articulation, patterns which reflected a similar style or *mode* in the way the Transcendentalists perceived the world. Each of the six operated out of this linguistic mode. Each saw the world in motion in a correspondence which set their word beside the New World celebrating itself in America.

In the following chapter, we continue the exploration of Transcendental language, now in its mature religious statement in the best-known of the Transcendental periodicals, *The Dial*. The details of this shared project and the purposive statements of its mission are rehearsed. Then, in the context of the air of destiny which surrounded its language, we study the mythic aspect of *The Dial*'s idiom for clues to its religious meaning. Here we find a New World commitment to the *yin* and *yang* of life, the female and male poles whose secret power lay in the balance between them. The Transcendentalists, we discover, expressed the qualitative dimensions of both of the poles but tilted their favor toward the feminine, or celebrated a muted androgyny in their symbolization. Their choice implied a judgment concerning the kind of motion which could bring America into correspondence with ideal and spiritual truth. At the same time their choice led them back from the heavens to the earth.

After the continual allusions to America, Chapter V deals directly with the new nation which formed the backdrop for the Transcendental adventure in language. It was, as the study shows, an America preeminently on the move, with a pace which corroborated the movement in Transcendental language. The members of the Club were well acquainted with the main features of the cultural landscape of their era and voiced their combined pleasure and displeasure at what they saw. They were often ambivalent as they viewed an Eastern seaboard speedily becoming industrialized and urbanized, often exploding out of established boundaries through the pressures of social ferment and the dis-ease induced by rapid and unprepared change.

What this chapter tries to suggest is an understanding of the similitude between Transcendental and American motion in the religious terms of the Transcendentalists; that is, in terms of correspondence. Too often, studies of the relationship between word and world have been disserved by analyses cast in the model of cause-and-effect relationships—the very pattern of causality which, as we shall see, the members of the Club sought to avoid. What is important here, however, is that correspondence can be a pragmatic tool for scholarship as well as an explanatory vision for religion. The academic study of religion has more and more become involved in hermeneutical issues which suggest the complexities of the interaction between "objective" realities and human subjectivity. Humans externalize their perceptions of the world by naming them. Once spoken, words begin to acquire a validity and life of their own, existing in objectified and "othered" modes and interpreting human action and idea by means of these modes. With the power and authority which such a condition implies, language is internalized again, having gained in substance and stature by its journey through the arena of public space.[9]

This model of cultural processes sets the familiar discussions of literary "influence" in a new context in which neither word nor world can be said to initiate in the old sense of cause and effect. We might say that, in this understanding, cause and effect have become "unprofitable servants," superseded by others which illuminate reality in a different and, at least for the present, more compelling manner. No doubt the Durkheimian sociological understanding of the dynamics of projection in the life of society has contributed to the persuasiveness of the new model.[10] No doubt, too, the nineteenth-century discovery of the unconscious has provided a groundwork without which the analysis could not proceed.[11] Finally, it seems probable that twentieth-century science, after the introduction of quantum mechanics and the theory of relativity, has also contributed to the attractiveness of this movement away from the strict dualism of cause and effect. But, more important than the correspondences of our model is its heuristic value in enabling us to perceive the extraordinary richness and complexity of what the Transcendentalists said and did amid the tensions which characterized their world.

Perhaps the surest expression of the ability of the Transcendentalists to deal creatively with that world was their implicit, and often explicit, prescription for its reconciliation. Chapter VI examines the prescription as expressed in the Emersonian notions of self-culture and of history. Both led Emerson and the other Transcendentalists finally to autobiography. In the framework of world religions, the Transcendentalists had blended the mystical quest of cultures based on correspondence with the thrusting individualism which characterized evangelical Christianity as well as America on the move. Their affirmation of America included a direction which would temper her impulsiveness and balance her urge for dominance and expansion. The corresponding motion of the Transcendentalists was neither complete nor absolute, for at some level the members of the Club had seen into the hidden depths of American consciousness and character and sought to balance them. Ultimately, they would measure America against immanental as well as transcendental truths.

This study is an attempt to clarify the religious nature of Transcendentalism. It should also have implications for the study of religion in general. Its exploration of the continuities and discontinuities between the Transcendental form of American religion and the patterns which are present in all religion can help us better estimate the tension between universality and particularity in which any religion lives. On another level, the discontinuities and especially the continuities between Transcendental religion and American life begin to suggest an understanding of religion as the very core of culture. While religion may immerse its devotees in a world of transcendence, it is also the way they orient themselves in the world of everyday. The immanental quality of Transcendental religion adumbrates a "real" religion which cannot be confined to church or even mountaintop and wild places in nature. It leads, by the force of its correspondential logic, to the railroad depot where goods are exchanged and earthly schedules kept. It points, in short, to a secular and pragmatic dimension to religious experience.

Finally, the Transcendentalists' experiment with language in community offers some hints about the essentially communal nature of all religion. Individualists though they proclaimed themselves, the Transcendentalists recognized their own individuality because they shared a consciousness which valued it. They ordered and expressed their sense of themselves in language which made and remade them a community. Even their "mystical" moments led them toward an All which absorbed them in the bonds of its unity. Religion for the Transcendentalists was ultimately never a solitary affair.

In the discussion which follows, notes have been kept at a minimum and a legacy of textual analysis gratefully presupposed. Thus, with Emerson, whose method of composition depended heavily on the repetition and reworking of phrases, sentences, and paragraphs from his journals or early lectures, only one formulation has generally been quoted without tracing the history of a particular linguistic expression. With the others as well, their expression has been taken at its word. In the beginning, we have been told, was the word.

Corresponding Motion

CHAPTER I

Child of
the Universe

THE TRANSCENDENTALISTS were religious people who shared with one another basic intuitions about the nature of the ultimate and the everyday. They were also and not surprisingly people who experienced the world in similar patterns. Since they numbered among their community Ralph Waldo Emerson, we can begin to understand their common religiousness by looking first at his proclamation of a new gospel in the days when the Transcendental Club was just coming into existence. It was his statement which seemed to provide a paradigm which the experience of the others either affirmed or echoed. And, according to Emerson, the proper manner of intuiting the world involved an awareness of correspondence. This worldview summarized his own religious experience and explained the workings of both cosmos and history.

From a global and historical perspective, the intuition of correspondence had a long and well-defined past in East and West. In fact, if one can judge by its sophisticated expressions in the earliest sources, correspondence seems older than the first written records of human history. Emerson himself was quietly aware of the religious tradition in which he stood and at times went so far as to cite his lineage. Yet, in the context of his contemporaries, his vision was new and revolutionary. As heirs to the Judaeo-Christian tradition with all that it implied of a marriage between Hebrew and Graeco-Roman sources, as heirs likewise of the philosophical tradition of the Enlightenment and early modern times, and finally as the

3

descendants of the Puritans, Emerson's neighbors saw the world from a different religious perspective—that of causality. Most comfortable separating sacred reality from the profane world around them, they clearly demarcated the sphere of religion from the contrasting realm of secularity. With the order and precision which this procedure brought to the world, Americans cleared a space to work toward the accomplishment of immediate and multiple goals. Still, they knew that God was present in the empyrean as first and final cause to which they could refer all things.

As different as Emerson's religious sense was from that of his neighbors, however, it was also in some measure different from traditional forms of correspondence. Curiously, the gap between the nineteenth-century American version of the experience and its relatives in diverse times and places suggested a tie between Transcendental religion and the orientation of other Americans. It became evident that Emerson and his friends were living out the theory of correspondence with reference to nineteenth-century America as well as the universal scheme of creation.

In *Nature*, Emerson articulated his understanding of religious correspondence. Once a "certain poet" had sung to him about the original condition of human life in which a man

> *filled nature with his overflowing currents. Out from him sprang the sun and moon; from man, the sun; from woman, the moon. The laws of his mind, the periods of his actions externized themselves into day and night, into the year and the seasons. But, having made for himself this huge shell, his waters retired; he no longer fills the veins and veinlets; he is shrunk to a drop. He sees, that the structure still fits him, but fits him colossally.* [1]

The "huge shell" of the world, then, was structurally identified with human form, although it was large, and humans had become small and shriveled. To use the technical language of the worldview of correspondence, the world existed as microcosm and macrocosm, and the two resembled each other even as they differed in scale. In the human microcosm, poet for Emerson meant priest; priest meant virtuoso in religious intuition and experience; and religious virtuoso meant one who as microcosm resonated totally to the structure and rhythms of the great whole. Hence, the "certain poet" knew and lived the cosmic truth. His ultimate reference was not aesthetics but sacrality, and religion was the matrix from which the form of poetry emerged.

Emerson began his discussion of correspondence by noting that temporal and local changes in nature corroborated human states of mind. "From breathless noon to grimmest midnight," each hour authorized a "different state of mind." A bare common brought perfect exhilaration; the woods gave perpetual youth. Both were no surprise, for all around field and wood suggested an "occult relation between man and the vegetable."[2] The relationship, for Emerson, might be discerned in four ways: through commodity, through beauty, through language, and through discipline, all of which, in the broad sense, might be considered the uses of nature.

Nature, first of all, bestowed advantages on the human senses in ways which provided the charter for pragmatic and thisworldly enterprise. Every piece of the natural world worked with other pieces for the profit of the human species. This was, of course, true in the great cycle of agriculture which depended on the circulation of light, air, and moisture. But if nature, even without culture, nourished human beings, she also offered numerous practical suggestions for imitation through technology, or, using Emerson's word, "art." Wind became steam for power; birds were reflected in the iron bars of the railroad and the coaches of its cars. The world was changed by this combination of factors so that even the poor man could acknowledge "cities, ships, canals, bridges, built for him." He was immersed in a web of relationships which seemed to imitate the cycle of nature, for in "post-office," "book-shop," "court-house," and even at home when his walk required snow-shoveling, he looked to the services of others.[3]

Secondly, through its beauty, nature applied a restorative to the human perspective: it brought a just proportion back to a body or mind "cramped by noxious work or company." "The tradesman, the attorney comes out of the din and craft of the street, and sees the sky and the woods, and is a man again."[4] Natural beauty corresponded to the beauty of the human will which acted rightly and in proportion to the totality of things, for "in proportion to the energy of his thought and will," a man took up "the world into himself." Moreover, the beauty of the harmonious working of nature correlated with the harmonious working of the mind. The human intellect reproduced the world in art, reflecting the absolute order of things in the work of the poet, painter, sculptor, musician, or architect.

But nature disclosed its paradigmatic character in another and third "use." Its operations shaped language, for words reflected the universal fitness and emblematic character of things. Words were "signs of natural facts"; "particular natural facts" were "symbols of particular spiritual facts"; and nature over all was "the symbol of spirit."[5] Emerson turned to the etymology of words to illustrate just how literally this was the case: right meant straight and wrong meant twisted; spirit meant wind and transgression meant the crossing of a line. He asserted a "radical correspondence between visible things and human thoughts" and encouraged the marriage of natural history and human history to bring fullness of life. The likeness went beyond thing and thought, for "the whole of nature" was "a metaphor of the human mind," wrote Emerson. "We are like travellers using the cinders of a volcano to roast their eggs. Whilst we see that it always stands ready to clothe what we would say, we cannot avoid the question, whether the characters are not significant of themselves."[6]

However, the culminating emblem of spirit was not language, for it was particular and partial. The climax of correspondence was wholeness, and Emerson found wholeness in discipline. Here he discovered the fourth and final way in which the universe supplied a model for humankind. In the midst of providing a macrocosmic referent for the microcosm, nature schooled the mind, the senses, the actions. It possessed an objectivity and a facticity which compelled attention and required compliance. One could not quarrel with the categories of space and time; water could not be woven, wool could not be sipped, and coal could not provide food. Hence, nature disciplined perception and thought by teaching distinction and separation of forms and properties. But, more important for Emerson, nature taught humans in every event and object the presence and power of will. From the human point of view, all things in nature were "moral" or "ethical." The complex interactions of "nature glorious with form, color, and motion" led to an ultimate unity and on the way hinted or thundered "the laws of right and wrong." Every natural process was a "version of a moral sentence," for the moral law lay "at the center of nature" and radiated "to the circumference." In short, at the apex of the structure of correspondence in the universe which Emerson contemplated was the model which nature gave for the living of human life. Nature became the point of departure for a life-orientation system; it was "ever the ally of Religion."[7]

A life-orientation system must be a pragmatic construct because it must be a useful guide for actual endeavor. Emerson's practicality ran through *Nature* from its focus on nature as a commodity to its final vision of nature as a discipline. But a vision, to be practical, needed also to possess the force to generate its own accomplishment. Useful nature needed to be powerful nature: it was not enough merely to see the utility of the macrocosm. Emerson recognized his understanding as a source, not only of perspective, but also of such power. "That which was unconscious truth, becomes, when interpreted and defined in an object, a part of the domain of knowledge,—a new weapon in the magazine of power."[8] It could lead to "the action of man upon nature with his entire force" and "Reason's momentary grasp of the sceptre." In more material terms, the results might be "the miracles of enthusiasm, as those reported of Swedenborg, Hohenlohe, and the Shakers," "Animal Magnetism," and "self-healing." Emerson's endorsement was not the quantum leap which it might on first glance appear; there was a logical progression which led to his enthusiastic statements. If every piece of the world was mirror and model to every other piece of the world, as correspondence taught, it followed that everything—with knowledge as the key—might be made to act on everything else. Such action exceeded the scientific canons of cause and effect and fit instead the definition of magic. The ultimate practical expression of the worldview of correspondence, magic meant the ability to manipulate the world for one's own benefit and to one's own purposes. It was power which moved in accordance with the laws of correspondence.

The knowledge which provided the key for the magical manipulation of the universe was, however, opaque and indirect. Instead of the linear logic of discursive thinking which found its most complete expression in the syllogism, intuition was required. There was not one way to link the pieces of the world; rather, there were many which one grasped by association in a great chain of homological thinking. The true naturalist had discovered that "there are far more excellent qualities in the student than preciseness and infallibility; that a guess is often more fruitful than an indisputable affirmation, and that a dream may let us deeper into the secret of nature than a hundred concerted experiments."[9] In order to be a magician, one had also to be a poet, a dreamer, and a contemplative. To locate and use the energies of the cosmos, one needed an inner sensor to receive the messages which the universe sent. In other words, magic (correspondential action) was based on intuition (correspondential thought). Here Emerson had supplied alternatives for the more usual Western understanding in which right action proceeded from a reasoned analysis of relations based on a logical structure to the world.

The worldview of correspondence which Emerson had discovered and articulated for himself and his Boston neighbors was, as we have indicated, at least as ancient as the earliest human records. In differing temporal, spatial, and cultural contexts, the understanding seemed to be similar. Structure and action in the human community replicated the structure and action of a vast natural or divine cosmos to which it was intimately bound and related. Human and transcendent cosmos were both made of the same "worldstuff" and programmed by their own internal forces to follow similar charts of existence. While very often the two worlds (human, and natural or divine) appeared spread in wild profusion, there was an orderly sequence of being and event in both. This order was certainly asymmetrical at some times and difficult to discern at others, but it continued nonetheless: almighty nature—and its human counterpart—lived according to intrinsic laws.

This understanding of the human community as a replica of the cosmos took two major forms. On the one hand, human society could be viewed as the "double" of a counterpart which was hidden from ordinary human sight. On the other hand, human society might be seen as a microcosm, a small world surrounded by a vast macrocosm out of which it arose and to which in some respects it ever returned.

First of all, in the model of "doubles"—common to the ancient Egyptian and Babylonian cultures, for example—the entire topography of the earth possessed duplicates, and exact counterparts of all that existed here stood also in other realms. More than that, the political hierarchy of human culture with a god-king at its apex repeated the socio-political arrangements elsewhere. The god-king became a veritable umbilical cord linking the life of two spheres, so that human society ever participated in the being of the hidden divine world.

Hence, the Egyptians conceived the earth as a flat circle with the rounded dome of the sky fitted securely over it to form a hemisphere. Beneath the flat surface of the earth, another hemisphere was fitted in the same size and shape. The underworld was, in fact, a duplicate of the upper regions with the same rivers and seas, mountains and valleys, fields and swamps. Deceased kings and gods lived in the sky of the upper world, while ordinary men and women who were dead lived below. The Nile which flowed through the land of Egypt had a heavenly counterpart, so that actually two Niles existed. According to the Pyramid Texts, a deceased king lived on earth and in heaven at once, and each human being possessed a spirit double, the *ka*-soul, which usually inhabited the upper realm.

The Babylonians also understood space in terms of counterparts. Huge cities possessed their starry doubles, and the Tigris and Euphrates were modeled on heavenly rivers. The earth was composed of two portions, an upper for the living and a lower for the dead. Similarly, human activity reflected that of the cosmos; the city-state established its political activity on a cosmos which was a prior political realm; the god-king in cultic festivals played the role of Dumuzi in his marriage to the goddess Inanna and by so doing released the power of nature for the needs of the state.

For both these ancient peoples, the cosmos which they contemplated was regular and predictable. It had been ordered out of chaos once at the time of creation, and it would continue to obey the hidden laws of its existence. Thus, because of this unchangeableness in rhythm, one could ascribe a static quality to the motion of the universe. In this respect, the traditional understanding of cosmic doubles would differ significantly from that of Emerson and the other Transcendentalists.[10]

The second understanding—that of the microcosm within an encompassing macrocosm—came closer to the religious sense of the Transcendentalists. Here, the human community was a circle at the center of the larger circle of a natural and spiritual universe. In many cases, this larger circle was a mysterious and hidden source of life which only became active and conscious in human culture. Human life, thus, was nature and spirit become conscious of itself—the form of being toward which the macrocosm potentially tended. The great unmanifest secret became manifest in human society by disclosing its inner content in the character of the community. The source of all things had its power because, as source, it held priority; but so too did human community which embodied the truth of the larger, hidden circle from which it emerged.

In the Hindu teaching of India, some of which the Transcendentalists would later endorse, we see an example of this kind of correspondence. The entire world system was an expression of *dharma* or universal law. Individual thought, existence, and social organization were real only insofar as they followed this law which supported the human cosmos. *Dharma* was the norm by which one measured and the model to which one conformed. The caste system of India was a human expression of the *dharma* of existence, and each caste lived by its own particular *dharma* because each shared an element of divinity. In the *Laws of Manu*, we learn how detailed could be the stipulations for caste existence in harmony with cosmic law— an existence in which each slightest gesture acquired an eternal meaning.[11] In this view, custom and propriety possessed a cosmic significance, and religion could be described as "proper practice," or relating to others "according to the 'natural distinctions' found in existence."[12] Social station and tradition were normative, since human society had been validated by the cosmos.

Although there were obvious differences between Indian and American correspondence—which we shall later explore—the Hindu example is significant for understanding the Transcendentalists. Like the Hindus, who highlighted the implicit unity of microcosm and macrocosm in an eternal divinity, Emerson and the others thought of the dualism of the manifest and unmanifest worlds as only provisional. At its core, the world·was one whole. Like the Hindus, Emerson and the Transcendentalists apprehended the oneness of the universe under the character of law. The moral basis of the human community was not an arbitrary invention but arose from the nature of things. If the universe was a model *of* human reality—a larger structure whose parts were similar, if not identical—it was also a model *for* human reality—a world which ever suggested proper directions for the incessant re-modeling of human existence in the midst of life.[13]

When one lived thus, according to "natural distinctions" which merged into an ultimate unity, and when one continually embodied the unity in the morality of instinctively right (in tune with the cosmos) being, then all human existence became religious. No one area of life could be cordoned off as sacred, and no one time could be set aside for religious and spiritual duties. Rather, all things were holy so long as an openness to the cosmic wholeness prevailed. From the Transcendental perspective, one did not need to attend a church in order to express one's religion; indeed, it seemed more correct to wander amid the manifestations of nature. It also seemed pointless to struggle to rid oneself of faults and blemishes and to work hard at "charitable" relationships. Rather, one should seek the moral expression which arose without thought or effort from a rightly ordered life. Disorder would always be evident in the lack of mental peace, in the failure of health, in the frenetic quest after fortune, in stepping out of "place." On the other hand, "real" religion meant life which quietly affirmed spiritual truth through one's duty in the midst of the ordinary. It followed that harmony with the cosmos led ultimately to the "secular" realm in which commodity and profit held sway. Nature had a pattern for the proper existence even of all of this.

Yet the insights of the worldview of correspondence extended further. As we have already implied in our discussion of "doubles," correspondence did not occur merely on a one-to-one basis. Rather, each piece of the world could participate simultaneously in the meaning of several spheres. The moon, for example, was like a woman in that both disclosed themselves gradually and in that both became new every twenty-eight days. The moon was like the rain which followed its phases in that both swept away old and outworn forms. The moon and the serpent participated in spiral form, and the undulation of both suggested the light/darkness cycle. Similarly, the moon disappeared, while the snake sloughed off its skin. The moon was the great spider, Arachne, because as the macrocosmic measuring gauge it wove the rhythms of fate, and the moon was Penelope, the weaver-woman and wife to Ulysses, because it bound together past, present, and future.

So too human experience was the many-faceted reflector of the cosmic secret. A child born under the sign of Leo shared the way of being in the world which Leo embodied, and a child hiding behind the sofa in a Puritan parlor after a naughty deed repeated the drama of Adam and Eve hiding from God in the Garden. If a child was stubborn, it was because all children in the family clan exhibited this trait; if a child was honest and straightforward, he or she rehearsed the expectation of adults in the ethnic group. The child's game of ninepins was linked to the original game which Rip Van Winkle had rolled in the Catskills, and the child's spinning top recalled the spinning of the earth. The universe, in sum, *answered*, and no part of existence was isolated from the process.

Finally, correspondence made it possible to collapse the power of space and time: if one possessed the saving knowledge, one knew that inner equaled outer, that space was coterminous with time, and that both could be made to disappear or, alternately, used to fullest advantage. Shamans and seers, saints and mystics could all act as cosmic sorcerers. In magic, the "normal" patterns for the operation of one spatial body on another gave way before the energies unleashed by correspondence. A magician was simply an adept who had learned to take active advantage of the basic unity of the world. Each person was, as Philo of Alexandria had written, a "miniature heaven" in that he carried around "within himself, like holy images, endowments of nature that correspond to the constellations."[14] One only had to know how and when and what to manipulate in order to obtain desired results.

In medieval Europe, for instance, magic was an ordinary manifestation. Serious Christian churchmen produced learned treatises on the phenomenon. Indeed, popular attitudes toward the sacramental system often made it difficult for ecclesiastical purists to decide the point at which magic ceased and prayer began. It was this sort of difficulty which disturbed the monastic solitude of Martin Luther on the eve of the Reformation. In the East, Chinese popular religion was only one example of how the theory of correspondence could be practically applied to manipulate the universe. Here, popular Taoism blended with Buddhism and some Confucian ritual elements to produce a worldview which understood the rhythm of the cosmos as an opportunity for magical action.

The experience of correspondence led notably to an interest and involvement with time. Coincidences were "meaningful." Like the Shakespearean tempest which preceded Othello's murderous rage, natural catastrophe was the concomitant to human restlessness and turmoil. On the other hand, natural calm affirmed a tranquillity in the affairs of men and women. As Carl Jung wrote in a twentieth-century version of the theory of correspondence, "synchronicity" rested on "archetypal foundations," so that clairvoyance and telepathy, which obviated separation in time (and space), were unexceptional.[15] Each moment in time possessed a characteristic quality which colored each event, such as a human birth, occurring in its duration. Time could be auspicious for one activity because of this quality it contained—or it could be inauspicious because its intrinsic nature was opposed to another kind of activity. Thus, to act in harmony with temporal patterns in the cosmos meant being able to discern the signs of the times. Methods for such discernment—horoscopes, almanacs, divination techniques—grew in number and refinement in many cultures.

Hellenistic peoples, for example, had to take the entire temporal scheme into account when contemplating a particular course of action. The scholar Franz Cumont tells us that haruspicy and augury, already a feature of early republican Rome, had developed to such a point that "people would no longer take a bath, go to the barber, change their clothes or manicure their fingernails, without first awaiting the propitious moment."[16] The Chinese *I Ching*, part of the Confucian canon, gave explicit formulation to the various patterns in the macrocosm and provided a developed technique for testing the time in light of a human problem or perplexity. Meanwhile, calendric prescriptions were a highly developed art. Every human activity from marrying to moving, cleaning house to embroidering, sowing and harvesting to grazing cattle, bathing to starting a business, had its appointed time; and it was the emperor's duty as Son of Heaven to study the heavens and provide the calendar through his designated officials.[17]

We see, therefore, that correspondence possessed a multiple signification. It meant that the nature of the universe held a religious primacy, and so the cosmos should be treated with great respect and reverence. It meant also that because human community was grounded in the nature of the cosmos, society itself acquired a greater "reality." This could be the occasion for extraordinary conservatism, but it could at the same time provide the basis for extraordinary security and self-assurance about human life in community. It provided, indeed, a highly positive estimate of the worth of human nature and grounded human moral response in clear and certain terms. Above all, correspondence meant that there could be no radical break between sacred and profane. The ordinary embodied the latent power of the cosmos so that everything became a sacrament and every duty a religious task. One could speak, in a sense, of a "polytheism" in which there were many centers of the sacred which ultimately fused in their macrocosmic Source.

It would be fascinating if at this point we could begin to trace the developments and nuances of the worldview of correspondence as it grew over the years in the East and the West. Yet a survey of this nature would carry us far from our involvement with Transcendental religion and lead, rather, in tangential directions. Therefore, let us single out some aspects of the Eastern and Western experience of correspondence which seem particularly germane. Emerson, later in his life, would delight in quoting from the *Bhagavad Gita* and the *Laws of Manu*, both important religious texts from the Hindu tradition to which we have already alluded. But, from the perspective of this essay, just as important for understanding the Transcendental religion of correspondence is the religious outlook of the Chinese.

It was among the Chinese that the worldview of correspondence completely encompassed a culture from the level of first principles to that of infinitesimal practical detail. Earliest archaeological finds contained evidence that the Chinese formed a connection between the action of the cosmos and that of human beings. Oracle bones, often tortoise shells or cattle scapula, were scratched with a question and then cracked by the touch of a red-hot implement. The pattern of resultant cracks was construed as an answer to the question, for, as in other cases of correspondence, participation in a common time meant that the human and the universal expressed correlative changes. Both Confucianism and Taoism, the two powerful and indigenous life-orientation systems of China, testified to the basic Chinese understanding of the sympathy of all things and the ability through knowledge to shape human destiny by tuning and adjusting to cosmic rhythms.

Thus, Confucian moral and ritual requirements rested on the foundation of correspondence. Successful human activity, for Confucius, must conform to *ming*, or the "total existent conditions and forces of the whole universe."[18] In the *Analects*, correspondence characterized every sphere, and Confucius exhorted his disciples concerning the knowledge which must inform a virtuous life by speaking of it in terms of the Mandate of Heaven, the rules of propriety, and the discernment of the feelings of other human beings.

In the matter of ritual, each detail was likewise woven with the thread of correspondence as, for example, when the three years' mourning for deceased parents was explained by the fact that a child did not leave its parents' arms until it was three years old.

Most interesting of the Confucian teachings, in light of the question concerning Transcendental religious language, is the principle of the rectification of names. The ethical imperative required that all spheres of the cosmos be brought into harmony, and human language was not exempt. Names were meant to designate existing actualities so that name and actuality in a set (sign and signified) faithfully reproduced each other. If names were true, then the realities would also be true. If language grew corrupt, so would the socio-political matrix whose disorder it shaped and reflected. When asked what would be his first measure in the administration of a country, Confucius replied that "it would certainly be to correct language."

> *A gentleman, when things he does not understand are mentioned, should maintain an attitude of reserve. If language is incorrect, then what is said does not concord with what was meant; and if what is said does not concord with what was meant, what is to be done cannot be effected. If what is to be done cannot be effected, then rites and music will not flourish. If rites and music do not flourish, then mutilations and lesser punishments will go astray. And if mutilations and lesser punishments go astray, then the people have nowhere to put hand or foot.*

The prince should "be a prince, the minister a minister, the father a father and the son a son." Ruling, indeed, was "straightening," and the ruler must "lead along a straight way."[19]

The Chinese example emphasizes the moral and religious impulse behind Emerson's concern with language in his proclamation in *Nature*. The poetic theory which he would evolve concerning the exact fit of words and things was based on the requirements of harmony with the moral law of the cosmos. If words did not accurately signify natural facts, spiritual truths would be lost as well. Like the Confucians, Emerson and the Transcendentalists who followed him would restore the human universe to harmonious action by restoring its language.[20] And further, the value which was placed on the shape and scope of language under this interpretation magnifies the importance of taking linguistic structures quite seriously in investigating Transcendental religious experience.

In light of this experience, the Taoistic tradition of China is similarly suggestive. Lao-tzu, the legendary founder of Taoism and author of its classic *Tao Te Ching*, was concerned with revealing the laws which underlay change in the cosmos. It was only by understanding these laws and living in harmony with them that life would be truly successful. The ideal of *wu-wei* or non-ado meant avoiding activity which was out of step with cosmic time and moving with the spontaneous flow of nature. The *Tao Te Ching* taught that

> *Man models himself after Earth.*
> *Earth models itself after Heaven.*
> *Heaven models itself after Tao.*
> *And Tao models itself after Nature.*[21]

Tao was the source of the One, and therefrom issued the two, the three, and the "ten thousand things" which were charged with the passive cosmic force called *yin* and the active cosmic force called *yang*. If one truly "knew" this harmony, one was in accord with the eternal, and this was the state of enlightenment. In the *Chuang Tzu*, the sage taught in similar fashion:

> *Wherever a parent tells a son to go, whether east, west, south, or north, he has to obey. The yin and yang are like man's parents. If they pressed me to die and I disobeyed, I would be obstinate. What fault is theirs? For the universe gave me the body so I may be carried, my life so I may toil, my old age so I may repose, and my death so I may rest. Therefore to regard life as good is the way to regard death as good.*[22]

Here, unlike the tendency toward stasis which often characterized the Near Eastern and Indian understandings of correspondence, the harmony of the spheres was viewed more clearly as a process of rhythmic alternations. There was a quiet and subtle dynamism in the Taoist *wu-wei* as life flowed between the female and male poles of *yin* and *yang*. There was an overarching sense of flux as the great alternation from life to death to life again acted out the ultimate mystery of the *tao*, the "source" and "Mother of all," in its manifest and unmanifest states. As season followed season in unending succession, growth, development, and maturity followed birth and were followed in turn by death. But, like the seasons which returned in an eternal cycle, death itself was not the end—only a new beginning. To attempt to stand still, to try to create a permanent structure was to fail to do the truth: it was living a lie. If to orient one's life rightly meant simply to imitate the macrobiotic pattern, then, paradoxically, correspondence meant that changelessness and change were intertwined. One could participate in movement in harmony with nature; one could not alter the basic structures or violate the essential patterns by motion which was violent or unorthodox.

Hints of a similar configuration of reality were present among the Transcendentalists as they groped toward an evaluation of themselves and their times. Often they would use "natural" language which clearly disclosed *yin* and *yang* values. Like the Taoists, the Transcendentalists searched for balance and yet favored the pole of femininity as an implicit corrective for the overemphasis of their culture on *yang* values—a situation which we will discuss later in the chapter on *The Dial*. Like the Taoists, the Transcendentalists described the correspondence of their world under the rubric of flux so that its movement seemed to be a significant statement of its religious meaning. But, as we shall see, there was something characteristically American in the movement the Transcendentalists perceived in the corresponding spheres of their cosmos.

In the West, the aboriginal inhabitants of Ralph Waldo Emerson's America shared a worldview similar to that of the Transcendentalists—a likeness which has not gone unnoticed by some twentieth-century followers of "nature" who have turned both to American Indian and Transcendentalist models for their inspiration. Perhaps long ago, when the aborigines had crossed the Bering Strait on a land bridge to the new continent, they had borne along with other cultural paraphernalia a sense of correspondence already developed in their old world. At any rate, in their creation myths and sacramental celebrations, American Indians saw themselves on a continuum with nature which had originated their being and continued to nourish it out of earth's body. An Indian might receive a name after an animal which was thought to have a kindred spirit. He might seek the protection of guardian natural spirits in ritual vision quests at the beginning of his career, and he might apologize to plants and animals before using their bodies for human sustenance.

When the white conquerors of the invaded land demanded that the Indians live on reservations, many Indians found that the square dwellings of the white enclosures violated their spirits. As Emerson and his friends would discover, the squares were not in accord with the circles which were part of nature and which the Indians imitated in their lodges and tepees. Shamans and medicine men who understood about the "great medicine" in the universe could activate their knowledge in their magical feats and cures. They could fly through the air at will, or heal the sick with marvelous potions. Natural forms of the world possessed the powerful energy of *wakan* or *orenda* in varying degrees, and holy men had learned to orchestrate the sympathy of the cosmic spheres to the advantage of themselves and their nations. The "spirit-bundle" of a warrior contained his own spirit-power, homologous to the power of his guardian spirit and bound up with the energies radiating from its material contents, the relics of memorable times and events. It was ironic that Emerson would exercise an Anglo-Saxon condescension toward the original inhabitants who had lived by the theory of correspondence long before he propounded it in his own version of "nature."[23]

Out of Europe and the deserts of Northern Africa, however, came a long tradition of correspondence of which Emerson was very much aware. For an example, Pythagoras, the ancient Greek philosopher, had proclaimed as the key to the proportionality of both microcosm and macrocosm the concept of number—a metaphysical reality containing an essence which all representative forms of a given quantity shared. Later, Plato based his ideal theory on the notion of a correspondence between two world orders, the realm of real and eternal Ideas and the realm of shadowy reflections here. Gnostics and Neoplatonists, centuries afterward, found themselves ready and willing to shape their own distinctive versions of this world picture, while, in medieval times, *correspondentia* became a favorite term for natural philosophers. Alchemists assumed that the process of transmuting base metals into gold meant a change, not only in the material world, but also in their inner beings, where the "gold" of personal divinity was distilled and experienced. Meanwhile, in the mystical teachings of the Jewish Kabbalah, the notion of microcosm and macrocosm, now identified with En Soph and the Sephiroth, flourished. Even as Western European intellectuals turned to a scientific worldview in the seventeenth century, the theory of correspondence continued to play a role in the speculations of respectable scholars, Francis Bacon and Gottfried von Leibniz among them.

In *Nature*, Emerson explicitly alluded to his Western forebears and recognized his links with the past. "These are not the dreams of a few poets, here and there," he wrote, "but man is an analogist and studies relations in all objects." And a few paragraphs further: "This relation between the mind and matter . . . is the standing problem which has exercised the wonder and the study of every fine genius since the world began; from the era of the Egyptians and the Brahmins, to that of Pythagoras, of Plato, of Bacon, of Leibnitz, of Swedenborg." "Prospects," a subtitled section of the long essay, seemed, rather, a consideration of retrospects. Emerson cited George Herbert, the seventeenth-century English metaphysical poet, and quoted a long portion of his poem ("Man is all symmetry,/Full of proportions . . ."). Thereafter, Emerson accepted without criticism Plato's evaluation that a poem was closer to truth than a historical study. The song which "a certain poet sang" was repeated—with its reference to Nebuchadnezzar as a symbol of the chaos which threatened the human condition. Salvation was at hand, though, and again one could look to the past for "gleams of a better light" which were the "occasional examples of the action of man upon nature with his entire force."[24] These examples embodied the magical principle: through miracle or charisma, the essential continuity between the human and the transcendent was realized, the channels were opened, and the stream of force from the human sphere could act upon the larger environment.

But the tradition in which Emerson stood and the religious position which he worked out for himself in *Nature* differed significantly from the normative or controlling worldview of the West. Despite a strong current of belief in the correspondence of the world, Westerners had largely identified themselves as people who stood over against nature. There had been a primordial rupture in the grand scheme of the universe, and it had obliterated the easy and unselfconscious life of union with the cosmos. Instead, selfconsciousness had supplanted it in the mode of a "fall" from grace—a fall only lengthened, as we shall see, by the Hebrew realization of linear pattern in history, the Graeco-Roman discovery of rational philosophy, and the combination of the two heritages in the long development of the Western tradition culminating in the Enlightenment and early modern times.

While it is difficult to generalize in view of the complexity of that Western heritage, it may be useful to summarize the fundamental assumptions of this Western mainstream as causality. In the causal view of the world, sacred power had given the original generative "push" to the world, so to speak, by creating it out of nothing. Thus, sacred reality had *caused* the profane world, but at the same time its essential being remained apart from the created product. Instead of the mythology of a microcosm in which the potential of the macrocosm became actual, in this mythology of sacred and profane, the realms were more clearly separated. Created existence, which was profane, was continually threatened by alienation from the "real" or sacred world, an alienation which the Judaeo-Christian tradition understood as sin and its Graeco-Roman counterpart saw as irrationality. The natural order as a whole lacked the vitality and coherence which were essential to its continued existence. At every turn, it could run itself down, decay, and die— returning to the conditions of chaos which had preceded the existence of ordered form. Yet hope was never far away in this exceedingly vulnerable creation, for one merely had to tap the essentially "real," the creative source from which life had originally come, in order to be re-energized with the strength and power which had characterized the world when it was new.

Therefore, one recited the particular story of the creative beginnings of a human community and enacted its significance through the celebration of ritual. In this way, one re-established contact with the sacred force which infused into the run-down forms all the power of the beginning time. Still further, the contact with the sacred did not come through mere memorial. In sacred time and space (both set apart), one lived the creation all over again. "Why *is* this night different from all others?" the Jewish boy asked his father at the Passover seder. And in the words of the Roman Catholic liturgy, the devotee prayed: "Come, Holy Spirit, fill the hearts of thy faithful, and kindle in them the fire of thy love. Send forth thy spirit, and *they shall be created*; and thou shalt renew the face of the earth" (emphasis mine).

Certainly, the cultural expression of the worldview of correspondence had also included the sacred *mythos* and its sacramental enactment in ritual. And, assuredly, the tale of origins and its solemn recitation implied, as in the worldview of causality, a distance which separated the sacred from the profane. But the correspondential *Weltanschauung* saw harmony not far away, its expression a natural human occupation, and the myth-and-ritual setting a way of bringing the natural and human worlds into a more intense awareness of their mutuality. One sees the process at work in the Hindu mythologies of origination from the body of the deity, that "All" which was "impounded in the first principle, which may be spoken of as the Person, Progenitor, Mountain, Tree, Dragon or endless Serpent."[25] One sees it as well in American Indian mythologies of migratory emergence out of the womb of earth or of origination out of nature through the action of animal earth-divers plunging into the waters.[26]

On the other hand, in the Edenic myth of creation, basic to the Judaeo-Christian tradition, we gain an insight into what the more pronounced sacred/profane dichotomy could imply for the human relationship to a natural cosmos. God dwelt far beyond earth-bound nature even as his power continued to cause it to be. Just as a great gulf extended between the divine and the human, similarly a huge distance stood between the human community and the rest of the natural world. Hence, God said to the primordial pair in the Garden: "Be fruitful and multiply; fill the earth and subdue it. Have dominion over the fish of the sea, the birds of the air, the cattle and all the animals that crawl on the earth" (Gen. 1:28). As if to reinforce the injunction, God then brought the birds and beasts to Adam to be named. When one remembers that for Hebrew thought, to name meant to control, the significance of the divine action becomes clear. Instead of perceiving nature as part of an answering macrocosm, the Western tradition saw field and stream, bird and beast, as part of a subordinate order of creation over which humankind was to exercise control. Nature was that which one mastered far more than that with which one lived in harmony. Unlike the tradition of correspondence in which it was possible to manipulate a more potent nature by uncovering its creative secret in magic, one dominated a lesser world by issuing the word of command.

The imperium which subjugated nature was only a short step away from a new emphasis on the human project which reached its clearest expression in the development of a sense of history. As the Hebrews shaped and expressed their understanding of the actions of their God, they fashioned for themselves and their progeny a model in which a transcendent and supernatural Yahweh could yet intervene in the world—now not so much in the realm of inferior and nonhuman nature, but more and more on behalf of his people. Thus, in the Bible, God acted in the public realm to create discernible, and sometimes striking, effects. So the Hebrews in the time of the Judges overwhelmed the city of Jericho because Yahweh, Lord of Hosts, fought on the side of Joshua and the people of his tribe. So the weapon of David, guided by the arm and power of God, could overcome the giant Goliath and his people, the Philistines. And so, in the clearest and most outstanding case, Yahweh had, before all this, led his people out of Egypt by separating the waters of the Red Sea so that they could pass and by drowning Pharaoh and his chariots as they followed. God had subsequently fed the Hebrews manna in the desert and likewise nourished their spirits with law in the Decalogue, both indicators of his continuing watchfulness and intervention for the renewal of Israel.

We have here at work a process which contained *in nuce* the creative and controlling restlessness of the Western tradition. There was a connection between the causal power of God and the effective action of the scions of Israel who aspired to make history. For history, even the "unscientific" history of the ancient world, was the story which traced the causes of public and witnessed effects. The model of a God who acted in history (a Cause producing "effects") not only suggested the dynamic of the relationship between the sacred and the profane but also emphasized the perception that the "real," the "true," the important story was that of the people who together formed a community. The action of this community became the story which gave meaning, and more significant action meant greater meaning. Hence, action in the world became a category for consciousness, a category which structured perception so that one asserted the truth of a phenomenon by proclaiming that it was indeed an effect (of a cause) which had occurred in the world "out there," in the presence of reliable witnesses. History, in short, became an absolute. Christians were only expressing this understanding of the ancient world with particular clarity when they insisted that Jesus was unlike the gods of the heathen in that he had lived, died, and risen in the flesh; that is, in the temporal and historical domain.

By contrast, the worldview of correspondence found the greatest significance in the patterned structure of the cosmos in which human culture replicated nature and the divine. Causal questions about the public order were simply not asked, or, if they were raised, were perceived as secondary—less important than the "mirror" quality of reality which expressed the most profound truth concerning existence. It is revelatory that neither Eastern nor Western Indians concerned themselves to any great extent with oral or written history. Similarly, the Chinese who possessed a modicum of historical writing did not perceive "making history"—in the Western style—as their major mode of expression. Rather, for the Chinese, history conformed to exemplary models which later generations acted out as they corresponded on a temporal plane to the great paradigms of ancestral times. Only in the West did the thrust of the cause-and-effect dynamic begin to suggest that men, by the labor of their hands, the strength of their weapons, and the conquering dreams of their restless spirits, were able to venture into a project that was *new*.

Therefore, it was also in the West that *gnosis*, or knowledge through intuitive understanding, gave place before a linear logic which used rational consciousness to posit a goal and make the necessary movements to arrive at it. Just as the sacred and the profane existed in a relationship of cause and effect, and just as human action exhibited a similar trajectory in history, so human thought was conceived as etiological; that is, productive of effects. In the order of logical action, the goal which was achieved was the necessary conclusion to a syllogism. As the sacred had empowered the profane, and as the action of making history had brought power to the fore in human relationships in the world, the vector of logic brought power to the realm of language.

Pre-Socratic Greek philosophy had been a search for the causes of things. Socrates himself seemed bent on the discovery of moral causes, and, although his student Plato explicated the correspondence between Ideas and their worldly copies, Plato's brilliant pupil Aristotle turned the West again toward the pursuit of causal questions. Aristotle's First Cause and Unmoved Mover was in due course baptized by Christian scholars and proclaimed the universal God. But more than that, Aristotle's method of procedure in the investigation of the world and the establishment of the natural sciences set the stage for much of what followed in the West. Aristotelian thinking moved from cause to effect with the presupposition that there was one correct answer to the question at issue. Here was a radical departure from the worldview of correspondence in which homologies for any given reality existed in a plurality of spheres, so that there could be and there were many correct answers, so that the answers existed simultaneously and coincidentally, and so that one was not understood as the cause of the next. Associative thinking had yielded before the onslaughts of discursive reason, and the latter became the ground of "reality" for the Western mainstream, while the former was fitted into the scheme as poetry, art, and fantasy.

But it was in the European Enlightenment of the seventeenth and the eighteenth centuries that the dual linear thrust of the West—in thought and in history—finally met and married. The encounter produced as its offspring the birth of modern times. As the men of the Enlightenment took up their cudgels against the past, they began to make the category of myth a significant tool for conceptualization. Myth, for them, designated a fantastic and supernatural story, marked by its superstition and *un*truth. As such it contrasted sharply with the Enlightenment understanding in which scientific reason was exalted to new heights as a criterion of truth and, therefore, power. Now, if one wanted to establish the validity of a proposition, one demonstrated with the new measuring rods provided by science in the service of inductive reason. The universe was conceived as a vast machine, the laws of which could be discovered by an analysis of its operations. Logic had found its partner in these instruments which could weigh and measure and sometimes break substances into component elements. Cause-and-effect thinking no longer needed to confine its deductions to the cerebral sphere, for the new (Enlightenment) science enabled thought to act upon the world in a compelling and more satisfying manner. One at last had proof of the lawful nature of things, and the nature of nature promised to be ever more pliant as its mechanical springs were discovered and transformed by enlightened reason.

As reason entered the early nineteenth century, it seemed almost inevitable that its confident stance before the machine of nature would lead it to assume an equally commanding posture in the midst of human society. A second new criterion of truthfulness and power was emerging with the victorious march of Hegelian history. The Idea was no longer content to act upon nature but became conscious of itself as transcendent Force in the workings of the human project. As Napoleon's armies swept Europe, so would the Idea become flesh in significant human enterprise—enterprise which resulted in territory and expansion, mighty empire and, finally, the triumphant nation-state. If there was here the "terror of history,"[27] there was also its awesomeness and fascination. As a numinous power, history swept along a culture and an age which saw in destiny the perfection of humanity and the birth of a secular millennium.

In sum, while the Enlightenment had begun by discovering myth, its impetus had bequeathed to the nineteenth century two new and invisible "myths." Like the myths of the past which the Enlightenment had disowned, these myths were true because they had effective power to order and express the meaning of the world.[28] Science and history, in Europe and also in its New World extension in America, had become twin vehicles for worldly regeneration. The old problem of the unequivocal sacred/profane dichotomy—with the creative tension toward dynamism it introduced—was now restated in the powers unleashed by scientific and historical action. When one felt destiny escaping and the world winding itself down, one did the truth in thisworldly action, conscious of the ever-present need to strive more earnestly and confident that such self-renewing action would bring the sacred to dwell within the human project.

In America, the Puritan forefathers of the Transcendentalists had, by their commanding presence, set the tone for much that would happen. Aligned to the developing tradition of Enlightenment reason, they founded Harvard University and a religious school system which was not inimical to scientific thinking and willing at least to make room for it. Aligned, further, to the already strong historical tradition of the West, they did not require the impulse of the nineteenth century to "make history" by beginning to subdue and conquer a continent. The Puritans attended to the duties which Jehovah had laid upon them in founding their city on a hill and accomplishing their errand into the wilderness. But in the process they also learned to separate the sacred more definitively from the profane by chaining Jehovah in stronger and more confident versions of the covenant.[29] Puritans became Yankees as they learned to celebrate secular success in trade and commerce more and more completely until, by the early nineteenth century, their heirs were experimenting with an American wedding of science and history in the incipient stages of the Industrial Revolution and the pursuit of manifest destiny.

It was into this world of science and history, as mediated by nineteenth-century America, that Emerson and the other Transcendentalists, not a little awed and fascinated themselves by scientific reason and Hegelian history, began to turn to the ancient truths of correspondence. We have seen that the controlling worldview of this new America was different as the West, in its dominant tradition, was different from the East, and now as the modernity of the post-Enlightenment era was different from its more subtle past. Yet, thus far we have been placing Emerson and the Transcendentalists uncritically in the tradition of correspondence. We have been seeing them for the most part in terms of continuities, and, in the main, we have overlooked the question of possible dissimilarities from the worldview of correspondence and of family relationships with the worldview of causality.

There was, however, a new emphasis in the ancient theory of correspondence as Emerson propounded it and as his friends would take it up and pursue it. In *Nature*, Emerson had spoken familiarly and comfortably of the "Final Cause of the Universe" toward which all existence tended.[30] While the goal toward which all things converged lay at the opposite pole from the efficient and generative causality which we have been considering, the notion of finality still implied a causal dynamic, and one which had been powerful in the Western tradition with its vision of an end to history. The general acquaintance of Emerson and the other Transcendentalists with the Western philosophical tradition meant that they had to a certain extent absorbed its dominant analyses and formulations; they were at home with the language of causality. Even more, the energy stimulated by the teleological impulse complemented certain other factors in the Transcendentalists' experience of the world, factors which our study will begin to take up.

Hence, the difference between Transcendental correspondence and other forms concerned the relative quietude in the traditional understanding of human society and the paradigmatic universe on which it was modeled. The rhythms were generated by the movement of the planetary stars and earthly seasons in regular and placid sequence, in accordance with the eternal harmony of the Indian *dharma*, or, as in the Chinese case, in terms of the tranquil dynamism of the *tao*. In the Emersonian cosmology which became the focal understanding for the Transcendental movement, there was a change. The cosmos to which the Transcendentalists became attuned in *Nature* was a world set in motion—and motion of a different sort from the peaceful rhythms in Eastern and Western correspondence until then.[31] For the universe of *Nature* had experienced the introduction of novelty. The movement was not merely the regular pattern of fixed stars, seasonal changes, or eternal principles. Rather, every natural piece of the world which Emerson contemplated seemed to evidence every sort of motion of which it was capable through its own power or through the impetus of external natural forces acting on it. In the introduction of his essay, Emerson set the tone for much of what was to follow: "Embosomed for a season in nature, whose floods of life stream around and through us by the powers they supply, to action proportioned to nature, why should we grope among the dry bones of the past, or put the living generation into masquerade out of its faded wardrobe?"[32] There were, he continued, "new lands, new men, new thoughts." Throughout, Emerson repeated his message of a ferment at the heart of things. "Nature is not fixed but fluid," his anonymous poet sang. "Spirit alters, moulds, makes it. The immobility or bruteness of nature, is the absence of spirit; to pure spirit it is fluid, it is volatile, it is obedient."[33]

Almost, it seemed, something in Emerson's human condition and that of his friends was setting the time which nature kept. There was a clue in his "philosophical" definition of nature. In the strict sense, different from the "common" sense of the word, he said, nature referred to everything which was not soul; "all which Philosophy distinguishes as the NOT ME, that is, both nature and art, all other men and my own body, must be ranked under this name, NATURE."[34] Under the general heading of nature then, one could subsume both the ordinary meaning of the term ("space, the air, the river, the leaf") and its philosophical meaning as art, which contained the notion of the application of human will to the raw material ("a house, a canal, a statue, a picture").

In other words, the nature which Emerson recognized included the products of human ingenuity. In nineteenth-century New England, these natural "arts" meant among other things, as we have already noted, the growing technological prowess of a post-Puritan culture fast immersing itself in the Industrial Revolution. Emerson's explicit reference to the canal suggested that he was aware of the implications of what he was saying, and the presence of technology in New England would be one among many signs of the new nature which he and his fellow-Transcendentalists confronted. If nature encompassed all of the developing realities of a cultural context—the "NOT ME" which Emerson designated—correspondence must extend to these. And, if the newly emerging America of the nineteenth century should turn out to be preeminently in motion, the Transcendental cosmos to which one attuned oneself would have to include the movement which was propelling culture. While the overt Transcendental message concentrated on nature in the commonsense and narrow definition of the term, the worldview of correspondence committed the Transcendentalists to keep in tune with the times. And the times contained novelty. We may hazard the guess that the New England Transcendentalists practiced correspondence in more ways than they preached. In fact, for Ralph Waldo Emerson and his friends, God seemed to be a God of Motion.

CHAPTER II

The Neighborhood of Boston

RALPH WALDO EMERSON and those of similar inclination did not go begging for intellectual and emotional support. On September 19, 1836, while the publication of *Nature* was sounding a new note in Boston religious, literary, and philosophical circles, Emerson and some of his friends assembled at the home of George Ripley for an evening of serious "conversation." For some time there had been talk of initiating a club of like-minded and like-spirited Bostonians, and now at last the project seemed to be getting off the ground.

At this first meeting there were at least six persons who were present.[1] Emerson had long known George Ripley casually because they were cousins and had mentioned Ripley's doings and his prospects in journals and letters. On one occasion their similar interests had become apparent, at least to Emerson. To his delight, he had found fifteen volumes of Goethe in a Boston bookstore, only to discover that Ripley had already borrowed two to decide whether or not he wanted to buy them. A closer friend was Frederic Henry Hedge, who seemed to have been a prime mover in getting the budding Transcendentalists together. Emerson had known him from Cambridge days, and later the two corresponded while Hedge ministered to a Unitarian congregation in Bangor, Maine. Once, after reading some pieces which Hedge had written, Emerson had enthusiastically proclaimed him an "unfolding man." Even nearer to Emerson, however, was Bronson Alcott, whom he had met only the year before. Both men kept journals in which their mutual admiration was evident. Soon Emerson had begun reading Alcott's manuscripts and journals and had visited his class at the Temple School, where he was an educational innovator. And Alcott had attended his friend's winter lecture series.

James Freeman Clarke, whom Emerson may have known at Harvard, had spent some time with him in 1832 discussing Goethe and German literature as well as the Englishman Thomas Carlyle, and after their meeting they had written to one another from time to time. Finally, Emerson had been acquainted with Convers Francis, the oldest of the gathered friends, because of ministerial duties. Francis had been delighted with sermons Emerson preached at Watertown, and subsequently the two men made plans to exchange pulpits for a Sunday.

At this first meeting, the evening's discussion turned on procedural matters, since the friends were contemplating other meetings. They planned future sessions, decided on a rotation of houses, discussed suggestions for invitees. At Alcott's house for the second meeting, Ripley yielded to senior Convers Francis as chairman, and the custom continued. Members considered "American Genius—the Causes Which Hinder Its Growth, and Give Us No First Rate Productions," while later sessions concerned "The Education of Humanity" and such diverse topics as wonder and worship, innocence and guilt, Emerson's journals, property, Harvard College, law, truth, and individuality. Meetings convened on an irregular basis, often when Hedge arrived from Bangor to visit. The gatherings appear to have been interrupted in 1837—but they resumed with a common enthusiasm. Called Hedge's Club and the Aesthetic Club on various occasions, the gathered clan has come to be known in the annals of American literary history as the Transcendental Club. In its time, the membership was a casual roster of liberal Boston, as locally celebrated individuals appeared and disappeared from one meeting to the next.

Although disagreements occurred between the more extroverted and more introverted members of the group, they were not serious enough to split the Club—at least until 1840 and thereafter. A consensus seemed to exist among the friends and their growing list of acquaintances, and the close agreement expressed itself in group projects which generated a common enthusiasm. *Specimens of Foreign Standard Literature* originated in this way when Ripley's gigantic translation series of significant modern French and German works called forth the talents and energies of Transcendental scholars. Later, the Club's master project and the climax of its experience as a community would be *The Dial*.

But the core of the Transcendentalists' project lay in the conversation which had become their *raison d'etre*. It functioned as a ritual by which they affirmed to one another their shared religious worldview. Coming from the Protestant and Unitarian heritage of the Word of God and the word of the sermon, they continued to hold language sacred, and, as Lawrence Buell has shown, the written word was the extension of Transcendental conversation.[2] Curiously, though, the religious experience of the Transcendentalists, which centered on their affirmation of correspondence and their celebration of the new faith in the ritual of conversation, emerged from their collective experience of *dis*harmony. In other words, what brought them to their "holy experiment" was a disturbing sense of alienation from the accepted verities in Brahmin Boston.

In the 1820s and 1830s Boston seemed a formal and conservative city with a wealthy upper class and an established aristocracy of prestige and community stature. Josiah Quincy, first mayor of the town and later president of Harvard, acknowledged the presence of "a decided first circle in the town, to which the barriers were not easily broken."[3] The first circle ruled the city, demanded conformity to its social ideal, and expressed qualms about new democratic ideas. "On Beacon Street, the theory was frankly asserted that social sanctions ought to be applied against any who strayed from the narrow path of good sound political, economic, and religious orthodoxy."[4] The rulers of the city were devoted to the past, and the virtuous citizen would bow before the system of law which had been inherited, content with his ordained station in society and suspicious of the new. Ironically, it was a society which by its reliance on tradition was implicitly acknowledging the harmony with cosmic law which its Transcendental heirs would promulgate as a new religious vision—and interpret so differently.

Intellectual interest seemed to be everywhere in Boston—the city of the Puritans who had founded Harvard College seven years after their arrival in Massachusetts Bay. Yet a few dissenting voices were raised concerning the quality of the native wit. Timothy Dwight, for all his admiration of Boston, deplored the education of people of fashion which was merely superficial. A young man educated in this way equated fashion, dress, and etiquette with learning, for "to mingle without awkwardness or confusion in that empty, unmeaning chat, those mere vibrations of the tongue, termed fashionable conversation, is the ultimate aim of his eloquence."[5] Years later, Emerson would remark in his journal that "from 1790 to 1820, there was not a book, a speech, a conversation, or a thought, in the State."[6] And one modern scholar of the period, Conrad Wright, has noted that he agrees with the general tenor of Emerson's remark. Wright has argued that no new ideas, for instance, were offered to counter the deism of Thomas Paine. The old and usual arguments of supernatural rationalism were simply rolled out and repeated endlessly, and "the pamphlets and sermons that resulted were uncorrupted by the slightest taint of originality."[7]

If Bostonians were placid in their intellectual traits, they seemed equally so in their emotional demeanor. William Tudor wrote of the New Englanders he knew: "There are no people more capable of measured excitement, or more steadily persevering; there are none who can be made to feel so much, and, at the same time, exhibit so little exterior emotion."[8] In an account of a sermon by William Ellery Channing, Francis Grund told how the listeners were obviously affected but left the church as soon as the sermon was over "with that peculiar English propriety and undisturbed countenance, which would have led an European from the Continent to suppose they had never been affected."[9] Alexis de Tocqueville, arriving in Boston without letters of introduction, noticed a coolness and frostiness in the social air.

Side by side with the studied external indifference was an attitude of opposition to change which meant, politically, that Fed-

eralist conservatism was gradually transformed to Whig tradi-
tionalism. Through it all, the hostility to innovation which had
characterized Puritan ancestors and Federalist forebears remained.
Grund found Daniel Webster's second speech on the sub-treasury
system particularly illustrative of the Boston character: "*Do we not see
the world prosper around us?* . . . Do we not see OTHER GOVERN-
MENTS, and OTHER NATIONS, enlightened by experience, and reject-
ing ARROGANT INNOVATIONS and THEORETIC DREAMS, accomplishing
the great ends of society?"[10]

Religiously, however, Boston had changed. It had evolved from
its original Calvinist, Puritan, and Congregational covenant theology toward more liberal and Arminian views. God became more
benevolent; salvation, more all-embracing; and people, more active
and enterprising in accomplishing their ultimate task—as well as
many less spectacular goals along the way. After the turn of the
century, liberal religion, or Unitarianism, became the official creed,
and its affirmation of human nature began to pose an implicit threat
to the inherited world, since an emphasis on human activity introduced the strong likelihood of change. But it would be some time
before the threat was perceived in all its practical ramifications, and
when that happened the Unitarians who had become Transcendentalists would be regarded as revolutionaries and her-
etics from tradition.

As Unitarianism emerged, it drew its strength from the conservative social classes of Boston: urban merchants, doctors,
lawyers, and professional folk. Liberal ministers seemed to have
more of the old, wealthy, and prestigious families in their congrega-
tions. With few exceptions, they were Federalists, and Daniel
Walker Howe's book, *The Unitarian Conscience*, is an excellent study
of the cult of stasis in the Unitarian Whiggery of the antebellum period.[11] This conservatism was only reinforced by the pursuit of morality so central to Unitarian life, for the moral imperative became a
dominant means of insuring order in the relations of people to one
another.

Furthermore, both Arminians and Unitarians showed a strong
distaste for religious controversy, preferring fellowship to doctrinal

precision and prudence to complete candor. Thus, caution seemed to dictate a good measure of early Unitarian sentiment in regard to slavery. Harriet Martineau, visiting from England, found that only Samuel May, Charles Follen, and William Ellery Channing had publicly reproved the slave power. "As a body," she wrote in 1837, "they must, though disapproving slavery, be ranked as the enemies of abolitionists." Her indictment continued with greater severity: "Seeing what I have seen, I can come to no other conclusion than that the most guilty class of the community in regard to the slavery question at present is, not the slave-holding, nor even the mercantile, but the clerical."[12]

Unitarian reserve meant likewise that liberal Christians did not proselytize much. "Zeal in this way would be extremely incongruous in them; it would be like eating an ice-cream with a hot spoon."[13] In addition, reserve meant an antipathy to innovation, and the continuity between Arminians and Unitarians suggests such a stance. Indeed, Conrad Wright has pointed out that "two generations of Arminians amassed the intellectual capital on which the liberals drew in the Unitarian controversy. Their accomplishment remained relatively unchanged until Emerson and his generation began to challenge its basic presuppositions."[14] For Harriet Martineau, though, the case was relatively simple: Boston churches were "far behind the country."[15]

Proper Federalist and Unitarian Boston lived out its days in the shadow of the university at Cambridge, just three miles away over West Boston Bridge. Fully one-fourth of its students were Bostonians, and the Unitarian clergy who filled Boston pulpits received their training there, along with a cadre of other students who would return to business, professional, or Brahmin life in the city. Some observers found in Cambridge a breeding-ground for the Boston aristocracy. When Samuel Osgood, of the Class of 1832, looked back thirty years to his student days at Harvard, he admitted that there was "a good deal of a certain caste or aristocracy in college, and that much prestige is given by high family, especially when associated with a noble bearing, and either with a commanding carriage or brilliant talents."[16] Because they were based on expensive habits, some college societies set their members apart from other students, and Osgood advised a young friend against joining a club which would separate him from most of the class. While objective scholarship has established that the young blades of the aristocracy were not typical students, Martineau seemed unaware of the great unwashed. Harvard, she said, would have its "aristocratic atmosphere" "much purified by a few breezes of such democratic inspiration as issue from the school-houses of some other country districts."[17]

But the key to a Harvard education—and many said to its ills—was the recitation system. Under this method, the student would memorize an assigned section of a text, and his professor or tutor would hear him recite. During the antebellum period almost every graduate recorded his distaste for the system in which "the Faculty were not there to teach, but to see that boys got their lessons; to explain difficulties or elucidate a text would have seemed improper."[18] Still, as Samuel Eliot Morison has observed, the fixed curriculum with its system of recitation did have a saving grace in that it was only minimally demanding. This often meant free time for the college or club library where a student could browse among the books and educate himself however his whims directed him.

Whatever may have been the correctness of this portrait of a staid and dignified Boston, unflappable in the winds of change, more important was its subjective correlative in the minds of the Transcendentalists. That is, Emerson and his friends *perceived* the Boston of their fathers and grandfathers as one of outworn rigidity. They felt themselves out of tune with its rhythms which seemed ponderous and heavy, and instead of assuming that they themselves ought to conform with custom and tradition, they came to the conclusion that something was wrong with the neighborhood of Boston. Gradually, and then more quickly, as their perception of the wrongness grew, they broke away from their accustomed world in the city. In this regard, a brief glance at the early personal biographies of the charter members of the Transcendental circle will be illuminating.

Emerson himself, coming from eight generations of "emphatically clerical stock," had been born at the center of the Boston inner circle. Education echoed his earlist social formation, as he moved from the aristocratic and traditional Boston Latin School to the world of proper education at Harvard. Seven Emersons in five generations had preceded him there, but looking back on his experience Emerson was decidedly unimpressed. He confided to his journal that at Harvard the young were "oppressed by their instructors." "Meek young men," he wrote, "grow up in colleges & believe it is their duty to accept the views which books have given and grow up slaves."[19] Indeed, the "entire ship" of a Cambridge education was "made of rotten timber of rotten honey combed traditional timber without so much as an inch of new plank in the hull."[20] Years later, a mature Emerson looked back on the classes in which Latin, Greek, and Mathematics

> *became stereotyped as* education, *as the manner of men is. But the Good Spirit never cared for the colleges, and though all men and boys were now drilled in Latin, Greek and Mathematics, it had quite left these shells high and dry on the beach, and was now creating and feeding other matters at other ends of the world.*[21]

Politically, Emerson mostly conformed to the conservative image, and James Cabot, an early biographer, tells us that he passed muster as a "good Federalist, like his father, and he never . . . would have met with exclusion from any society in Boston that he cared to enter."[22] In later life, he continued to support the Whigs and even to attend their conventions. Thus, in 1842, he was telling his journal that he had "many points of sympathy with the Whigs in these dregs of Romulus," and that he could not "for a moment permit these profligate Tammany Hall & Morning Post adventurers to represent the cause of humanity and love."[23]

Yet, by the 1840s, Emerson was finding the same dull dreariness in Whiggery that he had found in Cambridge education. The Whig seemed to be a hypochondriacal doctor, hovering over the patient, thermometer in hand: "The Whig assumes sickness, and his social frame is a hospital. His total legislation is for the present distress,—a universe in slippers & flannels, with bib & pap-spoon, swallowing pills & herb-tea, whig preaching, whig poetry, whig philosophy, whig marriages." "Universal Whiggery" became an

Emersonian whipping-boy, for it was "tame & weak." "Every proclamation, dinner-speech, report of victory, or protest against the
government it publishes betrays its thin & watery blood. It is never
serene nor angry nor formidable, neither cool nor red hot."[24]

Unitarianism for him was still more flaccid. Settled as junior
pastor at the Hanover Street Church of Boston in 1829, the young
Emerson found that his new duties, such as leading public prayer
and administering communion, left him restless and dissatisfied. Finally, in a misery compounded by the death of his first wife, Ellen,
he resigned from his church and, after a nine-month respite in
Europe, returned home to write and lecture, mostly from a secular
forum. His discontent stemmed from more than youthful wan-
derlust, and his friends began to understand that he had resigned his
pastorate, not because he was irreligious, but as a protest against
dead and dying religious forms.

He found the communion service "a document of the dulness of
the race," and pitied the minister who dared not invite the people to
the communion table because "the emptiness, the dry, sore, creak-
ing formalism is too plain than that he can face a man of wit &
energy & put the invitation without shrinking."[25] In a conversation
with Divinity School students, warning them against their future
profession, he did not mince words. "A minister nowadays," he
said, "is plainest prose, the prose of prose. He is a Warming-pan, a
Night-chair at sick beds & rheumatic souls";[26] seemingly a fit com-
panion for "universal Whiggery." "The present Church rattles
ominously," he wrote to Frederic Henry Hedge; "it must vanish
presently; & we shall have a real one."[27] Unitarianism was an
"icehouse" with "coldness continually increasing"; it was "cold and
cheerless the mere creature of the understanding." Its established
churches had become "old and ossified under the accumulation of
creeds and usages." Its soul was "stealing away," "forming itself a
new body, and leaving a corpse in their [the clergy's] hands."[28] "In
the dead pond which our church is, no life appears," he continued to
mourn.

Emerson's disgust was eminently an aversion to Unitarian
preaching. As early as 1823, he had written to a friend that he was

"tired and disgusted with preaching" which he had been "accustomed to hear."[29] But when the Reverend Barzillai Frost was ordained at his church in Concord, Emerson found the goad to his discontent. "The young preacher preached from his ears & his memory, & never a word from his soul," he complained. "His sermon was loud and hollow." One Sunday it snowed, and he confessed that the "snowstorm was real, the preacher merely spectral."[30] Another preacher warranted an uncomplimentary account of how "the dull man droned & droned & wound his stertorous horn," while a third provoked Emerson to describe his effort as "the most ominous shaking of Unitarian husks & pods out of which all corn & peas had long fallen."[31]

Emerson's closest friend, Bronson Alcott, shared many of his views, as well as sharing by adoption his Boston milieu. Alcott had grown up on his parents' farm in Wolcott, Connecticut; and, following a brief career as a peddler, he wandered into the teaching profession and then into Boston. Here he made a surprising number of contacts among the first citizens of the Brahmin caste, and by marrying Abigail May, he strengthened his new associations.

Alcott's relationship with the institutional church had never been so strong nor so emotion-laden as Emerson's. With an Episcopalian mother and a Calvinist father, he had finally been confirmed at St. John's Episcopal, but he never seemed to appropriate the tradition and the language of the church to any marked degree. He had been attracted to the Unitarian clergy on his initial encounter with their preaching at Boston but little by little had become disenchanted. Like Emerson, he objected to the deadness of traditional worship and its ministers:

> *The intellect of preachers seems still wandering among the mysteries of a dark and antiquated theology. . . . They lead us through a bewildering labyrinth of theory, of book-work, far away from the ever-present and all-pervading Deity. They lead us to what man has said and thought and recorded in books, rather than to what He who made man has recorded in living character.* [32]

Alcott had already repudiated his own casual religious heritage, decrying Philadelphia Episcopalianism as a "pompous, heartless form of worship" with "nothing natural, original, or spontaneous."[33] Later, during a European trip, he was irritated because St. Paul's in London contained "effigies and echoes of the Everlasting Word—its Christ a ghost, and its priests ossified at the heart." At Westminster Abbey, he found the service "imposing," but a "spectacle merely." "There is no worship in it. A pantomimic ritual. A masked show."[34] In his own way, Alcott attempted to initiate religious reform by holding Sunday readings at his Temple School. He had a church in mind eventually, as he explained to his diary:

> A church, when it shall come, will give me full scope. Unshackled by the time-worn forms and ceremonies that cramp and stupefy the mind in the discharge of worship; having young and yet unbe-guiled spirits, whose sense is clear, whose instincts alive; and hav-ing no predecessors whose forms can narrow my movements,—I can go on in the true spirit of induction, finding what is wanted by consulting the laws of the young mind. [35]

If Alcott never attended Harvard, he implicitly rejected it by challenging the Boston educational establishment with his program of reforms. The list was long and curious, but it included in the main an opposition to recitation, the introduction of an inductive method, and the promulgation of the concept of enjoying school. A headlong confrontation came in 1836 when he published his account of liberal education in the experimental Temple School. *Conversations with Children on the Gospels* ruined both the school and Alcott's career because its openness on the subject of human birth offended proper Bostonian tastes. "Variation from received tradition . . . really wrecked the Temple School, in the opinion of Boston," wrote his biographers.[36]

The *Boston Courier* ceremoniously reported that "a clergyman living no great distance from Boston, when asked his opinion of the *Conversation on the Gospels*, said that one-third was absurd, one-third blasphemous, and one-third obscene."[37] Alcott pasted the news-paper diatribe into his commonplace book and penciled beside it,

"Rev. Andrews Norton, D.D." Norton, often dubbed the "pope" of Unitarianism, was the head of the Boston clerical empire, whose collective wrath George Ripley underlined by warning Alcott that he was resented by the preachers of the city and that its teachers were decidedly hostile to him. Feeling ran so high that, at one Friday evening conversation which Alcott held, a mob assault had been planned. The scheme did not materialize, and gradually Boston began to quiet down.

Alcott's impatience with political conservatism was reflected in his involvement in radical cuases, including his experiment in a communist society at Fruitlands. His work as an anti-slavery crusader was especially noticeable. After his marriage with Abigail May, the sister of the abolitionist minister Samuel J. May, Alcott became acquainted with William Lloyd Garrison. In 1830, he heard Garrison speak at Julien Hall; told his diary that "his lecture was full of truth and power"; and dispatched a communication on Garrison's behalf to the *Boston Daily Advertiser*. The next night he recorded that he heard Garrison again, and a few weeks later he attended "a meeting of a few individuals friendly to the abolition of slavery to concert measures for the foundation of an Anti-slavery Society in this city."[38] It was the Preliminary Anti-Slavery Society, out of which, two years afterward, came the New England Anti-Slavery Society. Some years later, Alcott was arrested and jailed for refusing to pay his town tax—to a slave-holding government, as Franklin Sanborn remembered the incident.[39]

Indeed, Alcott's behavior consistently witnessed his repudiation of the status quo and his willingness to cast off the forms and customs of the past. An enthusiastic conventioneer, he at various times felt equally at home at the Convention of Non-resistants, the Convention of the Friends of Universal Reform, and the Come-outer Convention. When he traveled in Europe, according to the humorous account of his biographer, "Vegetarian societies claimed him; associations advocating 'Total Abstinence from Intoxicating Drinks' . . . snatched at him; advocates of bathing even as much as once a day greeted him as a brother; and all the enemies of private property saw that here was a man after their own hearts."[40] He at-

tended the "Anti-Corn-Law Conferences"; met with persons involved in Promoting Health and Chastity; presented himself at a
meeting of Chartists; and at Alcott House, named in his honor,
moved with the zealots of reform.

Emerson's cousin, George Ripley, formed the third in what
might be termed the radical axis of the Transcendental charter
group. Like Emerson, he left the Unitarian ministry; like Alcott,
he ventured a communitarian experiment—the well-remembered
Brook Farm. From his youth in Greenfield, Massachusetts, Ripley
had been exposed to the same forces of order and conservation as his
friends. Greenfield citizens were virtually all "Congregationalists in
religion, Federalists in politics, and native Americans of British
ancestry; the town had one church, school, political party, town
meeting, newspaper ('A Register of *Genuine* Federalism'), code of
ethics, and a single set of leaders who were dominant in every aspect
of community life."[41]

At Harvard, Ripley carried on the Greenfield tradition by
remaining a dutiful, obedient, and generally uncomplaining student
during strong uprisings in his rebellious Class of 1823. Marriage to
Sophia Dana cemented his position in Boston *haute culture*, but soon
an instinct for inner religious experience led him further and further
into a critique of the Brahmin circles which he had joined. The Unitarianism that Ripley had adopted toward the end of his Harvard
years and that he had supported in well-known pamphlets and sermons grew more and more weighted and dull. By the late 1830s, he
was telling John Sullivan Dwight that Unitarianism needed to shed
its emotional "coldness" and mental "blindness" to new ideas. While
Unitarians "stifled religion with abstractions," Ripley sought a
"church of humanity." True liberal Christianity "established the
Kingdom of God, not in the dead past, but in the living present;
gave the spirit a supremacy over the letter." Therefore, "man should
not live by creeds, forms, or precedents, but freely and spon-
taneously in accordance with the promptings of his own nature."[42]

From 1836 to 1840, Ripley engaged in a literary feud with Andrews Norton concerning the value of miracles as Christian evidence. Norton, as an advocate of Lockean sensational philosophy,

found the chief evidence for the truth of Christianity in documented miracles, while Ripley, as a Transcendentalist, found internal evidence from the mind and intuition much more persuasive. Yet, according to Ripley's biographer, even more was at stake, for "Andrews Norton's devotion to British empiricism and to neo-classical literature was indicative of a general outlook and a way of life in which stable social values, communal intellectual responsibility, rationality and common sense prevailed. Norton was emotionally frightened by 'German rhapsody and mysticism.' "[43]

Ripley attacked this underlying value structure. He understood that Norton's view stemmed from an aristocratic concept of culture, and he accused him of snatching Christianity from the hands of ordinary people and making it the property of a scholarly few. External evidence implied witnesses and learned interpreters; intuition dwelt democratically within every person.

Politically, Ripley soon parted company with his Federalist forebears. Through Orestes Brownson and George Bancroft, he came very close to active involvement in Jacksonian politics and, even more, considered the Locofocos not radical enough. Still, he had kept a strong distrust for professional politicians and therefore would not actively affiliate with the Democratic party. "By the infelicity of their position," politicians often lost "sight of the end, in the contemplation of the means." They thought only of policy but forgot humanity. When Ripley circulated the petition seeking "atheist" Abner Kneeland's pardon after the Massachusetts Supreme Court upheld his conviction for blasphemy, he took his own radical stand for ends and against means. Humanity ought to be free, and the means of law could not legislate belief and its expression.

The dream of freedom would become concrete in the cooperative venture at Brook Farm. Ripley would grow more and more restive in his pastoral duties at the "proper" church on Purchase Street with its deteriorating urban surroundings. His concern for the "mudsill" class would translate itself into an experiment in economic and social democracy which might be a straw in the wind of egalitarian change. Indeed, the list of social reforms which members of Brook Farm later supported sounded, as Charles Crowe has observed, "like a reform catalogue of the age replete with anti-currency men, labor reformers, Grahamites, hydropaths, Swedenborgians, and representatives of dozens of reform and religious sects."[44] Ripley invited speakers on all issues, and perplexed women's rights advocates found themselves greeted with alternate boredom and hostility by Brook Farm women who voted, held office, and performed equal duties beside men.

Visiting writers and reformers admired the Brook Farm school which educated the children of the elite in a sense of freedom and personal responsibility. A combination of theory with laboratory and field work aimed to elicit from the students a spontaneous involvement in the educational process; and, meanwhile, a program in industrial arts acknowledged the existence of the machine age which surrounded them. The school's approach to learning reflected the larger community where it was hoped that abolition of a division of labor would lead each community member to freedom. And ultimately, the web of reform activities in school and community would merge into the socialism of Charles Fourier. Brook Farm would end its days as a Fourierist phalanx.

James Freeman Clarke spent his youth in Newton, Massachusetts, and his *Autobiography* painted it in terms strikingly parallel to Ripley's Greenfield. The town was composed of farmers, "conservative in their habits and opinions. Like most of the people in the country towns of Massachusetts, they were Federalists, having a great horror of Jefferson and Madison." Clarke noted "little religious activity beyond going to church twice on Sabbath," in a setting in which "revivals were unknown," and "Sunday-schools had not been invented."[45]

When Clarke attended Harvard, he found education distinctly uninspired. Much later, in his *Autobiography*, he pondered the inability of his teachers to excite the simple human curiosity of their students. "We were expected to wade through Homer as though the Iliad were a bog, and it was our duty to get along at such a rate *per diem*." The teacher's gravest duty was to hear recitations; and, according to the sacrosanct liturgy of the recitation room, "to explain difficulties to the young men before him, to help them along by happy illustration and comment, to untie the knots too hard for their young fingers to loose,—this would have been thought almost improper." He regretted the three hours daily given to this process during freshman and sophomore years when "pencil in hand, he [the teacher] listened in silence to the student's translation or solution of a problem, and having affixed the proper number to his name, went on to the next." A student could not even learn from his fellow students, since few recited well, and Clarke complained of the "condition of mental torpor" which resulted.[46]

Fresh from Harvard Divinity School, Clarke had pooled his energies and literary talents with two other young Unitarian clergymen in the booster town of Cincinnati. The result had been the *Western Messenger*, a monthly devoted to "religion and literature" as well as the "spread of a rational and liberal religion"; that is, Unitarian Christianity. But, almost immediately, he became discontent with his Western ministry in Louisville, and the *Messenger* could not distract him from a parish he served only out of a sense of duty. Finally, in 1841, he would return to Boston and begin to experiment with a new religious society, the Church of the Disciples.

Clarke shared with the other Transcendentalists an instinct for smoking out dead wood and crumbling forms, whether Calvinist "dead Orthodoxy," which he hated, or the lifelessness he found in both liberal and conservative factions of the Unitarian church. Religion for him lay "not in the form but the spirit," but unlike Emerson, Alcott, and Ripley, Clarke had not given up on the church. In the years which would follow, his new religious society was meant to clothe the spirit in new forms—on the basis of certain principles he considered essential. The social principle was translated into frequent conversational meetings; the voluntary principle became the abolition of selling, renting, or taxing pews; the principle of congregational worship became a commitment to community hymns and prayers. The sermon with its docile and silent listeners was de-emphasized, while a democracy and equality of membership "to persons of all sorts and conditions" was encouraged. In fact, Francis Peabody later recorded that the Church of the Disciples was popularly dubbed the "Church of the Carry-alls"; and in his

"Professor at the Breakfast Table," Oliver Wendell Holmes painted a picture of the "Church of the Galileans," which Peabody considered a thin disguise for Clarke's congregation. [47]

Clarke's refusal to accept the status quo was especially evident in his stand on the issue of slavery. Once he had set foot on the soil of Kentucky, he confronted it face to face. Still in the stagecoach, he had "met four negroes *chained*, preceding a moving family." "It was the first time I had seen such a sight," he wrote in horror to William Henry Channing. [48] Clarke found a public voice for his outrage—in a three-night debate in which the anti-slavery forces won, in George Prentice's Louisville *Journal*, and in the pages of his own *Western Messenger*. One reason he left Kentucky was an unwillingness to rear his family in a region which permitted slavery.

Initially, for Clarke, anti-slavery did not mean abolition. He worked actively for a while in the American Colonization Society, but after returning to Boston his position would evolve in the direction of abolition. He would learn "to think otherwise of Mr. Garrison, and to cooperate with him to a considerable extent." Sermons would begin to include such themes as the "national sin of slaveholding," "the sin of holding in bondage three millions of our brethren," "slavery in the United States," the duty of abolition, and the wrongness of the annexation of Texas. [49] Although he had previously opposed the Whigs, he would vote, in 1844, for Henry Clay and against annexation, since the annexation of Texas would mean the extension of slavery.

Like his Transcendental brothers, Clarke's reform interests would continue to expand in an extending circle. The plight of prisoners later sparked him to ponder the best methods for influencing them to the good, and the abolition of capital punishment seemed to be one. The temperance crusade called him, and he quickly involved himself with the Washingtonian movement of reformed drunkards. He proclaimed the value of the Protective Labor Union and "constructive socialism," advocated women's suffrage and their education, and supported the peace initiative. He proudly numbered reformers among his friends and pronounced himself a Locofoco.

Unlike Clarke, who became noted in Boston for his social involvement, Frederic Henry Hedge expressed his impatience with the standing order in comparative seclusion. He was the scholar of the six, careful and prudential in intellectual or social judgment, fearful of the ultraist temptations of his times. His physical isolation (in Bangor, Maine) from the rest of the group during much of the early period of their interaction seemed a concrete symbol of his intellectual and emotional stance. Like Emerson, Hedge had inherited the mantle of Brahmin intellectuality with its dedication to proper and conservative themes. Perhaps more so: his grandfather, Lemuel Hedge, had been a Loyalist minister during the Revolution; his maternal grandmother was the daughter of President Edward Holyoke of Harvard; his father, the Reverend Levi Hedge, was professor of logic and metaphysics at Harvard and author of the duly-recited text, *Elements of Logick*.

After four years' study in Germany, Hedge matriculated at Harvard where he came under the influence of Edward Everett, who had also profited from a European education. A distrust of the "dogmatism of formal metaphysics" did not prevent him from reading deeply in the history of philosophy during these years, preferring Schelling, the romantic seer, to the systematic theorizing of Hegel and his disciples. Meanwhile, the arrival of Charles Follen as a teacher of German gave an impulse to the study of the language and literature of that country, and Hedge contributed to the emerging German enthusiasm by spreading a knowledge and love of the language among his friends.

All through the early 1830s, Hedge used his scholarly talent and his wide acquaintance with German metaphysical concerns to lay the groundwork for a Transcendental faith. Coleridge, Swedenborg, Schiller, and even phrenology received his attention in articles in the *Christian Examiner*. While others in the Transcendental movement were confronted and challenged by the emerging social reform movements of the decade, Hedge pursued his own more conservative ideas, and they seemed to lead to the delights of scholarship. Although later in life he would become almost a reactionary, now a search for life, an irritation at dry husks and outgrown forms, and an affirmation of progress informed his thought and feeling in a manner similar to that of his more active friends.

In religion, he used their language and their perceptions of aridity and death, but he applied the language to "sectarian" (non-Unitarian) experience. At its best, Unitarianism had meant that "dry bones" had been "covered with the flesh and blood of a more humane and practical religion." Instead of a "gaunt creed," it provided a "living faith."[50] Men like Channing should be celebrated because they loosened adherence to sectarian and rigid views. While Emerson could speak of "corpse-cold Unitarianism," Hedge found it alive and well. The corpse was only poor old Calvinism.

Hedge's disaffiliation with aspects of Boston Brahminism was expressed implicitly in his endorsement of the rising spirit of a new age. He viewed the practical genius of America with a strong sense of approval and praised the cult of self-education in the farmer, who was a "practical chemist," as well as the "mechanic in his workshop," the lawyer, the merchant, the banker, and the broker. He pointed with pride to the pragmatic tendency of American knowledge and inventiveness: there had been Benjamin Franklin and the capture of electricity, Robert Fulton and the application of the Watt steam engine to navigation, Eli Whitney and the cotton gin. He applauded "the aeronaut, who spurns the earth in his puffed balloon," and, in a Fourth of July oration, he speculated on how increased mechanization would shorten working hours; how wood, iron, and gas would take the place of manual labor. "Unseen powers shall labour and drudge," he prophesied.[51]

Hedge saw nineteenth-century America through progressive lenses: "A new discovery, another invention, and society, like a horde of wandering gypsies, must take up its march anew, and move its kitchen-utensils to the next resting place." His caution was lest practicality interfere with intellectual culture and progress ultimately be slowed: "The zeal for application is apt to interfere with the zeal for progress. . . . While the uses of knowledge only, are regarded, the kingdom of knowlege will advance but slowly."[52]

He agreed with the other Transcendentalists in some suspicion of materialism and saw a threat to liberty in the disparity between rich and poor and the "growing luxury of our cities." He felt a similar dis-ease in the presence of political ambition, the love of office and money, the American penchant for imitating other nations. But these qualifications on American experience did not prevent his being swept up in a wave of enthusiasm. The "surplus activity" of Americans was expended on trade instead of war, and "an abounding energy, a quick conceiving spirit of enterprise, and an indomitable force of purpose are ever goading us on to that which all prize." The national pursuit of wealth stemmed from vigor rather than concupiscence; and, he continued: "There is no sea which our flag has not explored. All the waters of the globe, from the arctic to the antarctic circle, are witnesses of our commerce. Paths of adventure . . . are familiar to our people."[53]

Finally, Convers Francis, the senior member of the Transcendental group, shared with the others a background in the environs of well-ordered Boston. As preparation for Harvard, he had attended Dr. Hosmer's Academy in West Cambridge and later described the institution in his *Autobiography:*

> *There was an air of aristocracy about it; sons of rich men from other towns came to it as boarding scholars; and only "the better sort," in the town, sent their children to it. It was quite a different thing from the common town school, where Tom, Dick, and Harry, everybody's boys, and everybody's girls, went as a matter of course. The academy was for the* elite.[54]

After his ordination to the ministry, Francis, in his political conservatism, followed the pattern typical of Unitarian pastors. His connection with the church brought him into touch with the political establishment, as at Brattle Street, Boston, where he preached before a congregation which included Daniel Webster, whose "presence seemed to give dignity even to a religious service"; and at Quincy, where on several exchange visits he "dined with the venerable Mr. Adams," once leaving a sermon for the old Federalist to read.[55] His own pastorate at Watertown put Francis near the pinnacle of the town's political hierarchy, for "Church and Town were still one; the minister was the Minister of the Town, settled by the town and paid out of the town taxes. All church business was transacted with the town business in Town Meeting. All Town Meetings were held in the Meeting House."⁵⁶

But Francis's sister was Lydia Maria Child, an ardent abolitionist; through his correspondence with her, Francis grew to learn more and more of the sufferings of the slaves and the work of the anti-slavery movement. She treated her brother to graphic descriptions of the oppression of blacks as well as perceptive social analysis. Slaves kept in Southern prisons existed under conditions "too loathsome and horrid for the worst of criminals," while the individuals who really promoted the mobs were "manufacturers who supply the South, merchants who trade with the South, politicians who trade with the South, ministers settled at the South, and editors patronized by the South."⁵⁷ Francis at least once cautioned Lydia to be prudent in her anti-slavery activity, but he quickly aligned himself with the forces promoting liberation. Theodore Parker, years later, wrote to his friend remembering that Francis "early took a deep, warm interest in the anti-slavery enterprise, when its friends were few, feeble, and despised"; that he "helped the great cause of human freedom, not merely by word and work, but by the silent and subtle force of example."⁵⁸ When abolitionist Elijah P. Lovejoy was murdered by a mob in Alton, Illinois, Francis "would not in conscience omit the notice of such an atrocity" and would make the outrage the subject of his Thanksgiving Day sermon for 1837.

The Watertown church which Francis led made a quiet and uneventful transition from Calvinism to liberalism over a period of time. Yet an undercurrent of the Transcendental radicalism which went beyond liberalism had surfaced already in Francis's youth, as his *Autobiography* reveals. "Many were the reveries, the dreamy, sweet thoughts, I had on the morning and night excursions in driving the cows to pasture, or bringing them home. The sky and the woods and the brooks came into the boy's soul, and shone and waved and rolled there; God was with him, and he was with God, though he knew not of it."⁵⁹ And, early in his ministry, he complained to his diary of problems with his preaching. While other Transcendentalists attacked the deadness of the Unitarian preaching they heard, Francis's attack moved against his own. He felt "cold and indifferent" in the very act of preaching and experienced "a total want of interest in the services, or, in the language of the Methodists, 'was shut up.'" Over a period of years the lament remained the same: "So I go from Sabbath to Sabbath, nobody caring what I preach, and to most of my people, probably, a post, if it could be made to utter any sounds, would do as much good as I do."[60]

Meanwhile, by 1836, Francis's growing study of German themes and literature informed his observation:

> *I have long seen that the Unitarians must break into two schools,—the Old one, or English school, belonging to the sensual and empiric philosophy,—and the New one, or the German school (perhaps it may be called), belonging to the spiritual philosophy. The last have the most truth; but it will take them some time to ripen, and meanwhile they will be laughed at, perhaps, for things that will appear visionary and crude. But the great cause of spiritual truth will gain far more by them than by the others.*[61]

By the tenor of his public speaking, he woud risk being counted in the camp of the new and heretical party. One journal entry summarized the fine line which Francis subsequently was required to walk in order to keep his respectability and his intuitions: "On Thursday I preached the lecture in Boston, and the sermon, I believe, gave some satisfaction to those who have been disposed to accuse me of the horrible crime of Transcendentalism!"[62]

Whether or not Francis's complicity was recognized on that occasion, what is clear about the crime of Transcendentalism is that it began in disenchantment. The life-orientation system which was normative in Brahmin Boston did not fit the forms of inner experience which Emerson and his friends wanted to see reflected in their world. Those who met in the Transcendental Club recognized themselves as a community which originated in a shared perception that something was amiss, that world did not agree with spirit, and that Boston violated inner being. In such a situation, correspondence did not mean a revolution in the self in order to be re-Brahminized;

rather, it meant a search for new forms of the world with which one could identify and to which one could realize correspondence.

How might the Transcendentalists proceed? In what way might they conduct the search for a world in which the various pieces fit together harmoniously? Surely there was at least one form of the world which they could shape to their spirits with hope of some success. The Transcendentalists would find that malleable structure in language. Words were internal in that they were formulated in the processes of individual thought. At the same time, they were external in that they were broadcast by being spoken and had been the gift of a cultural community to the individual who had learned to think and speak with them. Words, therefore, provided a bridge between inner spirit and outer world. Participating in both, they offered the one best hope for initiating the harmony which the Transcendentalists desired in the totality of things.

Furthermore, there was another reason why these New Englanders should begin to remedy their experience of disharmony by remodeling language. With their long and powerful tradition of intellectuality, as well as their inherent suspicion of feeling gone out of control, a lack of correspondence would be perceived first in those forms which were more intellectual. It is not surprising, therefore, that Transcendental discomfort with the inherited world should focus on a distaste for its language. The word which expressed the relationship between microcosm and macrocosm must be a true, that is, a *corresponding*, word. In this context, a search for the cosmos which reflected Transcendental inner being would begin with the promulgation of a new language.

This word had power, first of all, to bring order out of chaos, to name the confused and evasive subtlety of inner perception, and thus to pin down its meaning. Only by knowing the meaning, the pattern which had become the inner arrangement of the mind, could the possibility exist of discovering its correlate in the world. We have already spoken, in the introduction, of the threefold movement of externalization, objectivation, and internalization as a way of understanding the circular process of language.[63] For the Transcendentalists, hence, language would give a way to externalize and objectify private experience. Once this was done, the world as word could be internalized to authenticate structures of consciousness Transcendental. More simply, by speaking the word which reflected inner being accurately, inner meaning began to possess an externality, as objectivity outside the self. Since the word was now "out there," it could be used as a kind of sensor in the search for forms of the world which answered to an inner condition. And the sensor could attract these forms and meanings in a string of analogies in which the world mirrored itself on a multiplicity of levels. It was this new and weighted word which could then be internalized. The Transcendentalists, therefore, could become immersed in the intricate structure of the cosmos; they could acquire a security and a confirmation which, paradoxically, would make the conservatism of Brahmin Boston seem poorly grounded by comparison.

The word had power also to express that sense of the overwhelming fitness of things which the Transcendentalists had discovered. It was a nuanced word, colored with feeling—with hope, joy, antipathy, and ambivalence reflecting the uncertainty of the experience of the search. Thus, while the word brought order to the world, it did so only relatively. It also disclosed the ambiguity which is characteristic of "natural" patterns of thought. While scientific thought demanded precision, the word of the Transcendentalists would require looseness and flexibility. For this reason, it would take shape in those forms of language which most exactly rendered the tentative nature of perception: it would use the language of poetry in both verse and prose rhythms.

Finally, the word had power—although partial and incomplete—to communicate to other human beings the quality of Transcendental experience. Communication was important because there were many worlds of human meaning with which presumably it was possible to discover one's correspondence. Emerson and Alcott had shared this revelation as the secret energy of their friendship. "Alcott," Emerson once mused, "is a certain fluid in which men of a certain spirit can easily expand themselves & swim at large, they who elsewhere found themselves confined."[64] Communication was also important because mission and example were still values for these descendants of the Puritans who had gone on an "errand into the wilderness" and begun the task by building their "city upon a hill." The Unitarian moral philosophy, which had been the most recent conduit for these values, would not be lost on the heirs to Boston's Unitarian establishment. They would rework the message and transform it into their own. For, if correspondence was indeed the truth of things, the charter members of the Transcendental Club could do no other than preach and teach it by example.

In sum, the condemnation of "death" in Boston would lead to the search for a macrocosm which could harmonize with the consciousness of Emerson and his friends. The Transcendentalists would find a bridge into that macrocosm through linguistic structure. And since the dominant motif in the experience of these New Englanders was mental, the exploration could begin comfortably and easily. When the rectification of language had illuminated the microcosm of Transcendental inner experience and meaning, there would be a greater possibility of discovering those external spheres of the world with which it harmonized. As we shall see, the Transcendentalists agreed very strongly that their language must fit both themselves and their world, while their critics complained bitterly because that language jarred the sensitivities of the older residents of the neighborhood of Boston.

CHAPTER **III**

The Kinetic Revolution

In 1837, the scholarly and conservative Francis Bowen penned an article for the Unitarian *Christian Examiner*. "They have deepened the gulf between speculative and practical men," he wrote in horror, "and by their innovations in language, they are breaking down the only bridge that spans the chasm."[1] "They" were the Transcendentalists, and Bowen's remark was a feeble disclaimer compared to Andrews Norton's denunciation the following year. Writing in a widely circulated Boston paper in response to Emerson's "Divinity School Address" (15 July 1838), he first castigated an unnamed but clearly identified Transcendentalist.

> *He floats about magnificently on bladders, which he would have it believed are swelling with ideas. —Common thoughts, sometimes true, oftener false, and "Neutral nonsense, neither false nor true," are exaggerated, and twisted out of shape, and forced into strange connexions, to make them look like some grand and new conception.*

Norton continued the attack:

> *To produce a more striking effect, our common language is abused, antic tricks are played with it; inversions, exclamations, anomalous combinations of words, unmeaning, but coarse and violent, metaphors abound, and withal a strong infusion of German barbarisms.*[2]

56

Three days later, in response to Norton's diatribe, the newspaper published a letter by Theophilus Parsons ("S. X.") making a plea for responsible criticism of the "New School." If Norton were to be taken at his word, Parsons wrote, then "all who believed that the fountains of truth are neither sealed nor exhausted, are in fact directed to this new school as to friends who would favor progress." Once antiquity had been the acceptable standard of truth, but those days were past, and the human mind was now "abroad upon a pathless sea, and the waves are high, the sky is dark, and the winds are loud and angry. But for all this, beyond the clouds the sun still shines; and even the pathless ocean is bounded by the steadfast land; and who can fear the triumph or perpetuity of error."[3] Norton's reaction was angry and immediate. Two days after the Parsons letter, his condemnation appeared, telling readers: "A great part of the Reply consists of remarks concerning old and new opinions, somewhat too extravagantly and poetically expressed, and too much in the language of the New School."[4]

Transcendental innovators, like latter-day Galileans, could be recognized by their language, and good Unitarians would accordingly watch their tongues or pens. For the manner of Transcendental speaking clearly did not agree with that of former mentors such as Andrews Norton. Emerson and the other members of the New School did not think they had very much in common with the reactionary Norton, but at least they agreed with him on this one point: they were consciously speaking a different language, and Emerson, as we have already seen, had spelled out the theory which governed it. The worldview of correspondence meant that there was an essential, rather than an accidental, connection between a new word and a new apprehension of an object. Language clothed nature

> as the air clothes the earth, taking the exact form and pressure of every object. Only words that are new fit exactly the thing, those that are old like old scoriae that have been long exposed to the air and sunshine, have lost the sharpness of their mould and fit loosely. But in new objects and new names one is delighted with the plastic nature of man as much as in picture or sculpture.[5]

Yet the exact fit of even the newest word could hardly endure the moment, since the quality of the imagination, for Emerson, was "to flow, and not to freeze." All symbols were "fluxional"; all language was "vehicular and transitive." It was "good, as ferries and horses are, for conveyance, not as farms and houses are, for homestead."[6] In the old Greek myth, Charon the ferryman carried the souls of the dead across the River Styx to a land of mystery and terror. For Emerson, the right word played the role of Charon, ferrying the souls who rode with it to a land of heightened life in shared experience. But even with his new religion of correspondence to support him, Emerson recognized a separation between what he longed for and the place where time and again his own best language led him. For the most part, he felt, "a Lethean stream washes through us and bereaves us of ourselves." The linguistic Charon, who manned the boat and mediated the experience a person tried so earnestly to name, lay asleep in the vessel. "We come to speak with those who most fully accord in life and doctrine with ourselves, and lo! what mountains high and rivers wide. How still the word is to seek which can like a ferryman transport either into the point of view of the other."[7]

In admitting the inability to maintain the exact fit between word and thing and in acknowledging that even language on the move never quite caught up with reality, Emerson was revealing that he had been shaped more by his past than he himself cared to admit. Bound up with his experience was a sharply defined separation between sacred and profane as well as a correspondence between microcosm and macrocosm. Emerson and his friends were moving toward a goal, but they had not yet arrived. The language of motion which they began so eagerly to propound was tied to the motif of the journey, so that they experienced a separation between their ordinariness and their aspirations, and their movement seemed in part to be an old-fashioned pilgrimage.

Still, Emerson had stated that language must change with a changing world, and the law of correspondence meant that the best words should reflect nineteenth-century forms of the world. "Old scoriae" had to yield to new images which corroborated Transcendental experience, as Emerson's colleagues agreed. Clarke, for one, thought that "when men are compelled, by fear of denunciation, to speak their grandfathers' language instead of their own, their words seem empty to themselves." In the sixteenth century, it was a "hearty spontaneous faith which the first Reformers placed in their symbols," which "satisfied fully the want of *their* minds." But the past could not imprison the present or the future for "no human work, nor any human words can feed and nourish successive generations. Each generation looks with different feelings and through a different culture at the great truths of Heaven and Earth. They need a new language to express their faith. The old words do not satisfy them."[8] "The mind of a people imprints itself in its speech," Hedge argued, "as the light in a picture of Daguerre."[9] And Ripley deplored the reluctance of some to acknowledge the faith of others who expressed "allegiance to Christ in a language at variance with our own."[10]

Bronson Alcott, meanwhile, celebrated the energizing word, and Convers Francis found in the Gospel the "word of life" which would "go forth subduing and blessing the world."[11] Each in his own way was providing a clue to what was at stake in the shift to a new language. Emerson, their acknowledged leader, described his circle as the party of the future. In contrast to Puritan and Unitarian contemporaries who, he said, formed the party of the past, he hailed a new consciousness and proclaimed young men "born with knives in their brain." These blades of the movement, whetted on the documents of German idealism and British romanticism, had begun to express the "newness" in a language which suited their intuitions. Its content included traditional religious symbols used by their contemporaries as well as metaphors and similes taken from wild nature, long a source of inspiration for mystics and poets. It is true that the Trancendentalists emphasized the language of nature more than their immediate forebears, but this observation should not exclude another: Emerson in *Nature* had made it clear that in the strict sense the term nature included human beings and their technology, products of their "natural" brains. By implication, then, it included history and historical traditions. The Transcendentalists, who in many cases persevered in their Unitarian commitment, did not simply and completely throw off civilization in favor of the wilderness, nor tradition in favor of flower gardens and sunsets. What was new about their language in the context of Brahmin Boston was its *style* more than its content: it was written in the kinetic mode. From the churchly side, the Christian God along with his paraphernalia of word and sacrament joined the camp of motion. From the "natural" side, water became river, stream, current, ocean, and tide; light became burning flame or fire. Symbols—such as wind, breath, bird, or wing; path, journey, horse, and rider; bow and arrow; circle and circulation; string of beads, and changing garment; birth and nurtured growth—all proclaimed a new religion of process inaugurating a future of eternal energy.

Perhaps more than any of the other Transcendentalists, except Alcott, Emerson expressed the revolution in both style and content. The day after the charter meeting of the Club, he reported that the members had agreed that "no man should look at the spout but only at the flowing water." The metaphor was indicative, for Emerson's favorite form of expression for the flux of things was moving water. His writings and public lectures revealed his keen delight in it. More often than not, even when water was not specifically named, its presence in a religious context was evident. The source of language was thought, and Transcendental thoughts were "holy" when they came "floating up . . . in magical newness from the hidden Life."[12] Thought itself was but one facet of a total world "plastic and fluid in the hands of God," "ever flint" only to ignorance and sin. Nature was in "continual flux," and if a person did not resist "the law of his mind," the human being would be "filled with the divinity which flows through all things."[13] Sometimes the water ran in currents or streams identified more explicitly, as when Emerson discussed the synchronicity of thought in different parts of the world with Margaret Fuller: "And are you not struck with a certain subterranean current of identical thought that bubbles up to daylight in very remote & dissimilar circles of thought & culture?" Sometimes the very life of a person was the stream, as when he complained of his "strait limitations" after age thirty. "The stream feels its banks, which it had forgotten in the run & overflow of the first meadows." "When the tide ebbs & the stream of life runs low in the mud—Then we say We once have risen to yonder bank of rich flowers & have reflected a heaven of stars."[14]

Indeed, the river expressed Emerson's idea of how an individual human life fitted into the general schema of humanity and the larger one of the universe. Human life and thought were

> *a stream whose source is hidden. . . . When I watch that flowing river, which, out of regions I see not, pours for a season its streams into me, I see that I am a pensioner; not a cause but a surprised spectator of this ethereal water; that I desire and look up and put myself in the attitude of reception, but from some alien energy the visions come.*[15]

As each person received the energy, the mandate was not to stand fast but, rather, to flow with it:

> *Nature ever flows, stands never still. Motion or change is her mode of existence. The poetic eye sees in Man the Brother of the River, & in Woman the sister of the River. Their life is always transition. Hard blockheads only drive nails all the time; forever remember; which is fixing. Heroes do not fix but flow, bend forward ever & invent a resource for every moment.*[16]

Ego melted away into the supra-personal as Emerson confessed:

> *Above his life, above all creatures I flow down forever a sea of benefit into races of individuals. Nor can the stream ever roll backward or the sin or death of a man taint the immutable energy which distributes itself into men as the sun into rays or the sea into drops.*[17]

Like all rivers, his eventually met the sea. Conversation had its "tides"; the human heart could be "a sea that hates an ebb"; human life was a sea on which people might go "floating drifting far & wide." Time itself was a sea on which nations and races flitted by without leaving so much as a ripple, but the "tides of the Infinite" which rolled "their everlasting circles" lay within. "A man, I am the remote circumference, the skirt, the thin suburb or frontier post of God, but go inward & I find the ocean; I lose my individuality in its waves." It was more fitting to say "I become" than "I am." Sun, stars, and persons were "the first ripples & wavelets of the vast inundation of the All which is beyond & which I tend & labor to be."[18] Within and yet beyond, this All existed in continual but contrasting relationship with time and bounded human life. The finite was the "foam of the infinite," challenging each person to leave the shore. Emerson warned against the worship of "the dull God Terminus & not the Lord of Lords." "Dare rather," he urged, "to quit the platform, plunge into the sublime seas, dive deep, & swim far, so shall you come back with self respect, with new power, with an advanced experience, that shall explain & overlook the old."[19] Limitation led to the unlimited, the well-defined to the indescribable, and it was an error to "ask a description of the countries towards which you sail." "The only mode of obtaining an answer," Emerson said, was to "forego all such curiosity," accepting "in a trance of praise the great tide of Being that floats us into the secret of nature."[20]

The blowing wind intrigued him, whether he praised the lyceum circuit with its "charter like the wind," or proclaimed in time a drying wind for "the seedfield of today's thoughts which are dank & warm & wet & low-bent." The wind brought its secret of new life, so that "the old things rattle louder & louder & will soon blow away." And he confided to Thomas Carlyle that "the air we breathe is so vital that the Past serves to contribute nothing to the result."[21] All manner of Emersonian riders crept on the back of the wind— among them human experience:

> In its grub state it cannot fly, it cannot shine, it is a loathsome maggot. But suddenly, without observation, the selfsame thing unfurls beautiful wings and is an angel of wisdom. So is there no fact, no event, how intimate how great soever in our history, which shall not sooner or later lose its adhesive inert form, & astonish & rejoice us by soaring from our body into the Empyrean.[22]

The law had "eagle wings & its own path to heaven & to earth," and at least one person, Bronson Alcott, was "self poised, eagle winged, & advancing." But all people possessed wings and could therefore ride the wind:

> As the wandering sea bird which crossing the Ocean alights on some rock or islet to rest for a moment its wings & to look back on the wilderness of waves behind & forward to the wilderness of waters before, so stand we perched on this rock or shoal of time arrived out of the Immensity of the Past & bound & road ready to plunge into immensity again. [23]

The wind beckoned its message to others. There was the "noble steed" which countered the "numb palsy" with "revolution & regeneration," and the arrow of human endeavor which must not be scrutinized instead of its mark. In the spirit of the Industrial Revolution, there was the locomotive Destiny, which perhaps outstripped the wind in speed, and which "never seen, we yet know must be hitched on to the cars wherein we sit."[24] There were "the electrical currents which pass invisible through all things & thro' us, & then once interrupted break into dazzling light. Show they not me the force of a still nature in man."[25]

Manifestly, Emerson thrilled to speed, lamenting the tortoise pace of most human beings.

> Beautiful leaping of the squirrel up the long bough of a pine then instantly on to the stem of an oak & on again to another tree. This motion & the motion of a bird is the right perfection for foresters as these creatures are. They taste the forest joy. Man creeps along so slowly through the woods that he is annoyed by all the details & loses the floating exhaling evanescent beauty which these speedy movers find. [26]

He was astonished by "the irresistibleness of the fall of the lightning from a cloud," and decided the experience proved he had not tested "the possibilities of power & speed in the will or in moral nature." Paradoxically, mobility appeared to him as the only permanent state of his generation; form was fleeting, and "the necessity by which Deity rushes into distribution into variety & particles, is not less divine than the unity from which all begins."[27] It was significant that conversation at a Transcendental Club meeting awaited the rushing presence of the god:

> *In common hours society sits cold & statuesque. We all stand waiting, empty, knowing possibly that we can be full. . . . Then cometh the god & converts the statues into fiery men, & by a flash of his eye burns up the veil which shrouded all things & the meaning of the very furniture, of cup & saucer, of chair & clock & tester is manifest. The facts which loomed so large in the fogs of yesterday . . . have strangely changed their proportions all that we reckoned settled shakes now & rattles and literatures, cities, climates, religions leave their foundations & dance before our eyes.*[28]

"When a man rests he stinks," Emerson once remarked. He wrote in his journal that "if anything could stand still, it would be instantly crushed & dissipated by the torrent which it resisted, & if it were a mind, it would be crazed."[29] Clearly, he intended a contrast with the party of memory, and one suspects that a reference to Andrews Norton or other "stationary" Christians was implied. Emerson wrote to his friend, Samuel G. Ward, that "not in his goals but in his transition man is great, and the truest state of mind rested in becomes false."[30] Transition was the condition of nature, myth, and all of life.

> *Nothing is to me more welcome nor to my recent speculation more familiar than the Protean energy by which the brute horns of Io become the crescent moon of Isis, and nature lifts itself through everlasting transition to the higher & the highest. Whoever lives must rise & grow. Life like the nimble Tartar still overleaps the Chinese wall of distinctions that had made an eternal boundary in our geography.*[31]

Transition came from a divine imperative, for "the voice of the Almighty saith, Onward for evermore!" "God invents, God advances. The world, the flesh, & the devil sit & rot."[32]

Invited to speak on a number of public occasions, Emerson used the lecture platform to carry on his war with the "stationary" powers of settled Unitarian existence and spread his Transcendental gospel. In "The American Scholar," for example, the Universal Mind became "one central fire, which, flaming now out of the lips of Etna, lightens the capes of Sicily, and now out of the throat of Vesuvius, illuminates the towers and vineyards of Naples"; it was "one light which beams out of a thousand stars." Revealing the mystery of correspondence, mind and nature were intertwined:

> *There is never a beginning, there is never an end, to the inexplicable continuity of this web of God, but always circular power returning into itself. . . . Far too as her splendors shine, system on system shooting like rays, upward, downward, without centre, without circumference,—in the mass and in the particle, Nature hastens to render account of herself to the mind.* [33]

For the person in touch with the divine, said Emerson, the firmament flowed. If that person would be a scholar, he or she must possess an "active soul," which resisted being warped by an attractive book out of its own orbit and "made a satellite instead of a system." Inaction was "cowardice." The true scholar must cherish a "heroic mind," for action was "the raw material out of which the intellect moulds her splendid products." The scholar would rejoice that "the literature of the poor, the feelings of the child, the philosophy of the street, the meaning of household life, are the topics of the time." "New vigor" was signaled "when the extremities are made active, when currents of warm life run into the hands and the feet." [34]

The war between the New School and the old carried itself within Unitarian walls in the "Divinity School Address." Remarks deprecating traditional Christian institutions and doctrine, addressed to a senior divinity class and their faculty at Cambridge, could only be construed by the Unitarian hierarchs as open heresy. Despite Emerson's naive protestation of bewilderment, he had created an uproar. He told his audience that the Puritan creed was "passing away" without replacement. "The stationariness of religion" showed the falsity of contemporary theology. Yet "all attempts to protect and establish a Cultus with new rites and forms" were "vain," for "faith made its own forms." The remedy for dying forms was soul, which would render the forms "plastic and new." "A whole popedom of forms," he exhorted, "one pulsation of virtue can uplift and vivify." Since the pulsation did not come, contemporary Christianity rankled him: "The word Miracle, as pronounced by Christian churches, gives a false impression; it is Monster. It is not one with the *blowing* clover and the *falling* rain" (emphasis mine). Unitarian Christianity simply could not move with nature: it did not and could not ride the wind. Hence, Emerson was looking elsewhere for a true faith which would "blend with the light of rising and of setting suns, with the flying cloud, the singing bird, and the breath of flowers."[35]

Emerson had begun his annual custom of public lecture series because he needed money after his resignation from the ministry. During the winter of 1836–37, he spoke on the philosophy of history, and the twelve lectures offered him a broad framework within which to explain his new themes. Thus, in "Art" he told his listeners that all departments of life were "emanations of a Necessity . . . instant and alive, and dissolving man as well as his works, in its flowing beneficence." The creation of a work of art meant that "the iron lids of Reason were unclosed" and "the individual mind became for the moment the vent of the mind of humanity."[36] "Literature" meant that "the Drama, Biography, History, Songs, Law Reports, Sermons, Reviews, Newspapers are but the various pipes through which the same Musician bloweth."[37] The legal code of a nation, as evinced by "Politics," was "the high-water mark showing how high the last tide rose."[38]

"Religion" was, in essence, virtue, for "the world as it whirls round its solar centre sings this perpetual hymn and nature writes it in flaming characters of meteor, orb, and system on every far and silent wall of the Temple of Space."[39] The moving temple was inhabited by men and women of honor who, in "Manners," were described as "fountains." "Ethics" made clear that authentic fountains possessed a certain direction: "There is one direction to every man in which unlimited space is open to him. . . . On that side all obstruction is taken away and he sweeps serenely over God's depths into an infinite sea." The person bound up with evil was "not in the current of things, but an outlaw, a stoppage," and "the wheels of God must grind him to powder in their very mission of charity."[40]

During the following winter Emerson gave a course of ten lectures on human culture, and again the public forum provided a chance to shape and communicate an evangel in which God was in motion and flux was his clearest sign. In the opening lecture, traditional Unitarian moral concern outran the locomotive. Human aspiration was

> the centrifugal force in moral nature, the principle of expansion resisting the tendency to consolidation and rest. The first consequence of a new position is a new want. . . . We cannot go fast enough on our own legs, and so we tame the horse. The horse can no more equal the ideal speed, and so we forge and build the locomotive. The ideal still craves a speed like a cannon ball, a speed like a wish, and the inventive and practical faculties will never cease to toil for this end. [41]

In "The Head," the focus shifted to the intellectual life in which the intellect "pierces the form and overleaps the wall, detects the intrinsic likeness between remote things, and as a menstruum dissolves all things into a few principles."[42] In "The Heart," Emerson introduced the philosopher as the "soul of vegetation" who entered "the sap that bubbled up from the root," while for all people, culture opened "the pores of the soul," allowing the "generous blood to circulate from the heart to the extremities."[43] "Holiness" traced the divinizing process in which "the surges of everlasting nature enter into me and I become less and less a private will, more truly public and human in my regards and actions." The moments of surrender to this inspiration were "years of the mind." "The forms, the books, which are called religions are nothing but the monuments and landmarks men have erected to commemorate these moments, and to fix, if it were possible, their too volatile Spirit."[44]

The religious orientation which ran through Emerson's lectures gained final written form in many cases in his essays. In the first series of these essays, "History" acknowledged that changes came "in splendid variety," "all putting questions to the human spirit." To that of the formation of character, the wise individual would find an answer "in the running river and the rustling corn."[45] And in "Self-reliance," the "murmur of the brook and the rustle of the corn" echoed the independent voice of the person who lived with God. Intuition became the "fountain of action and of thought." The simple mind, which imbibed divine wisdom, saw "old things pass away,—means, teachers, texts, temples fall."[46]

The brief poem by Emerson which introduced his essay, "Compensation," told of the "wings of Time," the "changing moon" and the "tidal wave," the "electric star" and the "lonely Earth" which was a "makeweight flying to the void." For "all that Nature made thy own, / Floating in air or pent in stone, / Will rive the hills and swim the sea / And, like thy shadow, follow thee." Always, life was "a progress, and not a station."[47] "Spiritual Laws" repeated the perception, and "Love" was a kindled fire which lighted "the whole world and all nature with its generous flames." Meanwhile, "Friendship" transformed flame into jet as Emerson asked rhetorically, "What is so pleasant as these jets of affection which make a young world for me again?" "The systole and diastole of the heart," he affirmed, were "not without their analogy in the ebb and flow of love."[48]

In "The Over-soul," Emerson's gospel of motion received perhaps its most distinct expression. Immediately behind each person, the soul—clothed in the "web of events" as a "flowing robe"—was the empowering force. "When it breathes through his intellect, it is genius; when it breathes through his will, it is virtue; when it flows through his affection, it is love." Yet the soul participated in larger reality, and revelation granted "an influx of the Divine mind into our mind," "an ebb of the individual rivulet before the flowing surges of the sea of life." In this all-encompassing sacredness, true communion with one another could be found: "By the same fire, vital, consecrating, celestial, which burns until it shall dissolve all things into the waves and surges of an ocean of light, we see and know each other, and what spirit each is of."[49] "Circles," in turn, reiterated the thesis of continual motion which shaped the message of "The Over-soul." Emerson explained that human life was a "self-evolving circle, which, from a ring imperceptibly small, rushes on all sides outwards to new and larger circles, and that without end. The extent to which this generation of circles, wheel without wheel, will go, depends on the force or truth of the individual soul." There were "no fixtures in nature"; the universe was "fluid and volatile"; permanence, "a word of degrees." The only securities were "life, transition, the energizing spirit." "People wish to be settled; only as far as they are unsettled is there any hope for them."[50]

Introducing his second series of essays, Emerson presented "The Poet" whose eyes, "like meteors," "rived the dark," "overleapt the horizon's edge," and "saw the dance of nature." The poet was gifted in that he or she perceived the "flowing or metamorphosis" of nature with its evolutionary impulse to higher forms of life, inspiring speech to flow "with the flowing of nature." Moreover, the true poet did not spurn the new forms—such as factory villages and railroads—which nineteenth-century America had created: "Nature adopts them very fast into her vital circles, and the gliding train of cars she loves like her own."[51] "Experience" spelled out the metaphor of travel in what Michael Cowan has called "the essay's most compelling structural device."[52] Emerson described the life of each human being as a staircase with steps below and steps above; as a ship which sought to anchor but found the anchorage "quicksand"; as a "train of moods like a string of beads" which each person passed through. "Everything good is on the highway," he asserted. "We live amid surfaces, and the true art of life is to skate well on them."[53]

Travel characterized even "Manners," which "aid our dealing and conversation as a railway aids travelling, by getting rid of all avoidable obstructions of the road and leaving nothing to be conquered but pure space."[54] In the essay "Nature," the "foaming brook" inspired compunction, for "if our own life flowed with the right energy, we should shame the brook."[55] "Politics" shifted from the individual to the collective and reaffirmed the fluidity of society.

Only the young citizen misconstrued what was present, for he saw society "in rigid repose, with certain names, men and institutions rooted like oak-trees to the centre, round which all arrange themselves the best they can." The old statesman, however, knew the truth, "that society is fluid; there are no such roots and centres, but any particle may suddenly become the centre of the movement and compel the system to gyrate round it."[56] And "Nominalist and Realist" underscored the point: "The rotation which whirls every leaf and pebble to the meridian, reaches to every gift of man, and we all take turns at the top."[57] In the vortex, hierarchy and social station were unstrung; fixed order and settled existence sent spinning. Democracy and leveling, change and the flux of things were the new "lords of life."

When we turn to Emerson's friends and followers in the New School, the language of motion is equally apparent in varying formations and patterns. Both Bronson Alcott and George Ripley shared with Emerson a position on the more radical end of the Transcendental spectrum, and each of the two shared a number of similarities with the other. Both Alcott and Ripley were as involved as Emerson in public controversy. Both theorized extensively in private and in public, and both put theory into practice in their respective communitarian experiments, Fruitlands and Brook Farm.

Controversy had overwhelmed Alcott because he was a man in love with the symbolism of birth. There was the intriguing passage in his journal: "Fluids form solids. Mettle [sperm] is the Godhead proceeding into the matrix of nature to organize Man. Behold the creative jet! And hear the morning stars sing for joy at the sacred generation of the Gods!"[58] And there was his custom of sending birthday letters to his daughters as well as Christmas letters to remind them of the birth of Jesus. In *Conversations on the Gospels*, birth emerged as an important theme. Like the rose seed, Alcott told his young students, "so the seed of a human being is placed in the midst of matter which nourishes it, and it grows and becomes perfected." "Where is the Life that causes a seed to spring out and seek the light?" he asked. The answer lay with the spirit which "makes the body just as the rose throws out the rose leaves." The parents had "much to do in regard to the body of a child" because the body was the "soil of the soul." Yet it was God who worked on the body of the mother "in a mysterious way, and with her aid" to bring forth "the Child's Spirit in a little Body of its own."[59]

For Alcott, a contemplation of birth should lead to a disclosure of the nature of spirit. Based on this perception, it would be the task of education to lead forth the spirit implicit in the child and existing still in much of its original state of innocence. Education, thus, was an active and moving endeavor, a far cry from the humdrum of the recitation system of the Boston Latin School and Harvard University. Alcott explained his notion of education in *The Doctrine and Discipline of Human Culture* which appeared in 1836. Significantly, the title page bore the words of Jesus: "The wind bloweth where it listeth, and ye hear the sound thereof; but ye cannot tell whence it cometh nor whither it goeth; so is everyone that is born of the Spirit."

Alcott's reverence in dealing with the subject of birth did not prevent him from offending his neighbors' sense of propriety. In the eyes of conservative Boston, Alcott's candor was shocking, and to judge him by twentieth-century standards would be misleading. He should have been aware of his departure from the unspoken norms of the community. The fact that he preferred not to be, indicated his enormous attraction to the symbol of birth. He found the origin of the human person not just a fact to be assumed and ignored; it was motion and action, the "creative jet" which spoke the "energizing word" originally. Indeed, Alcott continued to hold to his perception despite the personal and social cost, and, as late as 1838, he wrote to Mrs. James Savage, the mother of one of his pupils before the publication of *Conversations* had closed his school:

> *Birth, to all pure and simple souls, is a joyous holiday, full of fresh and fair associations. And no eras of life are more befitting expressions of sentiment. Mr. A. hopes that the day is near, when life shall deem it not only a pleasure but privilege, to refresh its affections, and inspire its love, at the full fountain of the heart of childhood!*[60]

But his fascination with birth was only one example of Alcott's concern for movement and life in the general realm of education. Another favorite theme was spiritual culture, and in his mind this abstraction was decidedly kinetic. For Alcott, spiritual culture "lifts the body from the drowsy couch; opens the eyes upon the rising sun; tempts it forth to breathe the invigorating air; plunges it into the purifying bath, and thus whets all its functions for the duties of the coming day."[61] The movement corresponded to the activity of all creation, since "not only the whole universe is in motion, but every thing is in a state of change within it."[62]

Alcott interwove traditional gospel symbols with natural symbols of flux and flow in a worldview which shared basic perceptions with his friend Emerson. Yet, more than Emerson, he was using Christian language, and in doing so he was joining Ripley and the clerical Transcendentalists in the transformation of traditional symbols. The symbols which emerged had been part of the linguistic and conceptual heritage of Christianity but, under the impress of new historical realities, were bearers of new meanings and values which differed from those of the past. They allowed society to innovate with greater ease because they repeated the language which still carried the comfortable ring of the past. Thus, Alcott's language—and that of his friends who used Christian symbols in a new way—facilitated change within traditional religion. So in *Conversations*, matter was "like a great sea" moved by the living spirit which pervaded it. "Do you think God flowed through all the forefathers of Jesus down to Joseph?" Alcott asked his pupils. "Do you think his spirit flowed on through your ancestors and down to you?" He told them of a man in Boston whose spirit could "be made to flow out through his fingers, and make the sick person well." Another time, he recalled for them the effect the sight of the ocean had produced in him when he first saw it at the age of twelve, and again he painted the joy of country life where there were "living springs" from which water sprang up and was never dry. Water meant "Spirit pure and unspoiled," he told them. He asked, "Have you a living Spring?" and warned, "The waters become impure by standing still—by your not trying."[63]

The use of transformed symbols was as notable in George Ripley's controversy with Andrews Norton on the "latest form of infidelity." The public debate began when, in 1836, Ripley published a review of James Martineau's *Rationale of Religious Enquiry* in the Unitarian *Christian Examiner*. Ripley began his commentary by deploring the current state of theology: "The idea of infusing any fresh life into its aged veins has been deemed chimerical." Now "dry," "repulsive," and "perplexing," theological study should be "filled with the dewy freshness of the morning, it should breathe an atmosphere of unclouded light, it should move with the freedom and grace of conscious inspiration." With Martineau, Ripley shifted his gaze to the New Testament and to Jesus, whose soul was a "sea of light." He found the correspondence between the perfect moral beauty of the character of Jesus and the "most exalted ideas of divine perfection" a far better demonstration of divinity than "if we heard it thundered forth from the flames of Sinai, or saw it written by an angel's hand on the noon-day sky." Crowds were converted to Jesus, not because of miracles, but because "the hidden springs of faith within the soul" had been touched. The miracles of Jesus were the "free expressions of his character, rather than the formal supports of his mission," and the first Christian teachers, recognizing this, "stood upon the common level of humanity while the light from above was streaming into their souls." These individuals possessed hearts "charged and bursting with the flood of new and unutterable emotions which came pouring through them from the full fountain of Christ." "They could not but believe that the light which fell upon them was not from earth but from Heaven."[64]

The gist of Norton's angry response was that, by its appearance in a Unitarian periodical, Ripley's article had disturbed the standing order. Ripley's reply stressed the rights of free and open discussion: "I had thought that we had breathed the air of freedom too long, to substitute an appeal to popular prejudice in the place of reason and argument. The same course, Sir, that you have taken, has been pursued before against the innovator on traditional ideas."[65]

Norton's ire was rearoused by Emerson's "Divinity School Address" which had linked the Christian interpretation of "miracle" with "monster." When, on the anniversary of the address, before an audience of Harvard alumni, Norton took up his weapons to rout out infidelity, Ripley again responded in an open letter. Ripley claimed that he looked to Cambridge as the "fountain from which a bright and benignant light would radiate," while he understood the aim of its liberal scholars to be "to press forward in the course which they had begun, to ascend to higher views, to gain a deeper insight into Christianity, to imbibe more fully its divine spirit, and to apply the truths of revelation to the wants of society and the progress of man." He warned that philosophy (Lockean) would like to "smother the breathing life of heavenly truth," but he had hope in the great majority of liberal Christians who, "in the general fermentation of modern times," were "aware of the danger of artificial restraints." "A spirit is abroad, free, bold, uncompromising, and terrible as an army with banners, which is trying the opinions and institutions of the world as by fire."[66]

Norton responded in an angry pamphlet of his own in which he asserted that Ripley had been guilty of a personal rather than an intellectual attack. Not to be outdone, Ripley kept up the barrage with two more open letters, in the first of which he told his opponent that life was process and change was paramount: "The life of man is a vapor; the elements of nature are constantly changing their form; the whole universe is subject to perpetual decay and renovation."[67] In the second letter, Ripley concerned himself specifically with Friedrich Schleiermacher and Wilhelm De Wette and found that, as "exponents of the progress of opinion in German theology," they had inspired theology with a "fresh and vigorous life." He called the "law of gradual progress" the "great law of the Universe" and hailed "the full-orbed Sun of Righteousness and Truth" which "arose upon the world, in the soul of Jesus of Nazareth."[68] He differed from Norton not merely on the issue of Lockean philosophy as applied to Christian evidence: Ripley was preaching the gospel of motion.

Both Alcott and Ripley also expressed their Transcendental perception of ultimate reality in language which excited no strong reactions. In the private world of his journals and letters, Alcott's language went uncontroverted—except perhaps by the friendly criticisms of Emerson. In his exercise of the Unitarian ministry, Ripley steered relatively clear of sermons which might be considered sensational, and his editorial introductions and notes in *Specimens of Foreign Standard Literature* were generally well received by the Unitarian establishment. From the childhood years when he had discovered his identity by reading *Pilgrim's Progress*, Alcott's life had been a journey in the symbolic as well as the literal sense. The depth of his fascination with the theme was revealed in a dream:

> *Today, I had a dream of walking through the villages as a pedlar, holding communication with the people to whom I should thus gain access on the vital interests of life. . . . I see in the occupation of peddling many facilities for speaking that I could not enjoy in other relations. My epic would have a thread around which I could spin whatever of heroic action and utterance occasion should favour. It would be an* Excursion *realized in life.* [69]

He confided to Emerson his mode of address to his own soul: "Take passport then, my Psyche, and run on thy errand." Later, he praised his friend who "haunteth the same tracts of faery, goeth and returneth, knoweth the passway to the Island of Beauty."[70] Spirit, for Alcott, facilitated the journey over the bridge from time to eternity, for "Spirit restoreth and continually rebuildeth the bridge, that the terrestrial travellers may find footway over the stream on their way to the Country of Immortality." The past was but a roadsign to the future, for "traditions, creeds, systems, are to us but as waymarks, footprints, that indicate the career of the soul in its past sojournings to the beatific land of Truth; as inns and havens wherein we are not to tarry save as for a day and a night, not our goal."[71]

Like Emerson, Alcott appropriated the various symbolizations of natural motion to express his religious vision. Matter was in "constant flux—ebb and flow," "a mote floating in the beams of Spirit," casting its shadow "on the screen of Time." All people were emanations of a common Being, and the very atmosphere was "but the reflex current of all the living souls on the planet, returning on its ebb to be renewed and impelled with vital force in sustaining floods over the world, expired and inspired by the all-renewing Soul." Each soul was "shedding its slough and renewing itself," since "renovating ideas" were working in the heart of society, and old forms would be "cast off." Clad in its new garment, the soul of humanity would nourish itself on a new food instead of the "husks of doctrine." It would "find the living kernel, and feed thereon to fulness; for the day of false things draws to a close."[72]

The musings of George Ripley expressed the same juxtaposition of death and life. His general portrait of the religious person was a good example, since such a person could not afford to "be so occupied with the mere outside, the dry husk and shell of matter, as to lose sight of the Infinite and Divine Energy, from which it draws the reality of its being." For the believer, the divine voice would be "heard in the rushings of the wind and the whisperings of the breeze, in the roar of the thunder and the fall of the rain," while the godless person looked "coldly on" at a "mute and dead mass of material forms."[73]

A favorite metaphor for spiritual life was the fountain. Ripley saw that "in the light and strength of the Divine Spirit, which streams forth from the Primal Fountain, on all created things, its [the soul's] divine elements are quickened into life and activity, and it becomes a partaker of the divine nature." "Just as the stream partakes of the qualities of the fountain from which it flows," humanity possessed godlike attributes, and conversely the divine stream in human life could "be traced to no other source than to the Eternal Fountain of Truth and Good."[74]

In Ripley's ordination sermon for John Sullivan Dwight, he contrasted the rigidity of the past with the present state of affairs in the churches, where the discovery was being made that "other fountains also contain the waters of life."

> *A different state of things is now experienced among all the churches of the land. The unlimited freedom of thought which happily prevails in this community, produces a general fermentation; the ancient repose is disturbed; the stagnation of the past has given place to intense mental action; the doctrines of the theologians are*

brought before the tribunal of the people; a struggle has taken place between the old and the new; the most rigid creeds have been unable to prevent the progress of thought; so that there is scarcely a church of any communion, in which opinion is not divided, and the foundations of ages shaken to their centre. [75]

Later, when Ripley began to conclude that he must leave the Christian ministry, he shared his unrest with his congregation in a letter. He told his community that liberal Christians must be among those "sweeping away the traditions which obscured the simplicity of truth." The liberal clergy, he said, "could not linger around the grave of the past," and he confessed that he could not "stand still." In Ripley's vision of the church of the future, "there could be no cold or formal preaching; the instruction would be the outpouring of an individual soul." As for topics chosen, "the more exciting and soul-stirring the better." Committed to religious progress, exhorted Ripley, "we should let the dead Past bury its dead." "We should know where we were, by the divine peace and joy, with which our hearts overflow."[76] Some months after he reluctantly left Purchase Street, his own version of the church of motion commenced at Brook Farm. It was poetic justice that this new commune sheltered on its property a stream which gave it name and identity. Almost a century later, Zoltán Haraszti could still note "the brook, a few yards below, just beyond the road," where at evening one could "hear its murmur from the windows of the mansion, just as Hawthorne heard it nearly a hundred years ago."[77]

Like Brook Farm, Fruitlands grew first in the imagination. Alcott, during his trip to England, was writing home to his family concerning some of the qualities of his vision. He told his wife, Abba, he wanted to "import living minds into N. England to plant there the new state of things."[78] In another letter, he painted the landscape of a "second Eden" in which "the divine seed is to bruise the head of Evil, and restore Man to his rightful communion with God, in the Paradise of Good"; a place where "life and Immortality shall then come to light, and man pluck wisdom from the tree of life always."[79] Fruitlands would be a sun-sphere with Alcott its sun-hero, and he told Abba that "the sun shall rise fair over the hills, with promise on his wings: nor set more in despair—The dews shall bathe our feet as we tread the gardens and purity attend."[80]

When Alcott began to describe the actual site of Fruitlands, his fascination with running water was noteworthy. He told his brother Junius about the "many springs which descend from the uplands into the fields and meadows and pass off into the Still River which flows on the West of us into the Nashua." "There is a living fountain," he continued, "from which we may derive water for all household uses, for drink, cooking, bathing &c, and which may easily be carried to any apartment of our dwellings, and to the gardens, and pass thence into the rich peat lands near by to the river."[81] And in a birthday poem to his daughter Elizabeth, he expressed a similar enthusiasm for the "living water" of Fruitlands.

> *Works, wake, harmonious swell*
> *Along the deep sequestered dell,*
> *Along the grass and brake*
> *And where the cattle slake*
> *Their thirst; where glides*
> *Adown the sloping sides,*
> *   In ceaseless fret,*
> *   The wizard rivulet:*
> *And let the springing maize*
> *Join in the violin's note*
> *In hymning forth our praise*
> *From every jubilant throat,*
> *Our holiest joy to raise.*[82]

While Emerson and Alcott moved outside the sphere of Unitarian orthodoxy and Ripley trailed them, following in their direction by his decision to leave the ministry, the other charter members of the Transcendental Club were in varying degrees more moderate. Clarke, Hedge, and Francis all managed to achieve some sort of synthesis between their Transcendental gospel and Unitarian Christianity. They affirmed Unitarianism but did it in a way which transformed orthodoxy by their commitment to the theme of motion.

For James Freeman Clarke, the delicate balancing was part and parcel of tracts for the American Unitarian Association which revealed his reconstruction of traditional Christian symbols with kinetic material. In *Reconciliation by Jesus Christ*, Clarke began with a reminder of God's work in the natural creation: "The swarming insects who leap in the sunbeam; the free bird, flashing through the wood, or hanging high in the liquid firmament; the fish darting or gliding in the liquid wave,—all are provided for by the Universal Parent." Christianity echoed the movement of nature, for its word was "one which descended from the highest Heaven, far above the reach of the most soaring thought, with which man has ever penetrated the skies." Sin set up a "barrier" to the word and produced a "coldness of heart," which nature, with her "wheels [which] run on iron tracks," could never pardon. But the "awakened conscience" could expect a different reception from the Father, whose "sunshine would break in" at the return of the repentant sinner, and the result would be a renewal of the authentic spirit of Christianity, "love, flowing out of pardoned sin, love to God and man." For the future, "inward peace and joy with God" would strengthen the Christian to "run and not be weary in God's ways." Meanwhile, theology would furnish the "chart by which to guide ourselves through the intricacies of the wilderness, which the soul must traverse in its flight to God." There was only one caution: "We must not study the chart till we forget to go upon the journey."[83]

The journey motif was also evident in Clarke's tract, *Repentance toward God.* Life was a Jacob's ladder with the eye of God traveling along the gradation, "along this shining highway of spirits" in which "some had their faces toward him, turned upward and were ascending,—others had their eyes turned earthward, turned from him, and were descending." People must learn not to walk the broad and easy way, in another metaphor, but must leave "the religion of ceremony and form" and "walk in the Spirit." The lesson to be learned for the journey was that the doctrines of repentance and faith "moved the world then,—they move it now; they will always move it while man continues to be man." And while the human condition endured, each person would know what was required: "a radical change, not a superficial one."[84]

Individual change must proceed in tandem with institutional change, and in *Unitarian Reform* Clarke turned to the latter. He pondered the nature of the Unitarian movement and paraphrased a typical Unitarian proposition in this way: " 'Jesus Christ taught no formal system—the Apostles laid down no fixed standard of opinions—they taught the truth in a free, living manner, without any scheme or plan of theology at all.'" Clarke saw the first great object of Unitarian reform as "Christian Liberty," which meant living wholly free from "scholastic trammels." He praised the faith "that in the worst of men lay hidden and buried a divine spark to be kindled by love and truth." Put another way, loving sinners involved believing "that there is asleep, under their sin, a spirit of goodness which may be roused at last by our appeals and overcome by our love." He indicated his orientation toward a future of action and democracy as he summarized the Unitarian message:

> *Ours is the religion of the future, the religion of progress, the religion for the people. . . . With firm faith in the future triumph of our principles, in deep dependence on the mighty arm of Heaven, and in a strenuous endeavor to live as we profess, we can wait the hour when the truth of our principles will be understood and acknowledged.* [85]

When Clarke preached at the installation of George Simmons and Samuel Ripley in the church in Waltham, he chose the theme of the "well-instructed scribe" who brought from his treasure "things new and old." The semon tried to balance conservative with reform concerns, but Clarke emerged as decidedly on the side of movement and change. For him, conservatism meant gradual development, and Jesus was a true conservative who "saw that the development of events in their right times was the deepest secret of God, . . . who oversees the working of that universal system of things of which each event is a separate birth." Indeed, "Jesus, with all his gentleness, exerted an energy which broke down the most stony mass of bigotry which has ever in this world petrified around the form of true religion." He worked for the reform of mere externals, and "the word of Christ was a hammer and a fire to break in pieces this mass of formality." Like Jesus, the preacher's business was "action"; he stood in the pulpit "to *act* upon those before him." Correspondingly, God had "made man to improve, and subjected him to the law of progress." But a spirit was still abroad which had "sought to fetter the human mind" and which had "made long creeds and articles of faith, in order to rivet them, like manacles, on the intellect." Men still denounced "every innovation as heresy and infidelity." In the face of this paralysis, Clarke summed up his position. The largest danger was "listless conformity" and "dead orthodoxy," while reform had to "break through the soil of old custom, to force its way against the combined resistance of religious indifference and religious prejudice, to go sounding on its dim and perilous path where there are no landmarks, no foot tracks."[86]

At the death of William Ellery Channing, the saint of Boston Unitarianism and the bridge to its Transcendental dissidents, Clarke eulogized his memory before the congregation at the Church of the Disciples, praising Channing as a man "so full of spiritual life" that he was a "fountain of spiritual life to all of us." His life had "passed out of him in the form of thought, and had become a part of public opinion" so that, through thought, there could be continued communication with him. The words into which Channing's thought had been shaped "penetrated the recesses of the land. They passed social and sectarian barriers which they never had before." Channing's voice had "sunk deeper than any other into the foremost minds of the world—the men of the future," for he had spoken the Ideal which would characterize the "coming age." Other men in other ages had struck out toward that "fair Ideal."

> *Pursuing it, the May Flower sails with its little pilgrim company across the stormy Atlantic—pursuing it a Luther fixes his thesis on the church gate at Wittenberg—following such a vision, Xavier and Henry Martyn go to India with the everlasting gospel—*

and Father Marquette floats down the Mississippi, unvisited before by a white man's bars, and waves from his canoe the crucifix to the astonished Indians on the shores.

In the light of this vision, Clarke challenged a fitting response to the life of Channing: "Not with tears, but with upright actions, must we embalm his memory."[87]

Clarke expended considerable effort in writing for the *Western Messenger* which, in spite of its frontier location, occupied a central position in the evolution of the Transcendental movement. During the years of its publication (1835–41), the *Messenger* offered a capsule summary of the development of religious language from Calvinism to Transcendentalism. Articles on the new views appeared in the periodical, and Emerson was defended against his critics. His poems, as well as Jones Very's sonnets, made almost their first public debuts in the *Messenger*. Excerpts from addresses by Emerson and Channing were featured, while brief extracts from Emerson's writings began to be used as fillers.

In this context, Clarke's dawning awareness of his transforming use of old symbols became clear in his editorial comments. "A new spirit demands a new form," he reflected, "and the religious spirit of the coming generation needs something more than the Assembly's catechism can supply."[88] The awareness could be discerned in his unorthodox definition of Christianity: it was "each man's personal experience of the quickening and sanctifying power of Christian truth" and "something to be realised in the heart and life, not studied in a book."[89] Again, when Clarke mused on the influence of Unitarian ideas of truth and charity on Jacob Abbot, a Calvinist, he was sure that "God takes care of his word. The river which seems to lose itself in the earth shall doubtless burst forth anew in another region." For "the rain which cometh down from Heaven . . . watereth the earth and maketh it bring forth, and though lost to man's eye, is guided by the providence of God to the roots which it is to feed and nourish, till they give seed to the sower and bread to the eater."[90] In a letter to the Unitarian clergy on the subject of preaching law and gospel, Clarke revealed a concern for what would "excite love." In the existential situation, the "springs of life" were continually attacked by disease. Convinced of the sickness by a good physician, a person would try the prescribed remedy with the result that "love and gratitude gushes forth." While the Calvinist line of total conviction for sin was to be avoided, fault—the sickness—was still to be acknowledged; and "out of that small admission the whole river of penitence and faith might flow." Ultimately, the river came from the divine spirit which moved in the hearts of those who went to God through Jesus.[91]

Clarke's contemplation of natural symbols also revealed his fascination with the motion of water. "Viaduct over the Little Conemaugh, Pennsylvania," described the place where the Allegheny Portage Railroad passed the little Conemaugh: "Where, far below, the waters go, / The mountain spur bent round."[92] Another poem romanticized the pragmatic role of the Ohio River in settling the West.

> Flow on fair stream, through coming years;
> Flow on, in strength and beauty!
> If we, as faithful, do our work;
> True to our God and duty,
> Thou shalt not want thy poets, nor
> Be unrenowned in story;
> Not Tiber's wave, nor Yarrow's fount,
> Shall rival thee in glory.[93]

In prose, "The Land of Freedom" alluded to a future paradise by references to flowing water—fountains which "gushed from the rock, and filling marble basins, wound along amid beds of blue and yellow flowers" and streams which "trickled with a drowsy sound across the pebbles."[94] A rhapsodic endtime dominated "A Glance into the Future," where Jean Paul Richter's vision was reflected in the movement of the waters. "Strong attraction" of the sun and moon caused

> the oceans to roll together round the Equator—and then the whole atmosphere with its vapors rushes up from the poles after the

water, and still as the attraction increases, a frightful flood of
electric fluid pours and swells over all. The clouds, piled up in
mountain towers, stream quickly across the sky, and plunge into
the sea, and then rush upward again, while the lightning in burn-
ing wings flashes from Heaven to the Ocean and cleaves them
asunder. Look up to the Heaven, thou last man! All on thy earth
has disappeared—all its rivers have been swallowed up in its
sea.[95]

Flowing water in the poetry and prose of Clarke was accompanied by fluid light. Perhaps the clearest statement came in the
parousia speculation of "A Glance into the Future" where "the stars
and suns of the milky-way shall at last rush together in hostile
combat, and twist themselves into giant serpents, and a chaos,
worlds on worlds, roll and flame together." Here the bond between
light—the sun—and time—the duration of that which changed—
was expressed in the motif of intense movement. The connection
between them was, in associational thinking, a strong one, and
Franz Cumont, in his study of Mithraic sun religion, called the sun
the "physical manifestation" of Boundless Time, while ancient
statuary depicted Time with a serpent around its body to represent
the course of the sun on the ecliptic.[96] But, with Clarke, the regular
progression of light on a diurnal course seemed transformed by a
new urgency in which movement was not merely a corollary to
existence but its essence. And in the human world, light danced
also, as Clarke's parting tribute to his grandfather James Freeman
made clear. Freeman possessed "something of gaiety and excitement" which came from "fresh spirits sparkling up from the well just
unsealed by Nature's hand." In him "wit flashed and intellect
blazed, and knowledge and refinement poured out their rich colored
gems—while genius shook the atmosphere like thunder."[97] Freeman's holiness, in short, was a function of his correspondence to the
movement of nature.

Clarke's fellow-Transcendentalist Frederic Henry Hedge was
likewise fond of the vocabulary of motion; with Clarke he repeated
traditional Christian themes in the new language. It was not surpris-

ing, therefore, that Clarke's *Messenger* published a sermon by Hedge as an example of the best sort of preaching. "The Transfiguration" was structurally a Transcendental sermon since it was built on the theme of correspondence between the gospel narrative of the transfiguration of Jesus and the same phenomenon in the life of the ordinary Christian. But it also spoke in the language of the New School. When Christ had become transfigured, there had been a new revelation, and old religious truths were "radiant and beaming with that divine intelligence from which they spring." Similarly, a transfiguration in the life of the Christian made everything appear in a "new and clearer light." "The feature [*sic*] is unrolled before us like a chart, in which our own destiny, traced in lines of light, beckons us on beyond the kingdoms of the world." Spiritual excitement could bring each Christian to the transfigured Jesus, and, at this time, "the great objects of his kingdom would pass before us, no longer dim with earthly mists, but radiant with that pure light which flows directly from him the great Sun of Spirits."[98]

In another sermon, "Practical Goodness the True Religion," Hedge posed one kind of motion over against another: emotionalism, which was bad, was countered by moral action, which was good. In the enthusiasm of sectarian religion, there were "unnatural heats," and religion lived a "galvanic life." Yet Hedge feared "indifference and coldness" and prayed to be "inwardly and secretly revived." He disliked the evangelical revivals, not because they were revivals, but because they were "unnatural," and, in the people who made "practical goodness their road to Heaven," he could applaud the fitness of "religion carried into action."[99]

Hedge paralleled Clarke again in his memorial sermon on the death of William Ellery Channing. The tribute began with a celebration of faith which, he declared, caused "the wilderness to blossom and the earth to rejoice," the instrument for the discovery of "new laws, new continents, new worlds." True faith meant expansiveness and life, for it opened the mind to a "larger range and a livelier apprehension of all truth,—instead of confining it, as devotion to a creed does, within a given circle of ideas." And the paragon of faith had been Channing, sent by "the Father of lights" as a "burning and a shining light to go before us in the path of our destiny, revealing a farther goal than any we have yet attained, or, it may be, contemplated, in the march of improvement." The theme of moving light shone stronger as Hedge expatiated on Channing's ministry.

> *But, as light existed before the Sun, so truth floats vaguely in the mind of an age, and finds here and there a partial and imperfect utterance, before the man arises, whose office and privilege it is, to concentrate the vague conceptions of his time, and to ray them forth in statements which carry warmth as well as light, to all who have sense to see and hearts to feel.*[100]

Another address on conservatism and reform evoked Clarke's style and conclusions as Hedge played the role of enlightened referee, explaining conservatism and defending reform. But, unlike Clarke, Hedge made his focus the position a scholar should adopt toward both. Hearing his own voices, Hedge's scholar should function as a mediator and reconciler for more extreme positions, and Hedge, himself the selfconscious scholar, seemed to practice what he preached. "Where, in this heaving and shoreless chaos, shall I find the system and repose which my spirit craves?" he asked anxiously. Enlightened conservatism answered that "below the storm and the strife of the schools, there lies a region of perpetual calm, where rest the rock-foundations of Church and State, and where gushes in secret the everlasting fountain, which he who drinketh shall thirst no more."

As Hedge directed his remarks, he cautioned scholars as "fishers of men" against casting "secular nets in the muddy waters of political intrigue." Rather, the scholar should embark on a religious quest to "extend the path of discovery in any direction," even though this sometimes opposed his natural desire to cling to the limits of his own mind, " 'the butt and sea-mark of its utmost sail.' " Since it did not become the scholar to claim that "the bottom of the well where truth lies hid" had been discovered, the naturalness of evolution should be affirmed. "The history of the human mind, like all the processes of planetary life, has its appointed method, and is, from beginning to end, a series of evolutions, in which every phase is connected, by necessary sequence, with every other phase, and the first movement contains the last." It was the worldview of correspondence once again.

Hedge continued with his understanding that "a divine education" was evolving "in eternal procession, the divine soul," a process in which the various philosophies were simply factors by which the truth was "continually approximated and never reached." In this context, Transcendentalism, though it had its limitations, had given a "new impulse to thought" and had broadened the "horizon of life." It was an "observation of the heavens by which the wanderer, here below, is enabled to shape more correctly his terrestrial course."[101] Hedge's scholar, gently nudged by Transcendentalism as well as other philosophies, would move out from his old securities, but always gradually. He spoke the word of cautious development—never of revolt.

At the opening of a new lyceum in Bangor, Hedge aired the theme of the relationship of the quest for knowledge to spiritual goals. "Earth and sky teem with instruction," he told his audience, and knowledge was a threaded circle in which the student traced his line from part to whole.

> *He who understands one thing thoroughly, holds the threads of all knowledge in his hand, and if life were long enough, or circumstances and ability would permit us, to follow out to their extremities, the radii which centre in any particular branch of knowledge which we may have mastered, we might make ourselves masters of the whole circle of knowledge, without any instruction from other sources.*

Now Hedge turned to the American situation and commended the absence of hierarchical structure as an advantage. Democracy meant "a free and full development" of every person "where a levelling and radical spirit, of the true sort, has equalized the human condition by levelling *upward*." The quest for spirit was the implicit goal of knowledge. As that end drew nearer, "the outward form—the mere dead substance, grows less and less; action and life fill its place, till at last the whole of being appears to be but an aggregate of laws, and nature teems with spirit."[102]

Here and in other public addresses, Hedge was a spokesman for a civil religion which provided the occasion for him to preach the gospel of progress. In one Fourth of July oration, he looked only briefly at past history, dwelt lightly on the blessings of the present, and then turned full face toward the future, for which all else had been prologue.

> *When we contemplate what the last fifty years have done for human culture and human happiness, we involuntarily ask, what the next fifty, or the next one hundred, shall add to the account. It is not till within these centuries, that the idea of progress in human affairs, has dawned upon mankind. . . . that the earth, which witnessed the first unfolding, is destined to witness the final development of all that is in man.*

True, there had always been life, whatever the surface stagnation, and "with varying fortunes, in various lands, the unconscious race has crept or sped, but never staid." Now, though, there was a new impetus to the march:

> *Six thousand years, the sun and the stars have watched it moving; but never until now—with the momentum acquired in these latter years—has felt its motion. Now, first awakened to self-consciousness, Humanity is moving on, with new speed and conscious aims, to the fulfilment of its high calling.*

Then manifest destiny erupted for Hedge with a vengeance. The Anglo-Saxon race was

> *the moving force and the last hope of man. . . . climbing the Himmaleh [sic], piercing central Africa, stretching along the Mountains of the Moon, and overspreading Austral Asia, with their beneficent sway,—awakening once more the wizard Genius of the East, and carrying wherever the sun shines or the winds blow, the sacred gifts of Freedom.[103]*

Hedge was optimistic as he looked toward the coming time when "new inventions" would "remove from the lot of the poor, those obstructions which have hitherto checked the free circulation of social privilege and brotherly love." Biblically, he prophesied that "their desert" would "gush with new resources."

> *The very rock on which their feet now stumble, some kind prophet shall smite to healthful issues. For them too, shall be opened the everlasting fountains of intellectual life. The labouring man shall wipe the sweat from his brow, and steep his bread in the cooling wave; the meanest shall drink thereof and be filled.*

The future would bring perfection to humankind and, in almost Marxist terms, a withering away of the state. When that time came, the federal government would "dissolve of itself, as the capsule bursts when the seed is ripe."[104]

In a sermon in memory of President William Henry Harrison, the Transcendentalist minister brought together his civil and ecclesiastical concerns, highlighting his tribute with the theme of the journey. He chose as his text the verse of the Psalmist: "The steps of a good man are ordered by the Lord; and he delighteth in his way" (Ps. 37:23). Applying the verse to Harrison, Hedge told his congregation that when Harrison "had reached a station which brought him more prominently before the eyes of the world, it was only to exchange it, at the very entrance, for new and untried regions, in the onward progress of the soul." "The summit of earthly glory was, to him, but the mount of ascension to higher glories in heavenly places," and he had "passed again, by swift transition, to deeper shades than any [of] his beloved Ohio waters." Finally, Hedge turned to a closer scrutiny of Harrison's time on earth and cited the "moral beauty of his most active and exemplary life" which had been owned and acknowledged by the public, since "on the whole, the heart of a nation gravitates to individual worth, as inevitably as the earth to the sun."[105]

Convers Francis's Transcendental colleagues had paid tribute to his character when they selected him moderator of their Club, for he was above all a moderate. Still, his preaching revealed the transformation of traditional Christian themes which was characteristic of Transcendentalism. When his congregation at Watertown moved into a new meeting house, Francis greeted the occasion with a discourse on the significance of a Christian temple and shaped the old symbol of stability to suit his new insights. "Every moment of our lives, we breathe, stand, or move in the temple of the Most High," he preached, "for the whole universe is that temple." Francis explained:

> Ask of the bright worlds around us, as they roll in the everlasting harmony of their circles; and they shall tell you of Him, whose power launched them on their courses. . . . Ask of ocean's waters; and the roar of their boundless waves shall chant from shore to shore a hymn of ascription to that Being, who hath said "Hitherto shall ye come and no further." Ask of the rivers; and, as they roll onward to the sea, do they not bear along their ceaseless tribute to the ever-working Energy, which struck open their fountains and poured them down through the valleys?[106]

Revelation confirmed his interpretation, for the New Jerusalem had no temple—to signify that "the soul shall be emancipated into that world where her whole action will be the true worship, her whole growth the true service." Christian institutions found their true glory in "putting into active forms, and transmitting from mind to mind, from generation to generation, the living spirit, that animates the Kingdom of Christ in the soul."[107]

The Christian case was an instance of correspondence. Matter too was "mutable, transitory, in a state of flux and reflux."

> We stand before Nature, as before a passing show. . . . The bubble swelling and bursting on the surface of the water, the vapor ascending and vanishing in the thin air, the dust blown away by the wind,—these are the images by which man represents to himself his brief and broken life.

In this situation, it was "refreshing to mount on the wings of that faith, which springs from the constitution of the soul" to the "Fountain of life and blessedness." Ministry itself meant calling and direct

ing the sinner "to the purifying fountain opened in the Gospel," a
work accomplished in harmony with the first disciples who "gave
impulses, whose strong vibrations are now spreading through the
earth, so that the far distant islands of the ocean, and the tribes of
barbarous shores, are listening to the sound as it rolls on."[108]

A consideration of ministry allowed the institutional nature of
Christianity to emerge. Here Francis acknowledged that

> *a power which marshals the world forward on the path of
> improvement, is down in the depths and abroad over the surface of
> society, kindles the light of spiritual philosophy, tasks the most
> gifted intellects to follow its far-reaching revelations of truth, and
> holds under its reign the nations who march in the van of the
> world's progress.*

Dwelling on the role of the individual Christian in the corporate
identity, he continued:

> *Whatever may be the measure of our progress in the true spiritual
> life, it will correspond to the vast expansion of the Divine Nature,
> as the shadow on the dial corresponds in its motion to the sun in the
> heavens, though the shadow moves perhaps but a handbreadth,
> while the place of the great luminary changes by millions of
> miles.* [109]

Christians and their institutions needed grace, Francis reminded his
congregation, or they would "sink among the dead things of form,
instead of being instinct with a living power." And in a metaphor
which recalled the railroad, he spoke of "preparative influences,
which tranquillize and purify our trains of thought by taking them
out of their common tracks of worldliness." Too often Francis and
his people hastened along, "eyes on the ground" and "hands busy
among perishing things" when beauty and light were "bursting forth
in the upper region." But grace would bring the soul to that state
"when its movements are most free, as the motion of our globe,
swiftly as it careers through the fields of space, disturbs not even the
slender threads of which the spider weaves her web."[110]

After the death of Ezra Ripley, the venerable pastor of the First

Church in Concord, Francis preached to the bereaved congregation and used the occasion to describe the nature of personal authenticity amidst change. Conservative Ripley, "a living man and a living minister," cared about external forms because he believed them to be "the robe and defence of realities." Yet he would not get lost in the confusion of "lifeless arrangements" or be buried under "conventional devices," becoming "under the tyranny of custom a dead form." He would not "suffer his own individuality to be lost or shackled" by these forms and devices, for "his true soul shone over and spoke through them all. His action and speech sprung always from his own being, and meant what they purported to mean." Ripley was an authentic person amid a changing milieu, and he "never feared the law of progress."[111]

Francis, like Clarke, produced a number of tracts for the American Unitarian Association. In one of these, *Christianity as a Purely Internal Principle*, Francis defined the aim of Christianity as "to purify and sweeten the fountains in the deep places of the soul, that refreshing influences may thence go forth in a more hallowed life and more praiseworthy deeds." Behind and beyond the soul's fountains was the "Everlasting Fountain of truth" from which the gospel issued and Christianity spread, "like a secret and holy fire," warming and enlightening the "whole moral nature." Again, Christianity directed the warfare between sin and the soul so that the free spirit might "go on unshackled in its path of immortality." Thus liberated, the Christian could experience "a great many changes," knowing that the supreme change of conversion was the "business of a whole life" and that the choice of externals alone would mean "to feed upon the husk and reject the bread." Sectarians who engaged in bitter party warfare missed the point completely; they mistook external for eternal. "When the storm is abroad, they wrap around them more and more closely the mantle of the sect, and declare,— what they before never thought of maintaining—that it is the only Christian garment." Francis closed with a plea for moderation. Although the "religion of disputation and display" fascinated people, serving to "carry off the superfluous activity of stirring minds in outward excitements," no one could wish the opposite extreme, with the Christian community resembling a "stagnant pool" and "mantled over with collections of impurity."[112]

In another tract, *Christ the Way to God,* Francis began by noting the first stirrings of the sacred in the human heart, "where the spirit of wisdom and love is breathing around us, and the light of the upper world comes down in gentle shining, or broad flashing to the open eye,—where the seeds of all holy influences are broadcast, ready to spring up around us and yield a harvest of immortal life, if we will but take it." Just as the "heart beats, and the blood rolls through the system," Providence was always "around us and over us." Into this scheme of things entered Christ the mediator, a "channel for the conveyance of that holy power, by which the soul is saved from spiritual death, and brought into spiritual life." This was because in Jesus the "spirit of wisdom, love, and truth came from the Fountain of Inspiration," and so he "poured out that blood which became the seed of the world." The meaning of salvation was expressed in its motion, as Francis summarized:

> The ministry of Jesus can serve us only by kindling the life of God in our souls, only by rousing us from the death-slumbers of sin to a quickening sense of our eternal relations, only by imparting the energy which regenerates and sanctifies, which makes the word of God quick and powerful, and sharper than any two-edged sword."[113]

When Francis was chosen by Jared Sparks for a contribution of his mammoth Library of American Biography, he responded with *The Life of John Eliot, The Apostle to the Indians.* Here he reflected an attitude typical among contemporary Christians as well as other Americans by being condescending toward American Indians and assuming white Christian superiority. He regretted that Indian character had not been "developed in harmonious and well-proportioned movements," but thought the Indian a "stationary being" because he was "chiefly a sensual being."[114] The stationariness, however, could be reversed by Christian faith, as was evident in Francis's account of the conversion of Cutshamakin in which he described the "subduing spirit of love bursting forth in the bosom of the savage, like a beautiful wild-flower from the cleft of a rock."[115] The Indian confessions reported by Eliot showed that "divine truth was breaking into their souls, that some of its rays had struck through the darkness of barbarity." A seed had been sown and it "contained a vital principle, from which the tree of life might spring."[116] Eliot himself seemed a divine impetus to the conversion process, for in the encounter with a sinner "his voice swelled into solemn and powerful energy, and the heart of the transgressor shook as at the sound that rolled from Sinai."[117] In Eliot's letters on Indian affairs, Francis wrote, "his heart gushes forth in a mixture of warm zeal and gentle feeling," and his work among his people brought corresponding "fountains of life" which were "opened to refresh the waste places." But, though Eliot's words had "quickened many souls," ultimately the Bible was the "silent but quickening teacher of God's truth." His "expansive action in moral warmth" pointed beyond itself to the divine.

Convers Francis and Frederic Henry Hedge represented the opposite end of the Transcendental continuum from Ralph Waldo Emerson. Their "revolution," along with that of James Freeman Clarke, was assuredly very modest. However, from Emerson's most radical symbolizations of wild nature to Francis's, Hedge's, and Clarke's more moderate transformations of existing Christian language, a common denominator gathered the words of the Transcendentalists and separated them from the established language of Brahmin Boston. This common denominator was motion: though the content of Transcendental symbols dealt with conventional nature or Christian tradition, the mode of the symbols had changed so that the most salient characteristic of religious reality was that it moved.

There were other implications in the language of the New School. In the first place Emerson had expressed his reservations that human ability would ever capture the elusive quality of experience completely in language. The search for the *juste mot* was continual and unending, and the word as ferryman seemed never quite fit for its tasks. The dichotomy between sacred and profane, which the Emersonian theory suggested, had been visible in the language of his colleagues. Ripley, Clarke, Hedge, and Francis all made extensive use of the language of the Christian tradition, and in their appropriation of the past, however transformed, it was inevitable that they would absorb some of the worldview which grounded the religious experience of Christianity. In other words, if Christian life grew out of a profound sense of alienation from the sacred which demanded reconciliation and redemption, it reflected the worldview of causality. And, as we saw in the first chapter, the worldview of causality was different from the new religion of correspondence which the Transcendentalists were preaching. With the inherited tradition, even as transmitted by liberal Christianity, the members of the New School had absorbed a good dose of its religious sense. Sin was still very real; life was a journey on the right path or a climb on Jacob's ladder. The correspondence between self and world which the Transcendentalists sought had to take into account the fact that self limped a little. Even a Transcendental purist such as Bronson Alcott lived out his life as a "pedlar's progress," while Emerson often complained in the privacy of his journal's pages that he himself was "cold" and his emotional life a far cry from the fountains and streams he found in nature. In fact, it might be argued that the reason for the shift in Transcendental language from a corresponding word which mirrored the regular motion of nature to a corresponding word more intense and urgent had something to do with the basic assumptions of the Christian tradition. There was a distance (sin and alienation) to be closed and a goal (the sacred) to be reached. Once the efficient cause had brought the present state of affairs into the world, purposeful human activity was necessary. The linguistic cult of motion was related, in Aristotelian terms, to a final cause. It dealt with bodies in motion, the means to an end. So the language of the Transcendentalists was oriented toward the future and spun out the linear thread which would be woven into history. We shall return to this observation in more depth in the final chapter. For now, the hybrid quality of the Transcendental expression of correspondence is inescapable.

But the corresponding word of the members of the New School had a second implication. The theory of correspondence held that each piece of the world could be fitted to a multiplicity of spheres. Each piece was therefore discrete and individual even though it contained the pattern which shaped the whole. In keeping with this understanding of the nature of things, Emerson and his friends dispensed more and more with the Christian communal theology in which salvation came to each person as part of a special people. Emerson spoke of the self-reliant individual of the new age who was bound to no covenant, implicit to no community, woven only into the fabric of the universe:

> Be it known unto you that henceforward I obey no law less than the eternal law. I will have no covenants but proximities. I shall endeavor to nourish my parents, to support my family, to be the chaste husband of one wife,—but these relations I must fill after a new and unprecedented way. I appeal from your customs. I must be myself.[118]

His friends often expressed a similar view of the individual, immersed in the infinite universe, troubled about the problem of permanence and change, and bothered about the nature of personal authenticity. In the kaleidoscope, one could not depend on fixed relationships or secure associations. The corollary to motion was essential aloneness—even in the friendship of the Transcendental community.

Finally, the corresponding word was tied to a sacramental understanding of reality which has often been overlooked in the Transcendentalists. A sacrament can be any piece of the material world which points beyond itself to a larger and more powerful reality and at the same time contains the power and reality of the thing which is signified. In other terms, the sacrament is a power-object, and the sacramentalist sees the world charged with the raw energy issuing from many sacred centers. This means that the sacramentalist is always in some sense a polytheist. There are many gods in a world containing innumerable power-objects which really *are* what they symbolize. Now if, as the theory of correspondence maintained, each microcosm was a small-scale model which captured the power of the macrocosm, it followed that each individual portion of the world was a power-object or a sacrament. The reason that there was less need for completely separate space and time for myth and ritual in the religious experience of correspondence was that sacrament—and God—were everywhere and every time. This was true for wild nature, and it was true for human nature as well. In this view, the word was indeed a sacrament: Transcendental conversation was truly and not just figuratively a "ritual." It celebrated the correspondence with the macrocosm which could be discovered in the midst of ordinary life. This was why the word of the Transcendentalists, as Emerson preached, must always be spontaneous. In its unstudied expression, it celebrated the power of day-to-day existence which did not require salvation outside the natural world. Of course, the spontaneity of language was aspiration more than actuality in the Transcendental scheme of things, but even the hybrid nature of their experience, to which we have already referred, should not lead us away from one conclusion. Despite the conceptual monism which so many critics have accurately noted in the Transcendentalists, Emerson and his colleagues were experiential polytheists. Just as the Hinduism, which Emerson admired so enthusiastically, managed to contain both an austere monism and an exuberant polytheism, the Transcendental circle could be monistic and polytheistic at once. Each word—as well as each corresponding piece of the world "out there," as we shall see, was a sacred center, so that motion meant energy and power. Everything contained the secret of everything else; everything, therefore, *worked* on everything else.

CHAPTER IV

The Motion of
THE DIAL

IF THE WORD WAS SACRAMENT for the Transcendentalists, then it ought to be properly enshrined. Most of all, the spontaneity of shared conversation needed to be recaptured. One should not destroy the living and communal quality of this ritual, but instead record it so that in later and less "living" times contact could be made again. Here Emerson and his friends were playing good Judaeo-Christians, and, fearful of a separation from sacred reality, they sought to make the moment endure in their own sacred scripture. Thus, the production of *The Dial* was the most extensive group project in which the members of the Transcendental Club engaged. It was a cultural event which became an elongated "golden moment" for Transcendentalism as well as for the history of American religion and art.

As early as 1835, Emerson, in his correspondence with Thomas Carlyle, discussed the foundation of a journal and suggested that Carlyle cross the Atlantic to become its editor. But Carlyle's reluctance for an American excursion left the proposed editorial chair vacant, so that the project for a while seemed to be tottering on the edge of oblivion. Yet, in the casual gatherings of the members of the Club, enthusiasm for the journal received a new impetus when, in 1839, John A. Heraud began publication of the *Monthly Magazine* in London. Alcott, Francis, Ripley, and others approved warmly as the contents of the new British periodical were discussed, for Heraud's magazine resembled what the Transcendentalists had contemplated for themselves. The Heraud enterprise did not draw off American talent by providing an outlet for it, as they had thought. Emerson and Alcott both received delighted reviews in its pages, but Alcott was mistakenly saluted as the author of Emerson's *Nature*. And while the magazine promised eagerly that it would print the work of "new" New Englanders, nothing came of this plan beyond the publication of one speech by Robert Bartlett.

Perhaps the heightened anticipation followed by the letdown crystallized the sense of need for a new publication. Perhaps the English journal provoked an aesthetic envy in the Transcendental circle. Alcott, at least, mourned the absence of anything quite so good, even though an American journal was now being actively considered. "I question whether we shall find talent or spirit to equal that of our English brethren," he wrote in his diary.[1] Perhaps finally the appearance of an actual product from the British press proved the workability of the journalistic fantasy of the Transcendentalists. British success fanned Transcendental desire, and the dream began to hint of a chance for materialization. Emerson, in his opening message to the readers of *The Dial*, summarized the atmosphere of casual indecision and protracted communal wishing which lay behind the actual publication. The editors could not be accused of too great formality in the publication of their journal "but rather of a backwardness, when they remember how often in many private circles the work was projected, how eagerly desired."[2]

Plans had solidified at a meeting in September 1839, at the home of Cyrus Bartol. With Alcott, Hedge, Ripley, Theodore Parker, and William Henry Channing present, Margaret Fuller aired her views on the proposed magazine and how it should be conducted. Hedge had been asked to take the job of editor, but his conservatism led him to plead lack of time, and Fuller emerged with the position, although she was followed later by Emerson. The first issue was projected for April 1840. And, most important as a clue to Transcendental consciousness, Alcott chimed in during the course of the meeting with a suggestion for titling the new journal. It should be called the "Dial," the name he had given to his diary. "Dial" meant a sundial, and, with loyal adherence to their theory of correspondence, the Transcendentalists were quick to discover the cosmic implications of their choice. We have already seen that Francis likened the relationship between individual spiritual life and divine nature to that between a sundial and the sun. Alcott was fond of alluding to "Time's Dial," and in a letter to his brother-in-law referring to the new periodical, he inquired, "What of dialing? Do you discern the hour of the universe on our Famous Time Piece?"[3] James Freeman Clarke wrote to Margaret Fuller to second approval of the name. "I think it excellent," he remarked enthusiastically, "significant of those who believe in the progress of time and who watch it, not in the bustle of a city, but amid the flowers and leafiness of a garden walk. The name speaks of faith in Nature and in Progress."[4] Here, as elsewhere, the Transcendentalists' sense of time was tied to organic notions, an understanding which would lead them to certain prescriptions concerning the kind of motion or change they considered to be in tune with the periodicity of the universe. Now they would begin by imitating the movement of the cosmos in the quarterly appearance of a periodical.

The concern with time in its thrust toward the future was prominently displayed in the journal. Each issue bore on its cover the editorial creed: "*The Dial*, as its title indicates, will endeavor to occupy a station on which the light may fall; which is open to the rising sun; and from which it may correctly report the progress of the hour and the day." From the first, *The Dial* aspired to be a vehicle for the communication of those who affirmed a common gospel by speaking in the new fashion. Those who wrote in the journal, affirmed the editorial message, would be individuals whose hearts were "more in the future than in the past; and who trust[ed] the living soul rather than the dead letter." *The Dial* would "endeavor to promote the constant evolution of truth, not the petrifaction of opinion." On the frontier at Cincinnati, Clarke's *Western Messenger* corroborated. "'The Dial' marks an Era in American literature; it is the wind-flower of a new spring in the Western world,"[5] Clarke wrote, in an evaluation which was shaped by its kinetic content as well as its conscious articulation of Transcendental goals.

The preoccupation with movement was equally apparent in

Emerson's opening chat with readers. The editors, he told them, had obeyed a "strong current of thought and feeling" which had led them to counter "that rigor of our conventions of religion and education which is turning us to stone." He called it "the progress of a revolution." "Those who share in it have no external organization, no badge, no creed, no name. They do not vote, or print, or even meet together. They do not know each other's faces or names. They are united only in a common love of truth, and love of its work."[6] Always *The Dial* must stand for process and progress. It must be "such a Dial as is the Garden itself, in whose leaves and flowers and fruits the suddenly awakened sleeper is instantly apprised not what part of dead time, but what state of life and growth is now arrived and arriving."[7]

The shared gospel and revolution formed an underlying structure of consciousness, in other words, a mental base or foundation of very similar primary perceptions and value judgments. Upon such a base, diverse shapes and forms could rise on the phenomenal level— "special reforms in the state," "modifications of the various callings of men, and the customs of business," "a new scope for literature and art," "philosophical insight," "vast solitudes of prayer."[8] Gospel and revolution further were identified not only with editors but also with readers of *The Dial*. In a letter to Carlyle, Emerson described this audience as composed of religious people who hated ecclesiastical structure and who rejected old manners and mores without offering new ones. The "movement" for Emerson carried almost a messianic tinge: "Perhaps, one of these days, a great Yankee shall come, who will easily do the unknown deed."[9] Yet, whether or not the Transcendentalists were consciously aware of the fact, they *were* offering new manners and new mores. The rejection of any correspondence with the world of their immediate past was, as we shall see, interwoven with the discovery of a universe to which they found they could correspond.

Five of the six Club members whom we have been considering actually published in *The Dial*. Convers Francis, the one who did not, had taken part in preliminary discussions and supported production of the new journal. Therefore, in the pages of their *Dial* we can pursue the study of Transcendental consciousness through four years. During this extended "moment," the Transcendentalists did not so much develop as simply proclaim the nature of their revolution, and their language remained constant as it enunciated a view of reality in which motion was predominant. In overview, it is possible to describe this characterization of reality on two levels.

There was, first of all, a theoretical or conceptual level in which the language of process, life, force, energy, and emanation took the lead in expression. When more concrete language was used at this level, it tended to present a wholistic picture which mixed specific images freely to create an overall effect. In their use of language here, the Transcendentalists had blended a good dose of "linear logic" with their more mythic perceptions. They did not do this by couching their statements in syllogistic form as disciplined arguments but by being notional and abstract. In fact, one difficulty which critics have always had with their language—its vagueness—may be related to a problem which nagged the Transcendentalists. After years of education in discursive thinking, they were awkward in using the associative language their theory of correspondence called for.

At any rate, the Transcendentalists did move beyond this more theoretical plane to a second, an intuitional or poetic level, at which specific symbols formulated the meaning of life as change. Primarily, these symbols were natural forms of the world together with their respective series of associated meanings. The homologies which Emerson and his friends employed tended to be fairly conventional, and they often possessed archetypal dimensions. Moreover, since, for them, nature strictly understood meant all that was "NOT ME," nineteenth-century cultural forms were quickly linked to other, more traditional homologies. Nineteenth-century forms enabled the Transcendentalists to touch spiritual truth, for like every part of "nature," they were pieces in the macrocosm.

If mythic thinking characterized both levels of language which the members of the Club used, it follows that methods for the interpretation of myth will be helpful in understanding the Transcendentalists. Recent structural study has been helpful in illuminating systems of meaning which penetrate many cultures. After Immanuel Kant's critique of human reason, positing conceptual categories which, as part of mental structure, informed all discursive thought, it was easy to extend the Kantian analysis to mythic thought. One result in the West has been a new interest in theories of archetypal forms which are "culture-blind." Generally speaking, these archetypes are understood to exist in relationship to one another so that A is to B as C is to D, and E to F, until more and more aspects of the world can be included. Hard is to soft as active to passive and male to female. Sky is to earth as spirit to flesh and conscious logic to unconscious intuition. It is difficult to speak of controlling categories in such a context, since control implies normativeness and, in the worldview of correspondence, each piece of the world contains the germ of its opposite and the secret of the whole, so that it can be judge over every other. Still, in order to understand the meaning of myth somewhat "logically," it does become necessary to impose an order on the categories of experience which may appear to make some more central than others. So long as it is clear that this procedure is merely a heuristic tool, it can be a valid one.

Let us begin then with masculinity and femininity. These categories rise naturally out of human experience, and the oral and written recollections of humanity have everywhere demonstrated an awareness of sexual difference. Masculinity has often been linked to consciousness and spirit, while the feminine pole has been seen as the orbit of the unconscious and the material. In *Patterns in Comparative Religion*, Mircea Eliade discovered the cosmic equivalents of maleness and femaleness in sky and earth respectively.[10] In the sky, and especially the sun, Eliade saw a constellation of values which involved monotheism (the one sky over all), sovereignty and empire, military might, and linear logic (the comprehension of a systemic totality). The earth, on the other hand, provided the symbolic matrix for polytheism (many centers for the sacred), the cyclic rhythms of birth and death, and intuitive mental modes. To specify more, one need only extend the homologies in either direction. Thus, any form of light, a horse, an arrow, or the wind share the vigor of masculine consciousness, while water may recall the mysterious depths of the unconscious mind and the liquid womb of the female with its seeds of potential life. Clouds possess feminine softness, and vegetation is connected with (feminine) nurturing life. It is no accident that many languages have given gender designations to every portion of the world, for in the string of analogies every phenomenon finds itself in one orbit or the other—and even sometimes in both.

In these terms, a balanced cosmos means the presence and interaction of the opposite poles of existence which are, as well, poles of meaning and value. In both human community and the universe at large, correspondence includes the equipoise of the systems. As male complements female, sky bends to earth, activity requires passivity, and consciousness, the unconscious.[11] From the Transcendental perspective, a similar sense of the rightness of things would be part of the formula for the well-being of the era. Cosmic symbols which reflected either the masculine or the feminine pole, and sometimes participated in both, were used by the members of the New School. Cultural symbols, which were largely technological and gravitated toward the masculine sphere of influence, were used by them also. Always though, the Transcendental symbols suggested amid their harmony a concern for motion.

In the first place, the kinetic construction of reality ran through the more theoretical language which the Club members employed in *The Dial.* Both Ripley and Emerson used literary criticism to express their underlying worldview. Ripley found that literature reflected human life which did not "traverse an eternal circle" but instead advanced "in one endless career of progress towards the Infinite, the Perfect."[12] Similarly, Emerson reflected:

> *Every thought that arises in the mind, in its rising aims to pass out of the mind into act; just as every plant, in the moment of germination, struggles up to light. Thought is the seed of action; but action is as much its second form as thought is its first. It rises in thought to the end, that it may be uttered and acted.*[13]

Alcott testified that "both nature and man are ever making, never made."[14] People did not just speak: they held a "living intercourse" and felt the "quickening life and light," while Imagination sent abroad "her winged words." At the moment when the soul died, it could not be stuffed in a tomb, for "she eludes the grasp of decay; she builds and unseals the sepulchres," taking new form in bodies which were "fleeting, historical."[15] Meanwhile, Clarke looked at the movement in nature with "unfaltering eye" since he carried within him a "spirit conscious and active." Nature had been matched when soul stimulated soul and "pulses together beat."[16]

The Transcendentalists often evoked "life" and linked it with pulsation and germination. Alcott, for example, prophesied that "power which pulsates in all life, animates and builds all organizations, shall manifest itself as one universal deific energy, present alike at the outskirts and center of the universe."[17] Hedge rejoiced in movements "everywhere springing up," the "life, however spasmodic, of this generation."[18] Emerson studied Fourierism and found it wanting because it skipped the "faculty of life, which spawns and scorns system and system makers, which eludes all conditions, which makes or supplants a thousand phalanxes and New-Harmonies with each pulsation."[19] A human being was important because he owned "the dignity of the life which throbs around him in chemistry, and tree, and animal, and in the involuntary functions of his own body."[20]

Descriptions of life fanned out into "force" and "energy." Here "force" meant a more vigorous, thrusting, and defined form of life—masculine—while "energy" evoked a diffuse, generalized state which suggested underlying potentiality, unconscious power, and the feminine. For Alcott, the embodiment of force was the man of valor, "an augury of revolutions," who "revises men, time, life itself" and "overlives, outlives, eternizes."[21] For Emerson, the true poet was a being who possessed "thunder-tones, which cause to vibrate the sun and moon, which dissipate by dreadful melody all this iron network of circumstance."[22] Matter was not enough for the construction of the universe, but a "single impulse" was needed; "one shove to launch the mass, and generate the harmony of the centrifugal and centripetal forces."[23] At the other pole, Alcott found that solidity was an "illusion of the senses" since matter was "ever pervaded and agitated by the omnipresent soul."[24] Emerson discovered in vibrations of the human voice an "incalculable energy which countervails all other forces in nature, because they are the channel of supernatural powers."[25] Trade, politics, letters, science, and religion were all emanations, "rays of one sun," "instant and alive, and dissolving man as well as his works, in its flowing beneficence."[26]

Some language pictures, as we have remarked, reflected a generalized motion in which natural forms of the world were blended to convey one impression. For instance, something of the unpunctuated continuity of its rhythm was caught in Clarke's imagery of following the road westward:

> *Downward by gentle degrees, along the side of the mountain*
> *Winds our Simplon road, close to precipitous gulphs;*
> *Shooting up from below, spread the tops of the pine trees,*
> *Here a single misstep rolls us a thousand feet down,*
> *But, courage! trust to the driver, trust to the sure-footed horses,*
> *. . .*
> *Where below, like a map, lie many houses and farms,*
> *Over them all we look, over cornfields and meadows,*
> *Over the winding streams, shrouded with mantles of mist,*
> *Over an ocean of forests, up to the distant horizon*
> *Many a mile beyond, stretches our lengthening road.*[27]

The quicker the rhythm, the more highly it seemed to be valued. Emerson, in "The Snow-storm," celebrated "the mad wind's night-work, / The frolic architecture of the snow." Art would imitate slowly what the snow had done in a night. For the snow "driving o'er the fields" seemed "nowhere to alight." Because of it, housemates were "enclosed / In a tumultuous privacy of storm," and readers were invited to see the "north-wind's masonry," as he ran "speeding, the myriad-handed, his wild work / So fanciful, so savage."[28] Human as well as non-human nature corresponded to spirit. Emerson thought "the activity of the good [was] coincident with the axle of the world, with the sun and moon, and with the course of the rivers and of the winds, with the stream of laborers in the street, and with all the activity and well being of the race."[29]

In "The Sphinx," Emerson had written a poem which expressed the core of his religious understanding of motion. The theme was human self and ideal consciousness, which brought discontent, in contrast to the artless peace of nature. The Sphinx's "unanswered question" was humankind; the nature of the answer was conveyed by indirection in the kinetic imagery of the poem.

> *Uprose the merry Sphinx,*
> *And crouched no more in stone,*
> *She hopped into the baby's eyes,*
> *She hopped into the moon,*
> *She spired into a yellow flame,*
> *She flowered on blossoms red,*
> *She flowed into a foaming wave,*
> *She stood Monadnoc's head.*

Humanity and nature were cosmic twins, imitating each other. In humans, "Love works at the centre / Heart heaving alway, / Forth speed the strong pulses / To the borders of day." In nature, "The waves unashamed, / In difference sweet, / Play glad with the breezes, / Old playfellows meet. / The journeying atoms, / Primordial wholes, / Firmly draw, firmly drive, / By their animate poles."[30]

"Saadi" displayed the same proliferation of moving forms.

> *. . . before the listener's eye*
> *Swims the world in ecstasy,*
> *The forest waves, the morning breaks,*
> *The pastures sleep, ripple the lakes,*
> *Leaves twinkle, flowers like persons be,*
> *And life pulsates in rock or tree.*[31]

And in "Woodnotes," concrete imagery achieved metaphysical stature.

> The early genesis of things,
> Of tendency through endless ages,
> Of star-dust, and star pilgrimages,
> Of rounded worlds, of space and time,
> Of the old flood's subsiding slime,
> Of chemic matter, force and form
> Of poles, and powers, cold, wet, and warm;
> The rushing metamorphosis,
> Dissolving all that fixture is,
> Melts things that be to things that seem,
> And solid nature to a dream. [32]

The focus of the Transcendentalists seemed to narrow, however, to a relatively few cosmic and cultural symbols. As we have noted, some of these forms suggested the more masculine and forceful pole of the world. In this category, religious light was generally moving light. As an example, Alcott knew that the "prophet, whose eye is coincident with the celestial ray receives this into his breast, and intensifying there, it kindles on his brow a serene and perpetual day."[33] Saadi used the sunshine which had come into his heart to light "each transparent word."[34] Sometimes the light was lightning, so that, for Alcott, inspiration darted "like lightning, straight to its quarry," rending "all formulas of the schools as it illuminates the firmament of the mind."[35] More often, light was fire, and Hedge called the sun a "fireball," while Clarke found that the breath of God fanned the flame.[36] Meanwhile, Alcott saw the soul as a Prometheus which received divine fires and fashioned them into a human being who was both image of God and model for all other natural forms. Emerson called the heart of each Transcendentalist an "ark in which the fire is concealed, which shall burn in a broader and universal flame."[37]

Nature revealed its motion also in the wind. A striking aspect of the use of this symbol was its frequent association with the word in an atmosphere which suggested sacrality. Either the word was free, as the "breeze that flows cool and refreshing from the mountains, and invigorates their [people's] languid frames."[38] Or it was bound up with a poet like Saadi, whose words were "like a storm-wind" bringing "terror and beauty."[39] Or it was connected with prophecy, as Emerson's pine tree disclosed:

> *Song wakes in my pinnacles*
> *When the wind swells.*
> *Soundeth the prophetic wind,*
> *The shadows shake on the rock behind,*
> *And the countless leaves of the pine are strings*
> *Tuned to the lay the wood-god sings.* [40]

Finally, the wind became a God, and "To Eva at the South" told how the flowers, "tiny sect of Shakers," worshiped Zephyr and sang their hymn: "O come, then, quickly come, / We are budding, we are blowing, / And the wind that we perfume, / Sings a tune that's worth the knowing."[41]

The onward sweep of wind was paralleled by the rush of an arrow which reminded Alcott of a human soul, "quick with instincts of unerring aim."[42] The intellect was also like an arrow in Emerson's perception of wit, "a true shaft of Apollo" which traversed the universe.[43] In the horse of heaven, the thrusting power of wind and arrow grew stronger still. The tragedy for a genius, as Emerson saw it, was that he possessed one "wild" horse of heaven and one rather pedestrian beast of earth. Trying to drive such a team led only to "discord and ruin and downfall to chariot and charioteer."[44] A young poet's horses were "his own wild thoughts," which were not yet harnessed to the "team of society" to "drag with us all in the ruts of custom."[45]

The horse required a road, and the Transcendentalists understood life as a function of the path which was taken. Danger lurked on the "safe and approved path," while salvation beckoned on the solitary. For Ripley, a minister was wrong when he did not listen to his own ideas and inner voices. "He loves rather to ride in a troop on the dusty highway, than to search out for himself those green and shady avenues of truth."[46] Alcott advised that each person should "wend his course through this world of sense," taking his own route along "solitary by-roads,"[47] while Emerson located the hero's lonely path as "the highway of health and benefit to mankind."[48]

Technology in the nineteenth century brought an iron road and the pine tree of "Woodnotes" was transformed into miles of track:

> *Westward I ope the forest gates,*
> *The train along the railroad skates,*
> *It leaves the land behind like ages past,*
> *The foreland flows to it in rivers fast,*
> *I teach Iowa Saxon art.* [49]

In "The Young American," Emerson called the railroad an "arrow in our quiver,"[50] while in "The Tragic," he described fate as "this hideous enginery that grinds and thunders, and takes them [protagonists in Greek tragedy] up into its terrific system."[51]

The importance of personal charisma was suggested to Emerson by the nature of electricity. "Without electricity, the air would rot," he commented, and without the "violence of direction" which men and women possessed, there would be "no excitement, no efficiency."[52] The poet was a conductor from heaven to earth, "like the electric rod." In one lecture, he elucidated further:

> *There must be a few persons of purer fire kept specially as guages* [sic] *and meters of character; persons of a fine, detecting instinct, who betray the smallest accumulations of wit and feeling in the bystander. Perhaps too there might be room for the exciters and monitors; collectors of the heavenly spark with power to convey the electricity to others.* [53]

In considering another use of energy, Emerson explained how a mill was built "in such a position as to set the north wind to play upon our instrument, or the elastic force of steam, or the ebb and flow of the sea."[54] When later he spoke of "the mill of human ingenuity," human talent turned as it was played upon by divine forces.[55]

In sum, light, air, animal, space, technology—these cosmic and cultural symbols were translated to the printed page through the prism of Transcendental experience. The prism refracted in such a way that light became fire; air became wind; the horse pawed the earth and then sped off with its rider; space stretched into a highway or a railroad with its iron locomotive; and energy became electricity and steam.

When the Transcendentalists used the gentler symbols of the feminine axis, they expressed an equal dedication to motion. Here was pulsing energy more than tight-fisted force, diffused potency with controlled undertones which became more explicit in, for example, the flowing water images of fountain and river. Unlike the masculine symbols, the sexuality of which was largely implied rather than stated, the feminine symbols more openly disclosed their sexual content. For Emerson, nature was a maiden who must be wooed. Impulses drove young men away from society into solitude where they conversed with nature, and "courted [her] in a certain moody and exploring spirit."[56] The maiden married when Alcott spoke of the "sickle, marrying the soul and the soil by the rites of labor."[57] More often, the embosoming and mothering quality of nature was featured in Transcendental language. Emerson urged would-be reformers away from extremism and toward an imitation of the qualities of nature "which embosoms us all, and which sleeps no moment on an old past, but every hour repairs herself; yielding us every morning a new day, and with every pulsation a new life."[58]

Not only earthly nature, but also more abstract forms revealed their maternal inclinations. Alcott understood that "holiness embosoms him [a person] in the God-head," while "piety" embosomed "the fact that reason develops." Time was associated with mothering when the past acted as mother and nurse of the future. "Tradition suckles the young ages, who imbibe health or disease, insight or ignorance, valor or pusillanimity, as the stream of life flows down from urns of sobriety or luxury, from times of wisdom or folly, honor or shame."[59] Sometimes pregnancy and birth were used to describe human emotion and thought as when Alcott described a confinement of the heart: she was "great" and "big with the future."[60] Ripley observed that William Ellery Channing wrote "pregnant words" which embodied "the creed of the youth of this country, who are beginning, not so much to protest against the past, as to live in the present, and construct for the future."[61] "What is in, will out," summarized Emerson. "It [thought] struggles to the birth."[62]

Femininity was more subtle in the water imagery of the Transcendentalists. Water symbolized all-inclusive totality, the chaos from which form emerged: it was the source of existence which spoke of hidden power in seed and new birth. This androgynous and yet feminine quality of water led to its association with the unconscious in which, like a woman, it became mother to conscious life. Therefore, water became a great womb, giving rise to all being, both physical and spiritual. With an intuitive understanding, Emerson expressed his sense of the formless abyss from which forms came to be:

> And God said, Throb; and there was motion,
> And the vast mass became vast ocean.
> Onward and on, the eternal Pan
> Who layeth the world's incessant plan,
> Halteth never in one shape,
> But forever doth escape,
> Like wave or flame, into new forms
> Of gem, and air, and plants, and worms.[63]

The globe itself swam "so silently through the sea of space," and humanity arose from the pre-formal chaos: "Here on the surface of our swimming earth we come out of silence into society."[64]

Sometimes the Transcendental hero was a lonely sailor on the ocean of life. Clarke acknowledged that his fate was a solitary drifting "across life's many-tinted ocean." By himself, he would hear tempests and feel the water's "heavy motion."[65] In similar vein, Alcott thought of each soul as alone: it must sail the sea, steering and observing the heavens, to find its way back without the help of anybody else. And Emerson pictured the lonely voyager with his "new mind" as an adventurer who must put out into deep waters and leave behind the "gaping loiterers on the shore."[66]

The creativity and restlessness of water was expressed in the ebb and flow of tide. This understanding formed the basis of Alcott's ornate and extended metaphor on originality.

Most men are on the ebb; but now and then a man comes riding down sublimely in high hope from God on the flood tide of the soul, as she sets into the coasts of time, submerging old landmarks, and laying waste the labors of centuries. A new man wears channels broad and deep into the banks of the ages; he washes away ancient boundaries, and sets afloat institutions, creeds, usages which clog the ever flowing Present, stranding them on the shores of the Past. Such deluge is the harbinger of a new world, a renovated age. Hope builds an ark; the dove broods over the assuaged waters; the bow of promise gilds the east; the world is repeopled and re-planted.[67]

The intimate connection between time and tide was suggested; and the biblical language of ark, dove, and bow underlined the sacred quality of the water. Only what refused to be uprooted and clung to the shoreline was profane. The tide was a spiritual energy which "in eternal systole and diastole" incarnated nature in "mystic flow." Without it, the self ebbed back into "chaos and invisibility."

When Emerson, in "The Snow-storm," juxtaposed the river and heaven, both hidden by the snow, the conjunction expressed the religious overtones of a favorite Transcendental symbol. Sometimes there was the quiet motion of the "gentle brook, rippling the rocks along." Clarke noted that its "cool waters softly fall," while the valley was swept with the motion of time "into the opening day."[68] The poet's word also ran "like golden brooks through the dark forests of toil."[69]

For Emerson, the river could function as guardian spirit and teleological guide. It was the Beatrice of America, leading and nourishing at once. Asked how he found the sea from the forest, the peasant replied:

The watercourses were my guide,
I travelled grateful by their side,
Or through their channel dry;
They led me through the thicket damp,
Through brake and fern the beaver's camp,
Through beds of granite cut my road,
And their resistless friendship showed;

The falling waters led me,
The foodful waters fed me,
And brought me to the lowest land,
Unerring to the ocean sand. [70]

One of Ripley's favorite metaphors for spiritual life—the fountain—figured in *The Dial* when he warned a theological student not to be trapped in prevailing opinions but to "attain to a clear and living system of truth, which shall be to the soul what the blood is to the body,—a flowing fountain of inward strength."[71] In another critique, Ripley deplored the contemporary economic system which fostered intense competition. Its tendency was to "smother the gushing life of the spirit beneath a silver veil."[72] For Emerson, the fountain was a symbol of moral life: it was the "fountain of right" to which the brave ought to resort; a fountain of hope, present in human consciousness although no philosopher could locate it; a fountain of love which reformers had not reached because they stopped short at the intellectual recognition of social problems. In fact, "the origin of all reform" was "in that mysterious fountain of the moral sentiment in man." It was "new and creative," containing the supernatural, the place of "unbounded energy, unbounded power."[73]

In the water symbolism of the Transcendentalists, the conventional cosmic meanings were attached to a consciousness of water in a state of flux. It was never stagnant or standing still, and sometimes there was a flowing even when there was no observable water present. Emerson, for example, called a gift the "flowing of the giver" toward him, which corresponded to Emerson's own flowing toward the giver.[74] The source of the flowing was always divine energy, either directly or indirectly through nature, the mind, or the moral sense. For Alcott, the flux was the "plenitude of Life rushing gladly into the chambers of the breast," which transformed people into "incarnate Words,—prophets, silent or vocal, as the divine influx retreats to its source, or flows over their cloven tongues."[75] The setting for Emerson's "Woodnotes" was a charmed day in which "the genius of God" flowed. The task of a human instrument, such as a literary artist, was to not obstruct the flow through his own willfulness. The product then would belong as it should to nature. It would share "the sublimity of the sea and the sky" because it "flowed from his mind after the divine order of cause and effect."[76] Jones Very met this Transcendental specification because, as Emerson observed, most of his verses "rather flow through him than from him."[77]

"The soul of the Workman streams through us," Emerson wrote.[78] Still gentler, Clarke saw each individual floating in the Infinite Spirit "as motes in summer sky."[79] And Emerson celebrated nature's correspondence when he described the "softness and beauty of the summer clouds floating feathery overhead, enjoying, as it seemed, their height and privilege of motion."[80]

If masculinity and femininity were contrasting poles of meaning, between them lay a middle ground in which they could meet and marry. Religious traditions in both East and West had pointed to the reconciliation of opposites as the goal of spiritual endeavor. Humans imitated the mysterious unity of the cosmic spheres through the reunification of the separate aspects of their beings, while great symbols, such as the bisexual God or the mystical marriage, expressed a continuing theme in religious history. As the opposites merged in the macrocosm, so should the microcosmic world reflect the truth of things, and the members of the New School intuited this necessity. For the Transcendentalists, the integration of the divergent qualities of the world took place through the agency of motion, so that finally the Club members would blend the male and female character of the world by the general tenor of their prescriptions for the harmonious interaction of human and cosmic energy, prescriptions which we shall take up in more detail in the final chapter.

But advice began in symbol for the Transcendentalists. They reconciled the masculinity and femininity of existence first by seeing the world as qualitatively one, by identifying both poles of meaning with the dynamism of moving spheres. In practice, this meant that the members of the New School sometimes mingled the archetypal assignments of masculinity and femininity so that their world in flux possessed an androgynous character. Thus, Alcott, who liked to think of the soul as female, saw it also as a (masculine?) bow with arrows. "She is quivered with heavenly desires: her quarry is above the stars: her arrows are snatched from the armory of heaven."[81] It was evident that, for Ripley, there had been a "masculine" vigor about the energy with which water came from a fountain. And Emerson had, in an early lecture in 1834, personified water, as in some classical mythology, as "he."

> *It is surprizing to see how fast he can put on his masks, all new and all beautiful. Now he globes himself into a dewdrop. Now he reddens in the rainbow. Now he whitens into spray. Now he floats as a cloud. Now he shines as an icicle; now he crystallizes into the star of a snowflake; now he rolls as a wave, and then disappears from human eyes to make the transparency of the atmosphere.* [82]

Similarly, Clarke had seen the waters of the continent part "like brothers who roam far from the family home, / Some to the mighty Atlantic, some to the far Mississippi."[83] He had invoked the connection between a river and a human life when he portrayed a traveler gazing at the water: "Perchance he looks at the river which winds far below, vexed and foaming, / Childishly fretting around rocks which it cannot remove. / Ah! that river runs *westward*."[84] Still half-child, the river had to leave its ancient home to make its way in an alien world. Significantly, it followed the sun and the Western frontier. Its orientation was toward the future, and as a result, water had begun to express the thrust toward history and empire of a more masculine character.

The Transcendental concern for wholeness revealed itself also in the preference for the image of the circle. For Tantric Buddhists and mystical Taoists, for ancient Gnostics and modern-day Jungians, the circle, or mandala, meant the union of masculine and feminine, active and passive, conscious and unconscious in a completion which possessed a sacred quality.[85] Meanwhile, structurally, the line of the circle might be said to "flow." It had neither beginning nor end; disclosed neither source nor goal. It was self-contained, a totality—but a fluid totality.

Emerson's essay "Circles" had developed this theme. In *The*

Dial, he continued to use the motif, calling the poet a "wise harbinger of spheres," and the reformer a "fly-wheel in a mill, which
distributes the motion equably over all the wheels, and hinders it
from falling unequally and suddenly in destructive shocks."[86] Alcott
described how the soul worked "from center to periphery," round-
ing itself and completing its organizations.[87] Clarke showed that
when a person became feverish, the circle's movement was
disturbed. "Round and round within circled a whirlpool of
thoughts, / Round and round they went, his will had no power to
restrain them / Round and ever around some insignificant thing!"[88]
The answer to the riddle of the circle's roundness was the answer to
the riddle of the Sphinx—humanity itself. Emerson shared the age-
old religious vision and combined it with motion: "Profounder, profounder / Man's spirit must dive: / To his aye-rolling orbit / No
goal will arrive."[89]

  We have been following the associative chains of symbols which
shaped the language of the Transcendentalists into a proclamation of
motion. What we have not yet stressed, however, is that, like discursive thinking, mythic formulations could raise questions and pose
problems in the search for the meaning of life. Out of the symbols
used in *The Dial*, two related questions emerged. There was, first of
all, the problem of permanence and change or, more specifically,
what could be permanent in the midst of fluidity. Secondly, there
was the problem of the nature of authenticity, or what could truly be
called "real." The problems were related because the members of the
New School identified authenticity with an underlying permanence
in the flux. The twin formulation only underlined the seriousness of
the religious crisis in their minds.

  Although flux was sacred, even the Transcendentalists wanted
it to be grounded in some enduring form. On the conceptual level,
Emerson understood the soul as a permanent entity amid the im-
permanent senses. Ideal forms, he said, contained more truth than
the actual world because they did not change. And, in "The
Amulet," he sought a sign that love would remain the same.[90] Clarke
celebrated Nydia for the truth at the center of her being "which no
earth-mists had power to dim." He praised the marble bust of
Schiller because it expressed the eternal forms of Poet and Genius

which he had incarnated in his life.[91] Sometimes, specific symbols displayed forms of permanence in relation to the changes of nature. In his poem, "From Uhland: The Castle by the Sea," Hedge set the castle in a context of wind and sea: "The wind and the heaving sea, / Sounded they fresh and strong? / From the hall came notes of glee / Harping and festive song?" The movement of wind and sea surrounded the structural stability of the castle and became associated with the life and happiness within since, after the death of the maiden with golden hair, wind and water both rested "in slumbers deep." The change of death brought sympathetic non-motion to nature, and mourning was indicated because what should have been part of the flux had stopped moving.[92] Less complex was Clarke's picture of permanence and change in "Dream." He saw terraces supporting "noble statues," while majestic plants poured "streams of perfume round."[93] Emerson combined permanence with change when he wrote of "the river which ever flowing, yet is found in the same bed from age to age."[94]

Often a plant or tree expressed the rooted quality of permanence. But, almost always, natural forms suggested a context of motion—so that the plant or tree was not stationary, but rooted amidst continual movement. For example, Alcott addressed the heart as a "soul-flower, facing ever and following the motions of thy sun, opening thyself to her vivifying ray."[95] Emerson at times solved the problem by yoking a tree to a river. The spirit of the time, he observed, "has the step of Fate, and goes on existing like an oak or a river, because it must."[96] Both permanence and change, he seemed to say, existed necessarily. Both could teach him: "Listen what the poplar tree / And murmuring waters counselled me."[97]

In "Woodnotes," Emerson described a tree which suggested change as much as rootedness:

> *When the pine tosses its cones*
> *To the song of its waterfall tones,*
> *He speaks to the woodland walks,*
> *To the birds and trees he talks.* [98]

The pine tree later confessed what it stood for:

> *Change I may, but I pass not;*

Hitherto all things fast abide,
And anchored in the tempest ride.
Trenchant time behoves to hurry
All to yean and all to bury;
All the forms are fugitive,
But the substances survive. [99]

Typically, the tree corresponded to each human life which should also reveal a permanence in the midst of the passing show. For Alcott, a person must grow up "as the tree of the primeval woods, luxuriant, vigorous—armed at all points, to brave the winds and the storms of the finite and the mutable."[100] Emerson admired the "centred" individual, "grounded in the divine life by his proper roots," who would not be shaken in time of chaos.[101]

The Transcendentalists formulated the relationship between permanence and change in their quest for authenticity and personal integrity. What is the I of I? the Transcendentalists seemed to be asking. If I live in a changing world and if I myself am born, mature, grow old, and die, what is it that makes me the same person through these alterations? In this setting, a building became a fitting symbol for a person's inner spirit. Alcott spoke of the "citadel" of individual integrity, the "temple which the soul builds to herself."[102] Clarke turned to nature to find the image of his own spirit. He was like the ground in which roots were planted, yielding "precious vines" and "heavenly roses."[103] In these and other instances, the Transcendentalists were finding that what endured was the spark of the soul or the core of the self. It was the discrete particle which by itself contained the key to the whole without the mediation of covenant or historical community. The Hindu notion of the *atman* appealed to them, and their final answer to the question of integrity would be their own version of mystical theory and practice as taught by their leader, Emerson. In *The Dial*, the Transcendentalists were content to summarize their case in notions such as self-culture and the divinity of humanity. "I cannot find language of sufficient energy to convey my sense of the sacredness of private integrity," Emerson wrote flatly in one essay.[104]

When symbolic language was employed, it frequently emerged

in the pattern of the permanence-change motifs: what was unmoving was either combined with what moved or endowed with overtones of energy. Emerson spoke of granite which formed lofty mountains and yet lay deep in the earth beneath them; the "elemental reality" which permeated all political and personal relationships was like the granite since it "ever and anon comes to the surface, and forms the grand men."[105] He lectured on how people "drift like white sail across the wild ocean, now bright on the wave, now darkling in the trough of the sea." What made the situation endurable was that "underneath all these appearances, lies that which is, that which lives, that which causes. This ever renewing generation of appearances rests on a reality, and a reality that is alive."[106] In his poem "Fate," Emerson spoke of the "jewel" of uniqueness which each person possessed. What interested him was neither the material nor the color of the gem: even "pure water" would be acceptable. Rather, the jewel must "dazzle" him with its light.[107]

When Hedge discussed the scholarly vocation to fullness of life, he articulated his notion of integrity in terms suggesting its developmental nature. A satisfaction accompanied "the consciousness of progress, in the true direction towards the stature of a perfect man."[108] The "sanctity of the private heart" was a prominent theme for Alcott also. All outward change must be preceded by "renovation of being," for the change must originate within and work outwards.[109] Similarly, in his open letter to a theological student, Ripley congratulated the student on a purely self-motivated decision to embrace ministry and urged him to be, above all, true to himself.[110] Always, the permanent and enduring self was a self on the move. Alcott spoke for all of his friends when he found that reform, motion, and God were closely related. Reformers brought an end to stagnation, and this made them good. "They uproot institutions, erase traditions, revise usages, and renovate all things," he wrote exuberantly. "Extant in time, they work for eternity; dwelling with men, they are with God." Conversely, dogmatists were bad because they boasted of possessions which "skirt space" and they vetoed "all possible discoveries of time."[111]

Impatient with the formalism of Brahmin Boston, the Transcendentalists had instead chosen flux. The name of their *Dial* had been apt, indeed, for time and a futuristic thrust provided a categorical framework for the symbolization used by the Club members. "For Time's Dial is set by thee," Alcott confided to his diary, "and the orb of day wheels on his courses to illustrate the story of thy Soul."[112] In the eternal ordering of things, God had set the human heart, like a clock, to the future "by secret and inviolable springs." Because this was so, the moral imperative became "not to block improvement, and sit till we are stone, but to watch the uprise of successive mornings, and to conspire with the new works of new days." Government had been a "fossil; it should be a plant"; "new thoughts, new things."[113] The passage of days and seasons and a face set toward the future were twin desiderata. In combining these notions of organic time and human action, the Transcendentalists had expressed in their group project what they had all expressed individually. The kind of correspondence which they perceived in the cosmos was a hybrid sort: the placidity of the traditional cosmos with its harmonious spheres had a new urgency which suggested that humankind had not yet arrived at the temple; and the profane, which in essence was one with the sacred in pure correspondence, was now more radically separated from it. The "motion" of *The Dial* corroborated a new perception of religious reality.

Yet the urgency of human action, issuing from a system of values which included, as Eliade has shown, monotheism, might, empire, and logical thought processes, had been tempered in *The Dial* by a preponderance of symbols which were either feminine or sometimes an androgynous blend. With its choice of water as the primary carrier of the flux as well as its strong preference for symbols of nurture and vegetation, *The Dial* had skewed its motion toward the polytheism of many centers of the sacred, toward self-cultured individuals who lived amid the rhythms of nature, toward associative and intuitive thought. Curiously, as we shall see, the relativism of an American people concerned with making history ended by making history itself an absolute, while the conceptual monism of Transcendental believers led them to rejoice in the particularism and the polytheism of nature.

CHAPTER V

A Corresponding Revolution in Things

TRANSCENDENTAL LANGUAGE, as both the Club members and their elders had agreed, did not mesh very well with the more traditional speech of Boston. Yet, according to the principle of correspondence which had become the central tenet of the new faith, the Transcendental word should have been replicated in some part of the macrocosm. Emerson had made it clear that the macrocosm in question included nature and that nature in the "philosophical" sense meant all that was "NOT ME." Therefore, if there could be no correspondence with the formal world of Boston, there still should be some piece of the human, cultural world which Transcendental language reflected. By speaking their new tongue, the members of the Club had projected inner meaning into the world that was outside themselves, and now they could use their objectified word as a sounder to find that world to which their inner meaning conformed. While it is easy to see that non-human nature was related to the content of the Transcendental word, the question was, since a human world (proper Boston) had been rejected, what other *human* world corresponded? What other human world answered?

Outside the neighborhood of Boston, there was the world of nineteenth-century America in all the exuberance of its early national period. Indeed, the exuberance which characterized it may be the first clue to the shape of the macrocosm for which the Transcendentalists were searching. A great deal was happening "out there" in the America which was contemporaneous with the followers of the New School, and perhaps it could be summarized in words from a cultural celebration of the 1960s, the musical comedy *Hair*. "What have you got, 1967?" the year 1947 asked angrily. And 1967 responded rather arrogantly, "Well, if you really want to know, 1947, I've got life!" If 1836 had retorted in like fashion to 1806, it had every right to in its own context. Furthermore, if the Transcendentalists knew what was going on, they had every right to recognize some continuities with their own revolution. For, in 1836, many Americans were immersed in a period of intense social ferment and change. It seemed almost a dream that three decades previously, their world had been placidly agrarian, that Thomas Jefferson had hailed its stable agricultural flavor and purchased Louisiana to preserve it, that John Taylor of Caroline had theorized on the quality of rural virtue and the stuff of the agrarian dream. By 1836 the dream was phasing itself out with incredible speed. And, while the Transcendentalists could not discover the unspoiled pastures of wild nature hiding in the cultural transformations of 1836, they could discover that elusive quality they valued as highly. In short, what could appeal to the Transcendentalists about 1836 was that it had "life."

Men imbued with new energy were building mills, importing farm girls as operatives, and settling company towns. Others were dredging canals, harnessing steam to power boats, laying the iron and wooden planks which laced the countryside with a path for the speeding locomotive. The motif of speed was echoed in the cities which, with ever faster tempo, mushroomed in number and size. While rural migrants and hordes of immigrants settled the cities, others in prairie schooners moved through the plains toward the frontier. Democratic process took new turns in the Jacksonian era, and the economy spiraled, crashed, then soared to new heights. Meanwhile, as individuals attempted to grapple with the problems their age presented, a plethora of reform movements sprang up in a sub-culture of ultraism filled with unusual religious manifestations and communitarian episodes. Emerson had remarked "new thoughts, new things." It looked as if America, in 1836 and the years which ensued, was undergoing a corresponding revolution in things.

The revolution was first of all industrial, and it was as evident as the smoke from the new factory smokestacks. Before the War of 1812, manufacturing in the United States had operated on a home system in which each family used its own supplies and finished its own product. Homespun industry became household industry when merchant capitalists organized the process to some extent by parceling out work orders and sometimes distributing raw materials or supplies and tools. Then Francis Lowell's Boston Manufacturing Company began the transformation of raw cotton into cloth at Waltham, followed in 1822 by the Merrimack Manufacturing Company, at the new factory town of Lowell, which concentrated on calico cloth. A year later, the factory town of Chicopee was established. In the changeover, each separate process in the total manufacture of cotton commodities had been brought under a single roof and a single management. Victor Clark pointed to the significance of what had occurred:

> *The transfer of spinning and weaving in America from homes to factories was a greater change than their transfer from workshops to factories in Great Britain. No other industrial arts were so universally practiced by our people and no other were so suddenly taken from their hands. In spite of the occasional persistence of homespun in isolated districts until within recent memory, the short period between 1810 and 1830 saw the center of gravity of textile manufactures shift from the fireside to the factory. Not only did the household lose a traditional employment, but simultaneously industry—for the first time in our history—began to disintegrate the family.*[1]

Young female mill operatives came from local New England farms or small towns, remained for several years at a factory, and accumulated money to help out at home, to pay for an education, or perhaps to amass a dowry. Their goals accomplished, the girls would return to their homes, creating the phenomenon of a transient rather than a permanent mill population. Later, cheap Irish immigrant labor would replace the Lowell girls, and working conditions would become more grim. But even in the earlier period, when conditions in Massachusetts factory towns were semi-idyllic, the Rhode Island system employed entire families who learned what it meant to move from the farm and take up their lives in a new locale, working under harsh conditions as a "mill family."

Industrialization brought movement through its relocation of persons and entire families, its encouragement of transience, and its ability, through the introduction of a technology of interchangeable parts, to speed the pace of production radically. Mechanization had even further ramifications which heightened the mood of rapid change. New styles and patterns began to appear and disappear. "As soon as it was possible to produce goods mechanically with little labor, people became more fastidious, clothing was not worn so long, its texture was diversified, and considerations of fashion appealed to a wider range of consumers."[2] People were paced by machinery now; the artificial time of the clock replaced and transmuted the organic rhythms of nature with a new emphasis on speed. The growth of manufactures which so diversified material surroundings "substituted a thirst for change in place of an earlier love for fixed order and familiar ways."

> *The material environment, like the intellectual environment, of our forefathers was permanent. They lived in the same houses, used the same furniture, employed the same implements, wore the same clothing, and viewed the same scenes from youth to old age. Their minds reflected the conservative habit of their surroundings. A certain immobility of ideas and customs corresponded to the fixed features of their habitat.* [3]

This state of affairs had passed, whether for better or worse, for change had become a value, and newness a virtue.

Nineteenth-century roads and canals provided a complement to industrial production. The Cumberland Turnpike was extended across Ohio and Indiana to Vandalia, Illinois, by successive appropriations so that, along with other roads, it aided the flow of traffic westward. But with the spectacular success of the Erie Canal after 1825, a canal-building fever began to grip the United States, and by 1840, Americans had constructed 3326 miles of canals. The newly harnessed steam, which made canal and river transportation five times as fast as in the pre-steam era, brought with it a cult of speed almost fanatical in its intensity. This was particularly true in the West where the use of high compression made a condenser unnecessary and afforded an engine which was compact, inexpensive, easy to assemble, and—most of all—faster. Foreign visitors often recounted frightening episodes in which they were forced to contend with the American mania for speed and nonchalance toward danger. Baron de Gerstner could testify from personal experience to the American motto, "We always get ahead."

> *The Democrats here never like to remain behind one another: on the contrary, each wants to get ahead of the rest. When two steamboats happen to get alongside each other, the passengers will encourage the captains to run a race, which the latter agree to. The boilers intended for a pressure of only 100 pounds per square inch, are by the accelerated generation of steam, exposed to a pressure of 150, and even 200 pounds, and this goes sometimes so far, that the trials end with an explosion. . . . The races are the cause of most of the explosions, and yet they are still constantly taking place. The life of an American is, indeed, only a constant racing, and why should he fear it so much on board the steamboats?*[4]

The doom of the canals, however, was sealed just one year after the completion of the Erie Canal when the tiny horse-drawn Granite Railroad, the first in the United States, began to run near the home of the Adamses in Quincy, Massachusetts. In 1828, the Baltimore and Ohio steam railroad would win its charter, and two years later thirteen miles of track would extend toward Ohio. From 1830 to 1840, the railroad grew from infancy to a formidable economic presence, a situation which was reflected in the fact that Massachusetts had added 267 miles of track to its three of 1830, while the nation as a whole could boast of 3698 miles. With a fever of haste and a scarcity of capital, roadbeds were constructed mostly of wood, and a special American locomotive had to be designed which would be light and flexible. Not surprisingly, such locomotives would also travel faster: John Bloomfield Jervis's Brother Jonathan could speed to sixty or eighty miles an hour, while Joseph Harrison's Mercury outdid the Brother Jonathan in its ability to maintain the speed steadily, traveling 37,000 miles at sixty miles an hour with a train of passenger cars. The mad pace of the Boston and Lowell Railroad brought discomfort to at least one distinguished European visitor, as Charles Dickens recorded in his *American Notes:*

> *It [the train] rushes across the turnpike road, where there is no gate, no policeman, no signal: nothing but a rough wooden arch, on which is painted "WHEN THE BELL RINGS, LOOK OUT FOR THE LOCOMOTIVE." On it whirls headlong, dives through the woods again, emerges in the light, clatters over frail arches, rumbles upon the heavy ground, shoots beneath a wooden bridge which intercepts the light for a second like a wink, suddenly awakens all the slumbering echoes in the main street of a large town, and dashes on haphazard, pell-mell, neck-or-nothing, down the middle of the road. There . . . on, on, on—tears the mad dragon of an engine with its train of cars; scattering in all directions a shower of burning sparks from its wood fire; screeching, hissing, yelling, panting; until at last the thirsty monster stops beneath a covered way to drink, the people cluster round, and you have time to breathe again.* [5]

Unnerving though the new technology might be, it represented "improvement," and, partly encouraged by the improved means of transportation, the great Western trek gained momentum, as would-be settlers poured across the continent. From 1810 to 1830, two million people migrated from the Eastern states, while by 1840 one out of every three persons lived across the Appalachians. "All was motion and change"; Frederick Jackson Turner wrote, "restlessness was universal." [6] Editors continually waxed eloquent about how short a time it took before a wilderness could be transformed into a settlement. One man from Virginia moved to Ohio in 1819, to Indiana in 1825, to Wisconsin in 1835, and then in 1849 complained, "I reached the Pacific, and yet the sun sets west of me, and my wife positively refuses to go to the Sandwich Islands, and the bark is starting off my rails, and that is longer than I ever allowed myself to remain on one farm."[7]

Meanwhile, the cities multiplied in number and in size. In 1820, only 7.2 per cent of the population had lived in cities of 2500 or more, and over half of all city-dwellers were clustered in the six largest cities: New York, Philadelphia, Baltimore, Boston, New Orleans, and Charleston—all thriving seaports. But from 1820, urban growth became a booming reality. During the forties, city population rose 92.1 per cent, while the total United States population increased only 35.9 per cent.[8] New York City, which had passed 130,000 in 1820, contained a population of close to 350,000 in 1840. In Boston, the situation was similar as the population grew from 54,000 to almost 120,000 during the same time span.[9] Migration combined with the rise of the steamboat and the use of the canal to induce a phenomenal growth in Western cities. In the Ohio Valley, the economy had blossomed into cities like Cincinnati, Pittsburgh, and Louisville, and the Lake Erie economy fed Toledo, Cleveland, and Detroit. At the juncture of the Missouri and the Mississippi, St. Louis throve, while an infant Chicago began to stretch itself along the Midwest plain beside Lake Michigan.

Beginning with the horse-drawn omnibuses introduced in cities like Boston and Philadelphia, rapid transit systems facilitated the urbanization process. Then, in 1838, the Boston and Worcester Railroad issued its first annual commuter ticket, and not much later a special commuter train connected Boston with West Newton. At the same time, sanitary and health conditions in the urban centers rapidly worsened. The cities grew at a pace which did not allow for a sensible perception of and planning for crowded conditions, poor sewage and lighting, the rise of crime, and other ills.

Slums like Half Moon Place in Boston were tenanted by Irish immigrants who numbered among droves of foreigners pouring into Eastern cities and compounding the problems. Here, shacks and shanties appeared indiscriminately and incongruously, while the Cholera Commission reported that a large part of the area was occupied by continually overflowing privies and "ill constructed worn out sinks and drains, into which are hourly thrown solid substances, of all sorts, which choke them up." Whole families were crowded into cellars, some of them "divided off into one or more rooms, into which hardly a ray of light, or breath of air passes."[10] The immigrant population grew at over twice the rate of the native-born, so that disorder soon became a fact of life in urban America. The Irish—whose rowdyism and drinking habits were often deplored by Protestant evangelicals—organized themselves into street gangs and were quickly countered by native-born gangs. Even in 1835, there were tales of Irishmen driving Whigs from polling places in New York and fighting off the mayor and the sheriff's posse with the Irish brand of confetti—brickbats. While, in 1820, most urban newcomers had been rural migrants, the percentage of foreign-born new residents grew steadily, doubling every decade. Tensions increased and with them the number of violent incidents. The usual procedure for restoring order was calling out the militia, with soldiers an ordinary sight in Eastern seaboard cities.

The influx of foreigners created an abundant supply of unskilled labor to replace an earlier scarcity. At the same time, the factory system had begun to wrest autonomy from independent artisans by making them part of a larger complex. Conditions which seemed plausible in a rural setting—such as the sunup-to-sundown day—grew more and more burdensome in an urban environment. Under these circumstances, labor began to organize, and soon Workingmen's Parties would prove a political force to be reckoned with.

It was the era of the common and ordinary citizenry. In 1828, General Andrew Jackson, hero of the battle of New Orleans, celebrated the new mood in America by his election to the presidency. While the powerful mourned, humbler people rejoiced in the democratic aura which surrounded the man from Tennessee. Although it is surely a romanticization to say of Jackson that "the people called him, and he came, like the great folk heroes, to lead them out of captivity and bondage,"[11] he did replace old hierarchies with newer, less decentralized units. His redistribution of federal offices, the "spoils system," permanently instituted the practice of rotation in office and brought some decentralization, some change in the direction of greater interaction among disparate people, and some democratization in the upper echelons. His war against Nicholas Biddle and the Second Bank of the United States, whatever its merits or demerits, effectively defeated the institution, and, until the rise of the independent treasury, state banks spread the banking business of the government across a wide geographical area.

At the same time—and independent of the "democratic" persona of the chief executive—political and electoral reforms were initiating a more populist style in politics and encouraging the emergence of new institutions. Even before the election of 1828, most states had extended suffrage to all white males who were taxpayers, while South Carolina was the only state which did not choose its electors by popular vote. Concurrently, party conventions replaced legislative caucuses as the normative means for party management. At least one student of the political forms of the Jacksonian period has called these changes a "hidden revolution."[12] Whether or not they actually made the political process more democratic, they were basic innovations which brought the "newness" into the political arena.

The "newness" also had its effect on the business and economic world, an effect which was jolting during the financial crash and Panic of 1837. Contractions in the business cycle such as this one seemed to affect the American economy periodically. The contraction would be preceded by a long period of expansion in which note issue rested on a smaller and smaller specie base. Speculation would grip the banks which floated ever more notes, largely to finance investment crazes in Western lands. Meanwhile, more and more banks sprang up to reap the financial fortunes accompanying the inflationary spiral. The bubble would inevitably burst; and, in a familiar pattern, runs were made on banks demanding specie payments which were almost non-existent. The banks took action to suspend payment, and the economic cycle plunged to its nadir. The drama was repeated in 1819, in 1837, and in 1857. Michel Chevalier, visiting from France in the mid-1830s, remarked that while the French queued up at the doors of theatres, the Americans were fonder of lining up at the doors of banks. The American, he said, needed "violent sensations" to "stir his vigorous nerves." "He launches with delight into the ever-moving sea of speculation. One day, the wave raises him to the clouds; he enjoys in haste the moment of triumph. The next day he disappears between the crests of the billows; he is little troubled by the reverse; he bides his time coolly and consoles himself with the hope of better fortune."[13] Still, it was the "heyday of the entrepreneur," and Chevalier accurately assessed that "some individuals lose, but the country is a gainer; the country is peopled, cleared, cultivated; its resources are unfolded, its wealth increased."[14]

The movement and change which characterized the larger aspects of the American political, social, and economic scene were paralleled by a social ferment operating on a less universal scale. Speculative and technological fever did not exhaust the energies of some Americans. Rather, their restlessness found issue in crusades of conscience which were directed toward one or another abuse that must be obliterated or necessity that must be instituted. This might be termed a more "social" kind of motion than the largely impersonal activity of building and planting a country. Movements for individual reforms seemed to originate in the crisis of conscience of a few—whose resulting energy then was channeled as external force to supply a need in society. The reform activity of the era was indeed so widespread that it created a sub-culture of ultraism. The black and the Indian; temperance, peace, and women's rights; schools, prisons, and asylums—all received the influx of the reformers' energies.

Social reform often echoed the enthusiasm of religious ferment. The ultraist spirit fanned the great revival fires such as those of the "burned-over district" in western New York state, while some came to believe that the millennium was imminent, and others embraced the spiritualist teaching that they could communicate with those who had passed to a world beyond this life. At the same time, a popular interest in mesmerism and Swedenborgianism, both nineteenth-century forms of the occult, complemented the spiritualist manifestations.

Still others followed the call of newly evolving religious communities. Like most of the religious phenomena of the era, these communities seemed to act as surrogates for the stable covenant community of the mainline Christian churches which, in an age of fragmentation, was beginning to lose its power for some. The Mormon church was only one example of the direction a new community could take. Combining elements of ecclesiastical structure with more purely communal aspects, such as the pooling of financial assets and polygamous marriage, its history in the first half of the nineteenth century was one of migration. Other native American communities, such as John Humphrey Noyes's Oneida Community, experienced a migratory phase. Meanwhile, foreign groups, such as the English Shakers and the German Rappites, now in the New World, moved to new locations to contribute to the American communitarian tradition.

American religious sects grew more secular as their communities succeeded, and hence they provided continuity with groups such as Robert Owen's New Harmony Society. It was an unintended comment on this continuity that Robert Owen purchased the land and buildings of the Rappites in Harmony, Indiana, for his own experiment. Even failure of Owenism did not dampen a revival of communitarianism in the 1840s. The theories of the French socialist, Charles Fourier, together with those of his compatriot, the Conte de Saint-Simon, were popularized in America by such men as Albert Brisbane, Horace Greeley, and Parke Godwin. Encouraged by a vocal press campaign, Fourierist phalanxes arose in numbers in the area surrounding New York City. At Red Bank, New Jersey, and at Rochester, New York, strong associative communities developed, while a cluster sprang up near Cincinnati. Interestingly, the most famous exponent of Fourierist principles was Ripley's Brook Farm. Here the "Age of Reason in a patty-pan" had progressed through four years when, by the vote of its trustees, it became a Fourierist phalanx. For the next several years, Brook Farm was the feather in the cap of American Fourierism. But, like the other American phalanxes and like the Owenite communities before them, Brook Farm Fourierism was destined to disappear. Associative communities usually lasted from ten to thirty years, so that they were but slightly longer variations on Owenism; like the many changes of the time, they came and went.

From the Industrial Revolution to Jacksonian politics to burning revival fires and communitarian Utopias, the context of the casual gathering of Transcendental spirits was a veritable kaleidoscope of movement and change. Chevalier remarked on the quality of American life in the 1830s:

> *If movement and the quick succession of sensations and ideas constitute life, here one lives a hundredfold more than elsewhere; here, all is circulation, motion, and boiling agitation. Experiment follows experiment; enterprise follows enterprise. Riches and poverty follow on each other's traces and each in turn occupies the place of the other. While the great men of one day dethrone those of the past, they are already half overturned themselves by those of the morrow. Fortunes last for a season; reputations for the twinkling of an eye. An irresistible current sweeps everything away, grinds everything to powder and deposits it again under new forms. Men change their houses, their climate, their trade, their condition, their party, their sect; the States change their laws, their officers, their constitutions. The soil itself, or at least the houses, partake in the universal instability. The existence of social order in the bosom of this whirlpool seems a miracle, an inexplicable anomaly.* [15]

Hence, the activity of the new America might be said to answer the quality of Transcendental language. Both the Transcendentalists and the new America participated in a certain style of intuiting and expressing the nature of things, and the style for both was motion. But, how aware were Emerson and his friends of the answer of America? Was there an overt connection between the perception of events or involvement in them and the language of the new religion? Often the Transcendentalists have been cast as fuzzy "mystics" who walked through their own era with a case of myopia that left them in a genteel fog. Arthur Schlesinger's *Age of Jackson* provides a classical example of this kind of criticism, and every respectable high school anthology of American literature has contained its subtle or not-so-subtle innuendo concerning the impracticality of the Transcendental coterie. In truth, they seemed an eccentric bunch, so that in many cases the correspondence between the joke and its Transcendental butt was clear. Yet, as we have already seen to some extent, there was an active Yankee hiding inside many of the Club members. The non-action of the Transcendentalists was not total, and, when it did occur, it was not inactivity but rather another *form* of action. Even more, while the suggestion has been so far that the members of the New School were at least minimally aware of what was going on in their world, the record reveals just how deeply impressed they were by a consciousness of the events which made their time an era of social revolution.

Some of the Transcendentalists had firsthand acquaintance with parts of the process of industrial transformation. Francis recalled an early phase in the development of the commercial bakery when he worked for his father, who had grown famous in the vicinity for Medford crackers. The trade was a household industry, and at the bakehouse Francis had become an "expert in the business." He could "*break* and *mould* and *flat* and *dock* as well as the best; but *rolling* and *setting* were reserved for more practised hands."[16] Clarke's father had converted an old grist mill in Newton into a bleaching factory for beeswax and then into a plant to manufacture drugs. The impression on young Clarke must have been vivid, for several years later he recounted a dream he had once had in which he was in his father's factory during an "important chemical process." "Immense wheels were rolling, chains were rattling, and liquid fire was spouted up through curiously bent tubes, while torrents of a melted and heaving mass seemed to dash itself about by an internal force which was with difficulty restrained by the machinery."[17] Meanwhile, Alcott, rather unenthusiastically, had been employed at Silas Hoadley's clock factory for nine months.

From his youth, Emerson had been casually exposed to the factory system. He had written once to his brother William about a "walk to Mr. Lovejoy's Factory," and later, he visited Shepherd's factory at Round Hill and a lead mine, which he described in detail.[18] He marveled at a new machine at Waltham "to watch the watchmen of the factory. Every hour they must put a ring on to the wheel or if they fall asleep & do not, the machine will show their neglect & which hour they slept."[19] At Bangor, Maine, he became enthusiastic over the "noble sight" of the ten-sawed mill and proceeded to describe the lumbering operation in some detail.[20] The spring of 1837 found Emerson "gay as a canary bird" because he had learned that "the destiny of New England is to be the manufacturing country of America." "Where they have the sun, let them plant," he decided. "We who have it not, will drive our pens & waterwheels."[21] There were "great advantages" that arose from division of labor,[22] and the manufacturer was bound up with nature, for factory bell, city clock, and shining sun all asked, "What doest thou?"[23] It was this "prospective working of nature" toward culture and the transcendent idea which ennobled the factory system. Without it, he could see "nothing agreeable to the imagination in the din and smoke of so many trades as turn the streets of a city into the wards and apartments of a great factory."[24]

Alcott remembered the installation of Parson John Keys in 1814 as synchronous with the appearance of factories. "Up to his time the pursuit had been mainly agriculture; but now new industries had sprung into existence in neighboring towns, and drawn the young people away by the offer of better wages or more agreeable pursuits."[25] A growth in clock manufacture had come when Seth Thomas standardized parts, and soon Alcott's sisters were spinning clock cords, while Thomas's employees came to the family farm to look for mountain laurel or "ivy" which they needed to make clock pinions. Ripley's Greenfield had boasted a grist mill, an iron foundry, and a nail plant while he was growing up. Likewise, Francis, as a child, could not have escaped an awareness of industrialization. There in Menotomy was the factory which manufactured wool and cotton cards by a machine which combined several operations in one—the chief factory of its kind in the United States. Francis must have agreed with his sister's remarks when she wrote to him in 1840, "Is not the idea of this present age written in the fact that any man can have his likeness taken in a minute by machinery?"[26] As for the "scholar" of the group, Hedge, as we have seen, made the theme of an expanding industrial America a frequent motif in his public addresses.[27]

The transportation revolution did not escape the notice of the members of the Transcendental Club either. Emerson, their leader, was captivated by it. "I never was on a coach which went fast enough for me," he wrote in 1834, while on another occasion he told his journal that he admired "three advantages of civilization: the post office, the newspaper, and the road."[28] In a letter to Carlyle he complained of his isolation and suggested its solution: "I live so much alone, shrinking almost cowardly from the contact of worldly and public men, that I need more than others to quit home sometimes, & roll with the river of travellers, & live in hotels."[29]

The railroad held Emerson the most. During his European trip, he had recorded how he "went to the railroad & saw Rocket & Goliath & Pluto & Firefly and the rest of that vulcanian generation," which "should not go faster than 15 miles the hour, it racks the engines so to go faster."[30] He probably had his first experience of riding the road during the same trip. Later the impact of speed on his consciousness was often apparent in letters in which he noted exactly how fast his train had gone. Beginning in the winter of 1842, a projected railroad through Concord occasioned a steady stream of references in letters by Emerson. He told his brother William that "the great Locomotive Demon remembers us or we are mindful of him so far that all Concord is agitated this day & for weeks past with project of a railway from Boston hither & so on to Fitchburg. This day a man begged of me to subscribe to its stock—today in vain."[31] A year later, the Concord woods were "full of engineers & their 'tail' contractors for the railroad." Emerson disliked the interruption of his peace and quiet.[32]

Mostly though, Emerson thrilled to the new experience and vividly described his sensations. Boston from a stage coach presented a "ludicrous pathetic tragical picture," but "get into a railroad car & the Ideal Philosophy takes place at once."[33]

Matter is phenomenal whilst men & trees & barns whiz by you as fast as the leaves of a dictionary. As our tea-kettle hissed along through a field of mayflowers, we could judge of the sensations of a swallow who skims by trees & bushes with about the same speed. The very permanence of matter seems compromised & oaks, fields, hills, hitherto esteemed symbols of stability do absolutely dance by you. [34]

There was a fondness for the railroad—"The Americans take to the little contrivance as if it were the cradle in which they were born"[35]—and an ecstasy:

> *I hear the whistle of the locomotive in the woods. Wherever that music comes it has a sequel. It is the voice of the civility of the Nineteenth Century saying "Here I am." It is interrogative: it is prophetic: and this Cassandra is believed: "Whew! Whew! Whew! How is real estate here in the swamp & wilderness? Swamp & Wilderness, ho for Boston! Whew! Whew! Down with that forest on the side of the hill. I want ten thousand chestnut sleepers. I want cedar posts and hundreds of thousands of feet of boards. Up my masters, of oak & pine! You have waited long enough—a good part of a century in the wind & stupid sky. Ho for axes & saws, and away with me to Boston! Whew! Whew! I will plant a dozen houses on this pasture next moon and a village anon; and I will sprinkle yonder square mile with white houses like the broken snow-banks that strow it in March."* [36]

If there was fear in this description, it vanished when Emerson summarized: "Machinery & Transcendentalism agree well."[37]

Clarke was fascinated by his experiences with transportation on his Western journeys. From the Ohio River, he wrote to Margaret Fuller that he had "felt very vacant and unindividual" until he "got upon the Newcastle Railroad, where, by steam, we travel sixteen miles in an hour and ten minutes." He continued graphically: "We flew through the rain and lightning, four enormous carriages, chained together, and crossed the Chesapeake amid a continuation of the same storm."[38] Likewise, Clarke seemed to revel in the steamboat and bragged in another letter to Fuller:

> *If my handwriting is even more irregular than usual you must attribute it to the great shaking which an engine driven by six*

> *boilers keeps up in the Chief Justice Marshall, on which steamer I*
> *am at present speeding back from Cincin[nati] to Louisville. She is*
> *a large Mississippi boat, and her upper cabin, 70 feet long, glitters*
> *with brass and mirrors and curtains and carpets, so as to be rather*
> *imposing. She is not so large, though, nor so splendid as several*
> *other boats that have lately gone down to N[ew] Orleans.* [39]

Once, in New Orleans, Clarke preached aboard a steamboat, and "sometime, by way of variety, and sometimes from necessity," he traveled in canal boats.[40] At Niagara Falls, he described his experience in a weigh-lock on a canal boat, while several times he spoke of steamboat disasters, such as the explosion on the Moselle in which one of his parishioners lost her husband. In the *Western Messenger*, he editorialized: "What is the cause of the explosions and burning of boats on the western rivers?" "The rage for money-making," he answered, "which rushes on, reckless of danger, and careless of human life."[41]

"A Trip to Owensboro" caused Clarke to remark again on steamboat explosions, since the disaster on the Moselle and a similar one on the Orinoko had not decreased the amount of steam travel. "Impressions made on our community are almost like those stamped on water. They pass away immediately and leave the surface of the popular mind as before." But on the same trip, Clarke noted the coal bands near the town and nodded his approval to Robert Triplett who was "making a rail road, by which the coal will be brought to a point on the river where there is a fine harbour."[42] His friend Ripley agreed on the advantages of the railroad. In a description of the location of Brook Farm, Ripley pointed with pride to the fact that it was "situated in West Roxbury, three miles from the depot of the Dedham Branch Railroad, and about eight miles from Boston." It combined a "convenient nearness to the city with a degree of retirement and freedom from unfavorable influences, unusual even in the country."[43]

Alcott was also directly confronted by the "newness" in travel. When he and his cousin set out for Charleston in 1820, they sailed with about one hundred Connecticut men and boys who were going to work on a canal project at Columbia, South Carolina. The Alcotts could find no work, though, and decided to walk the six hundred miles to Norfolk, Virginia, following the canal while they could. Alcott's rootlessness—he lived in thirty different houses during his married life alone—meant that he traveled a good deal. Peddling was a novitiate for the rest of his life, as he rode the Great Western Turnpike, slept in hotels, and took passage in steamers. The Alcotts lived in Concord while the Fitchburg Railroad was being built and could not have escaped the local excitement and upheaval. And although Alcott thought the "demonic man" was the appropriate railroad builder,[44] from Fruitlands he eyed a more suitable estate for his new Eden at Leominster. Among its other virtues, it was "within two miles of the village." "The rail road depot," he added, was to "come within a mile of the house."[45]

The realities of trade, commerce, and finance were equally visible to the "transparent eyeball" of Emerson and the other Transcendentalists. As an adolescent, Emerson had visited Boston's Long Wharf and noted the changes: "It was but a little time ago, when there was nothing but water to be seen there; & now, a long block of 30 stores fills up the places."[46] In "The Present Age," he characterized the time as an "era of Trade," and in another lecture, he enumerated some of the commodities which came to Long Wharf—seal, otter, and ermine from the Rocky Mountains; seashells, strombus, turbo, and pearl from the Gulf of Mexico; green eggs from Labrador ducks.[47] He commented on the fragility of the economic venture, remarking that New England trade

> saves itself by extreme activity. It takes banknotes, good, bad, clean, ragged, and saves itself by the speed with which it passes them off. Iron cannot rust, nor beer sour, nor timber rot, nor calicoes go out of fashion, nor moneystocks depreciate, in the few swift moments which the Yankee suffers any one of them to remain in his possession. In skating over thin ice, our safety is in our speed.[48]

Emerson was somewhat ambivalent about what he observed. In "Woodnotes," he advised that merchandise, churches, and charities should be spurned, while on other occasions he was optimistic that trade would lead to liberty and peace and would result in the abolition of slavery. In fact, trade was attractive because it did not set up permanent patterns but rather was "continually falling, like the waves of the sea, before new claims of the sort."[49] When he himself was involved, however, in the Panic of 1837, his tone grew more worried. Correspondence with his brother throughout the year centered around the issue of money—stocks, loans, guarantees, interest, income, making ends meet. In his journal, he mourned of "cold April; hard times; men breaking who ought not to break; banks bullied into the bolstering of desperate speculators; all the newspapers a chorus of owls." There were, he said, "loud cracks in the social edifice.—Sixty thousand laborers, says rumor, to be presently thrown out of work, and these make a formidable mob to break open banks & rob the rich & brave the domestic government."[50]

Ripley's pastoral response to the Panic of 1837 has been preserved. Here, he reflected on "The Temptations of the Times" in a fashion which seemed to foreshadow his Brook Farm venture. He told his congregation that the crisis they were all experiencing should not be considered merely one of "signal commercial difficulties" but one of "peculiar temptations as regards our religious and moral condition." Ripley warned of the danger "from the indulgence of a spirit of restlessness and improvident concern," from the temptation to "hazardous experiments," from a "blind adventurousness upon uncertain risks." Regulated rather than restless motion was needed. It would be far better if people would be "content with the slow and regular, but almost certain gains of thrifty enterprise and persevering industry, instead of aspiring to these huge fabrics of wealth which are built up in a few years, and in a few hours blown down." Yet Ripley looked with hope to the day when "the dark cloud which hovers over us will break in blessings on our land," and he saw "progress" as the goal, through the experience of dependence on one another. The crisis, teaching the importance of each person to the community's welfare, would bring a "quickened sense of responsibility" and make them all "more strenuous" in doing their duty.[51]

Travel articles by Clarke scattered throughout the *Messenger* often pointed to his sensitivity to trade and commerce. In an open letter from New Orleans, he eulogized the bustling emporium, "this great mart to which all our western produce pours down—this sacred Venice, city of the waters."[52] Similarly, "A Visit to Mobile" confronted Clarke with railway, steamboats, and a city where "the steam presses are puffing and screaming before the dawn and long after dark, and . . . Sunday is often no day of rest to them." "The chief aim of man in Mobile," he said, was to "buy, sell, pack, press, speculate in and talk about COTTON."[53]

If Clarke seemed ambivalent, Alcott was decidedly negative in one comment which appeared in the *Boston Quarterly Review*. Perhaps it was the slavery of blacks to which Alcott was alluding, perhaps the slavery of all:

> *Bread! there is alway enough and to spare in the granaries of Providence. But covetousness has driven long a prosperous business in the world; monopolized the hunger and thirst, the nakedness and exposure of mankind; and held a market for selling the flesh and blood of human beings. Bodies are everywhere bought and sold. Mammon, in league with slaughter, carnage, lust, forestalls the breath of souls; the Babe even at the breast is mortgaged to cancel the debts of the needy. Air, light, fire, fuel, water, earth, home, the grave even; heaven, hell;—all, are stock in trade of the house of Mammon, Beelzebub & Co.; which emboldened by its gains, plots always speculations, daring and impious, appropriating the universe to fill the vaults of Plutus. God and the world, all things are coined, all things sold.*[54]

Money and banks led inevitably to the city. The Transcendentalists, who regarded Boston as their hub, were quick to see its possibilities and its problems. Thus, for example, in an early sermon, Emerson was elated by its cosmopolitanism as he exhorted his congregation:

> *Look at the great throng the city presents. Consider the variety of callings and pursuits. Here is one man toiling with a hod on his shoulder; and another with his saw and tools; a third with his*

> *books; a fourth driving bargains at the corners of the streets;*
> *another draws a map; another is hasting to his entertainment and*
> *to dangerous pleasures; another is led to the jail between officers;*
> *another takes his seat on a bench to judge him.*[55]

Emerson was more concrete when he told Carlyle that the population of New York had jumped in forty years from 20,000 to 350,000. "The city has such immense natural advantages, & such capabilities of boundless growth," he wrote, "such varied & ever increasing accommodation & appliances for eye & ear, for memory & wit, for locomotion & lavation, & all manner of delectation."[56] But Emerson was not unaware of the misery which the city contained. He knew that

> *the eye that sees the morning sun shine on long streets of decorated*
> *dwellings is apt to forget how many obscure garrets, how many*
> *damp basements are here and there found amid this magnificence,*
> *that contain victims of great suffering, poor men and women*
> *reduced by consumptions or bedridden with rheumatism, or worn*
> *with fruitless labors to meet demands the quarter day.*[57]

Alcott, too, responded to the quality of city life and formed varying opinions depending upon the city. Boston was his alabaster shrine, and he praised its morality, "more pure than that of any other city in America."

> *There is no city in this country in which there is more mental and*
> *philanthropic activity than in Boston. The better mind and*
> *conscience of this continent are there. Philosophy and literature, if*
> *not adequately cherished and cultivated, receive more attention*
> *than in other cities. . . . It is the place, I think, for all generous*
> *efforts to improve humanity to be located.*[58]

Yet, on an early morning walk at Lynn, the city revealed another side. Alcott had a "vivid experience of the bald ugliness of life in cities when thus contrasted with the fresh grace of existence amidst the scenes of nature."[59] In London, he told his diary: "The din and huddle about me pain and confuse my senses."[60] A year later, his denunciation was more strident: "Not in the stir of towns, of bales and banks, chapmen and publicans, breathes Honesty, but harvests indigenous bread from virgin soils, midst hills and waters."[61]

Meanwhile, as we have seen, the deteriorating condition of the city neighborhood in which Ripley's church stood forced him to confront the issue of urban life in changing places. Conditions grew worse after the Panic of 1837, and Ripley finally announced to his congregation that he could no longer be still amid the pain and misery of the working classes which surrounded the church: the city and its urban poor had made their impact on his consciousness. Yet he could celebrate the city on occasion, as his remarks in New York City in honor of Charles Fourier's birthday made clear. This was a "great and populous city, devoted to the pursuits of commerce and the acquisition of wealth." It was a city "absorbed in the busy rivalries and competitions of life."[62]

Clarke, in turn, was horrified at the moral deadness of life in Louisville where "duels, dirkings, shootings, beatings to death, etc.," occurred daily, "and no one troubles themselves about them."[63] Although his congregation came from the "better families," Clarke began to learn the seamy side of Louisville life among the poor by the river. With some women of the church who were interested in welfare work, he visited Mother Safely's—a shack by the river where a widow rented rooms to transients. Here, one tenant, an extremely sick girl, was a disinherited orphan whom Clarke visited until her death. There were immigrants in Louisville too, and Clarke added to his list of social commitments by joining the Immigrants' Friends, founded to aid a group of Polish immigrants on their way west to Illinois.

Similarly, Emerson acknowledged immigration and its attendant difficulties. He thought the Irish population "the most laborious but neither the most moral nor the most intelligent."[64] He noted especially that their movement into Concord to build the railroad threatened the economic stability of local farmers, because their wages were so low. Emerson wrote of his impressions:

> *If you look at these railroad labourers & hear their stories, their fortunes appear as little controuled as those of the forest leaves. One is whirled off to Albany one to Ohio, one digs on the levee at*

New Orleans & one at Walden Pond; others on the wharves in Boston or the woods in Maine, and they have too little foresight & too little money to leave them any more election of whither to go or what to do than the poor leaf which is blown into this dike or that brook to perish. "*To work from dark to dark for fifty cents the day*" *as the poor woman in the shanty told us, is but pitiful wages for a married man.* [65]

Although Emerson could reflect that "this stern day's work of 15 or 16 hours" was "a better police than the Sheriff & his deputies to let off the peccant humours," he deplored the fact that so many Irish immigrants had drawn a lot which included low wages, exploitation, and excessive work. [66]

Two decades earlier, the phenomenon of Western migration had impressed Emerson. He had told his journals of the "vast rapidity with which the desarts [*sic*] & forests of the interior of this country are peopled." Patriots were fearful that the nation was growing "*too fast* for its virtue & its peace," and through the rough characters who led the emigration, the axe was "laid to the root of the forest," the Indian was "driven from his hut & the bison from the plains." [67] Wilderness activity was ominous. Even Unitarians at their meetings were becoming concerned about settling the frontier, and Emerson wrote that "*The West*" was the "leading topic at all such meetings." [68] He was interested in Alexis de Tocqueville's calculation that the population at the Western frontier advanced "every year a mean distance of seventeen miles." [69] Vaguely threatened by the process, Emerson shaped his metaphor accordingly. "The frontier region of effects" was the place of "the fugitive and fleeting effects which have no real being when once the divine wave of Truth which they incrust has ebbed." [70]

From childhood, Clarke had known that the Hulls, his maternal grandparents, had lived on the frontier at Detroit. In his own vocational decision, the frontier loomed large: "I was afraid that if I were settled in an old-fashioned Unitarian society I should gradually subside into routine; while in the West there would be no routine, but I should be free to originate such methods as might seem necessary and useful."[71] He liked the extempore style of Western speech and praised the annual summer "political barbecues, where leading speakers discussed with each other the public questions of the day." The fine art of "stump-speaking" was practiced here, just one example of Clarke's theory that pragmatic and aesthetic values were related.[72] The provisional quality of Western life was exciting. "Everyone who comes to the West has to run a risk," he told Margaret Fuller.

The political sentiments of the Transcendentalists were generally tied to their interest in various kinds of social reform, both of which we have discussed in some measure. For all the Transcendentalists—with the exception of Hedge who remained aloof—reform interests were interwoven with daily life to the point that a separation of this or that aspect is difficult. On the whole, Alcott, Ripley, and Clarke took the lead in activist roles, while Emerson and Francis, although they did get involved, were more hesitant. Emerson provided the rationale for those members of the Club who did not plunge headlong into reform activity when he argued that each person must accomplish self-reform before the general conditions of life in society could be changed. As he anguished about whether or not to join Ripley's Brook Farm, Emerson wrote:

> *I wish to break all prisons. I have not yet conquered my own house. It irks & repents me. Shall I raise the siege of this hencoop & march baffled away to a pretended siege of Babylon? It seems to me that so to do were to dodge the problem I am set to solve, & to hide my impotency in the thick of a crowd.* [73]

The non-action of Emerson and his colleagues who gravitated toward a life of scholarship, teaching, and preaching was a schema for *inner* action which would be given substance in the mystical theory and practice of Transcendentalism. It would provide the blueprint for spiritual action which was the core of the Transcendental faith, however outwardly expressed.

But the concerns of his age forced the reluctant Emerson out of his solitary quest for self-culture and into the public arena. In this, he was somewhat paradigmatic, supplying in visibility what he lacked in enthusiasm. Hence, Emerson the leader can provide insight into the reform involvement of most of his friends. Moncure Conway, an early biographer, has called Emerson "the first American scholar to cast a dart at slavery," noting that, in 1831, Emerson "admitted an abolitionist to lecture on the subject in his church, and in the following year another was invited to his pulpit." Conway went on to underline the importance of the date since this was "six years before even Channing had committed himself to that side," at a time when Garrison was "regarded as a vulgar street-preacher of notions too wild to excite more than a smile."[74] Samuel May had been the abolitionist, and his address occasioned full press reports, which linked Emerson's name with the cause. The following year Emerson opened his church to the Society for the Abolition of Slavery, and its annual meeting was held there.

Emerson rubbed benign shoulders with a collection of abolitionist types. He approved of Samuel May, introduced Lydia Maria Child to Thomas Carlyle, breakfasted at his home in Concord with George Thompson, hosted the Grimké sisters, and admired William Lloyd Garrison. When Elijah P. Lovejoy was shot to death by a mob at Alton, Illinois, in 1837, some Boston citizens, headed by William Ellery Channing, were refused the use of Faneuil Hall for a protest meeting. Despite his reserve, Emerson departed from the text of a planned lecture to express his outrage: "It is but the other day, that the brave Lovejoy gave his breast to the bullets of a mob, for the rights of free speech and opinion, and died when it was better not to live."[75] In November 1837 he had already delivered an address at the Second Church on the subject of slavery, and James Cabot reported his remarks: "I regret to hear that all the churches but one, and almost all the public halls in Boston, are closed against the discussion of the question."[76] In 1844 at the Concord Courthouse, Emerson delivered an address which commemorated the anniversary of black emancipation in the British West Indies.

Emerson confronted the Indian question in similar fashion. When the Cherokees were forcibly removed from Georgia to be resettled in Indian territory in accordance with a treaty to which they had not assented, Emerson was disturbed. "This disaster of the Cherokees" blackened his days and nights. "I can do nothing. Why shriek? Why strike ineffectual blows?"[77] Yet he agreed to address a citizens' meeting in Concord on the Cherokee Indian case, and the next day he sent an open letter to President Martin Van Buren on behalf of himself and his friends. Moreover, Emerson watched the development of the other main reform movements of his day and commented freely on their evolution.

Temperance was an example. In his journal, Emerson solemnly noted statistics on alcohol consumption and cost. He mentioned a lecture by Father Edward Taylor on temperance and remarked that the issue was "a question which rides the conversation of ten thousand circles, of every Lyceum, of every stage coach, of every church meeting, of every county caucus."[78] He deplored the "fritter & degradation of man which we see everywhere in the stage coach & bar room," yet found that the Temperance Society had made the bar a "cold place."[79] He himself went so far as to give a speech before the Temperance Society in the village of Harvard.

The peace movement received Emerson's approval as well. He listened to William Ellery Channing speak before the Peace Society and afterwards summarized his argument for his own journal. He admired Joshua Blanchard, "that faithful man whose whole life & least part is conformed to his Reason who upholds the Peace Society & works at the Bank Sundays & eschews the Communion & sweetens his tea with Canton sugar out of hatred to slavery & thinks Homer & Shakspeare [sic] to be the strongest War party."[80] In 1838, Emerson lectured on war to the American Peace Society, and thereafter the address was quoted often and extensively. Similarly, he listened with openness to the views of Horace Mann concerning a common school system and, acknowledging the existence of the movement for women's rights, decided that "a certain awkward consciousness of inferiority in the men may give rise to the new chivalry."[81] After he attended the celebrated meeting of the Friends of Universal Progress, the Chardon Street Convention of 1840, his amused description of the participants became canonical.

*Madmen, madwomen, men with beards, Dunkers, Mug-
gletonians, Come-Outers, Groaners, Agrarians, Seventh-day
Baptists, Quakers, Abolitionists, Calvinists, Unitarians, and
philosophers,—all came successively to the top, and seized their
moment. If not their hour, wherein to chide or pray or preach or
protest. The faces were a study. The most daring innovators, and
the champions-until-death of the old cause, sat side by side.* [82]

Whether or not each of the Transcendentalists could be
classified with the "most daring innovators" of Chardon Street (Alcott had issued the call at the Convention, and Ripley had also been
present), the evidence does warrant several observations about the
members of the New School and their relationship to the revolution
in nineteenth-century America. First of all, the Transcendentalists
were aware of the general scope and magnitude of the changes which
were sweeping their era. In other words, not only were these
transformations objective realities, but they were perceived as such
by the members of the Club. Even Hedge, for whom we possess the
least biographical information during the period, left an impressive
record of public statements which indicated his mindfulness and
overall approval of the tenor of his times. And Francis, who gave less
public indication of his familiarity than any of the others except
Hedge, corroborated it in private correspondence and diaries as well
as in public declarations and activities supporting the anti-slavery
cause. [83]

Secondly, the Transcendentalists were somewhat ambivalent
about the substance of what they perceived. They marveled at the
wonders which technology could produce, yet they feared being
overpowered by the logic of the machine. They hailed the advantages of urban life but deplored its crime and squalor. They
credited the commercial ingenuity of their fellow New Englanders
yet feared that, as Emerson once put it, things were "in the saddle"
and rode mankind. They disliked the Whigs but could not be totally
converted to Jacksonian democracy. Finally, they affirmed the ideals
behind reformist activities but were divided among themselves on
the question of direct involvement. Still, their enthusiasm for the

"newness" in whatever field suggested that they were fundamentally on the side of the new America. Beyond substance, though, Emerson and his friends affirmed the *style* of the new America. They made the affirmation directly in exuberant remarks such as Emerson's "Machinery & Transcendentalism agree well." And they stamped their approval indirectly by their continual avowals that they were perpetrating a revolution, that they were converts at the shrine of "novelty," and that they were discrete particles in a universal flux without a bond to any traditional community.

But a further process was at work among the Transcendentalists. As we have applied the theory of correspondence, we have already made a connection between the new world of America and the new word of the Transcendentalists: in style, they both chose the dynamic over the placid, the moving over the stationary. Even more, since Transcendental structures of consciousness were grounded in the theory of correspondence, and since the members of the Club revealed themselves as committed more to associative than discursive thinking, the Transcendentalists were probably practicing their new religion in further ways than they realized. In other words, the theological dictum which identified God with motion and its moral counterpart which equated action (outer or inner) with the good may have been indirectly communicated to the Transcendentalists via the messages they received from their own times.

In a review article for *The Dial*, Emerson unintendingly presented a vignette which summarized this creative process. When commenting on *The Worship of the Soul* by Samuel D. Robbins, he quoted Robbins directly in a pattern which suggested Emerson's own method of discerning the nature of the world. The Robbins of Emerson began his book with a historical and contextual observation, the tendency toward revolution he had observed in his contemporaries. People were "outgrowing the tyranny of forms, and overleaping all former barriers." After an extended discussion of this interpretation of events, Robbins made an appeal for adherence to the Christianity of Jesus. The language in which his exhortation was couched was familiar: "the age will never arrive when men cannot draw from the fountain of God's truth, the waters of life and salvation."[84]

Let us remember that it was Emerson the reviewer who selected the quotations from Robbins's book. What was interesting about the selections was that the Robbins of Emerson passed from a discussion of revolution in the world, i.e., violent movement and change, to an apology for the Christian message cast in the vocabulary of motion. Over the synapse between the two observations—the presence of revolution in the world and the need for Christianity in the spirits of individuals—came the distinct impression of a connection being made, an analogous underpinning seen in the realities of outer and inner world. In other words, the Robbins of Emerson had associated the two phenomena by seeing the second, Christianity, in language which suggested the dynamic nature of a world in motion, in this case through revolution.

Robbins may or may not have made the transition as directly as did Emerson's review. The point is, however, that the article provided a capsule summary of the Transcendentalists' own mental world. Emerson was indirectly admiring himself and his friends in their *modus operandi*, and that mode was such that they could learn a lesson of newness in the America which they encountered. There was a connection between the structure of events and the language of ideals: the Transcendental affirmation had extended to imitation.

CHAPTER VI

Desiderata

EMERSON introduced his second edition of *Nature* with a few lines of poetry:

> *A subtle chain of countless rings*
> *The next unto the farthest brings;*
> *The eye reads omens where it goes,*
> *And speaks all languages the rose;*
> *And, striving to be man, the worm*
> *Mounts through all the spires of form.* [1]

The verse was perceptive, for Emerson had succinctly stated the double consciousness which made it possible for Transcendental religion to be linked to the new America. The language of ideals had begun with one worldview and, in order to maintain it, had ended by endorsing a second. Meanwhile, the structure of events disclosed the second worldview in the apparent sequence of historical causation. First of all, Emerson's "chain of countless rings" proclaimed the identity of microcosm and macrocosm in their essential nature. Hence, there could be omens for the eye of the beholder and, hence, the rose could speak in every civilized tongue. In addition, the worldview of correspondence implied that there was a connection between the inner self and the human cultural world, so that the secret of the self could also be discovered "out there."

Yet the structure of events had invited a different sense of the nature of things which suggested, in traditional religious form, that

God and humanity were separated by the double barrier of a profound difference in nature (infinitude/finitude) and a profounder difference occasioned by history (the Fall). Now in transformed and secular dress, it suggested that humanity was separated from its goal of worldly perfection but that the gap between present and future could be bridged by progress. The present age taught that the worm had not been content to remain a worm. Dimly aware of the disparity between what it was and what it could be, it had begun to strive and, in so doing, to climb through "all the spires of form." The worm wanted a human nature, while human beings sought a divine one. Paradoxically, nineteenth-century correspondence taught that the nature of things was evolutionary and developmental, that the worldview of causality was correct.

The connection between the language of ideals and the structure of events, therefore, meant that the former led to the latter. It followed that, since the structure of events called for action, Transcendental believers would find themselves drawn into the search for the norms of action. The prescriptions for self and society which Emerson and his friends would support would grow out of their efforts to reconcile the disagreement between the harmony of corresponding spheres and the nervous energy of the new America, between life in the contemplative present and life in the active future. Emerson as leader would take the initiative in formulating the law for self and society which could bridge the gap between the poles and bring about a union of opposites. In conversations of the Club members, in shared journals, in public lectures and writings, and in the group project of *The Dial*, the message would become communal and collective, the teaching of a new Transcendental religion.

Emerson's prescriptions for each individual were summed up in his mystical theory and spelled out in his notion of self-culture. His remedies for society arose from a discussion of the collective existence of selves in the flow of history. Finally, both mystical self-culture and collective history were collapsed by Emerson into autobiography, the inner story of a self in time, which proved the ultimate reconciliation of opposites and the source of a lifestyle for the new America.

Mysticism, as we have already suggested, was in some forms the individual analogue to collective correspondence. Since a harmony existed between different microcosmic and macrocosmic pieces of the world, correspondence included a basic optimism about the natural possibilities of human beings. That is, since each piece of the world—in this case each human being—was in secret essence like the power behind the whole, it was possible for each human being to realize that basic identity and celebrate it. The Hinduism which Emerson found so attractive spoke of "realized beings," who had discovered by experience that the *atman* (individual soul-spark) was *Brahman* (the power behind the universe and the source of life).

In this kind of mysticism, a person remained no longer a discrete and separated particle of the world but merged into the ultimate reality. He or she became absorbed in the power of the whole, so that there was, for the space of the experience, no more "I" as an ego-based individual but only the "I" of the cosmos. Another way of saying this was to speak of the dissolution of the boundaries between subject and object. In ordinary existence, no matter how close humans came to one another, even in the communion of friends and lovers, a sense remained of being individuals and historical selves, born in a certain space and time and bearers of inherited traits and acquired characteristics. But in this mystical experience, the biographical sense evaporated. It was *maya* or appearance, as the Indians claimed, and the truth of identification supplanted it. No longer was divine power an Other; instead there was only one "I" in the world, the "I" which was at the heart of things. Through the transformation of the experience, the mystic was that "I," and this *was* that.

Since normal human faculties—senses, emotions, conceptual thought processes—operated out of a recognition of distinction between self and world, they could only interfere with the realization of this type of mystical identity. Thus, mystics of many cultures were adamant in insisting that what they experienced was beyond their ability to express. In fact, "beyond" was a favorite word for many mystics who spoke of the direct and unmediated quality of their experience: no word, no thought, no passion, or sense perception—no mental or physical or psychosomatic category—separated them from the reality they discerned in the cosmos. At the same time, these mystics spoke of their experiences as transient, "highs" from which they had to descend to become, once more, biographical individuals. They talked about the passivity which was part of the experience as it unfolded—no matter how many years they had toiled in preparatory exercises. Mysticism was a small death from which one returned, a love-death, ecstatic and transforming, so that life after this death was never the same as before.

Mystics were alone at the heights of their experience though they might be physically in the presence of a crowd. Yet mystics usually learned how to pursue their quest from a spiritual master, whether guru, sheikh, or confessor. The first steps along the path were taken as part of a school, and over the centuries the schools developed a wide repertoire of techniques which might assist the would-be mystic. Almost like a sex manual, the mystical manual sought to capture what was elusive and triggered by mystery. In the process, various schemas were developed which in one form or another were followed by mystical aspirants.

Sometimes, it was a seven-stage schema based on the ancient theories of the Babylonians who believed the soul traveled through seven spheres to the seven planetary gods after death. In mystical theory, the journey had become an interior and present one in which various stages achieved would lead, it was hoped, to corresponding states. Sometimes, it was a variation of the three-part schema in which the mystic passed through stages of purification, illumination, and union. During the stage of purification or purgation, there was an emphasis on techniques either of sensory deprivation or sensory overload. Meditation, fasting, and self-discipline, or ecstatic song, dance, and sexual activity equally might purify the mystic from attachment to the periphery of things and lead to a centering of forces and a knowledge of self. Then came the state of illumination, when enlightenment, as it was often called, brought a noetic experience in which self-knowledge merged with divine knowledge. Sudden and incisive, the light of this stage was dissolved in the culminating experience of union. Inner became outer, and the mystic became the pulse of the world.

At times, the stages of illumination and union were so interwoven as to be incapable of separation, and mystics spoke of the quality of the knowledge which possessed them. Like everything else about the final phases of the process, it was "beyond." It did not come by way of linear logic, but welled up, or in, from regions unknown. It was *gnosis*, sacred, secret, and saving knowledge which came all in a flash and split the normal shape of the world to reveal the innermost mystery of things, incommunicable save to one who also knew. Emerson and his friends, coming from their own "noetic" atmosphere in New England, would make much of the gnostic aspects of this kind of mysticism.

Mysticism, therefore, was very far from a catchall term for vagaries of whatever sort. Whether in response to a harmonious cosmos or in other forms which we have not discussed, such as an experience of the Void or immediate communion with a personal deity, mysticism did not mean simple clairvoyance or magic or unexplainable occult events. It was not a label one put on any unusual experience which could not be otherwise defined. The mystics understood their experience with precision. Their insistence on their inability to talk about it was equaled by their willingness in countless words and many documents to do exactly that. Emerson was no exception here, so that when he spoke of mysticism, during the years of the Club and throughout his life, he had a specific form of experience in mind. Even a casual reading of his journals and essays reveals certain patterns which thread their way through and yield a summary of Emersonian mystical theory. Generally, these writings suggest that he sought the same goal of union/identification as many more traditional mystics, but he differed with them concerning the means as well as the outcome of the experience.

Emerson parsed his definition of mysticism out of Greek etymological roots. *Mystes* derived from the Greek μυω, one who mused or meditated on ideas which could not adequately be expressed in words dealing with sense images and intellectual concepts.[2] The object of the mystical quest was understood by Emerson both cosmologically and ontologically. God was in the universe— nature was his projection; and God was in each human person. If an individual reached one God, he reached the other. "Man stands on the point betwixt the inward spirit & the outward matter. He sees that the one explains, translates the other: that the world is the mirror of the soul. He is the priest and interpreter of nature thereby."[3] Emerson spoke of the ancient theory that the human mind was a portion of God which had been separated for a time from the infinite mind and at death would be reabsorbed into the world soul. He called God the substratum of the soul and described how the God within worshiped the God in the universe. "Is not that the solution of the riddle of sympathy? It is one of the oldest principles of philosophy that like must beget like, & that only like can know like. It is worms & flesh in us that fear or sympathize with worms & flesh and God only within that worships God of the Universe."[4] The more a person knew his or her own soul, the more intense was the love for outward nature. The very act of worship declared that God was not one, that at least two Gods, an ontological and a cosmological, must be reconciled.

The reconciled God was identified by Emerson in various terms. It was the Whole and the All, the Unconscious, the Intellect and Reason. Each of these applied to a reality which was within a human being and at the same time distinct from him or her. There was one Mind in all individuals, and true human progress was from the individual to the Universal or the All. Human reason was the same as the divine essence; *compounded* nature brought separation from God.[5] Here Emerson followed Samuel Coleridge's reading of Immanuel Kant and saw Reason as "an instantaneous instreaming causing power," the pure Intellect of God as it entered the human sphere.[6] Indeed, "the intellectual power was not the gift of God, but the presence of God."[7] Distinguished from Reason, the Understanding was intellect manifested in human thought. It represented the human power over nature; it was practical wisdom, but the Intellect was always its "head."[8] Even the genius of a Shakespeare or a Plato could not be compared to this light of Intellect. "Higher yet, shall I say, is it to prefer the idea or power to the thought—that is, to the idea once individualized or domesticated in one man's mind, as Shakespeare or Plato."[9] When Emerson pointed to the self in self-culture, it was the self which participated in universal Reason that he had in mind.

His twin conception of the mystical goal was obviously a function of the theory of correspondence. A person could know the laws of azote because he once was azote. He or she was "only a piece of the universe made alive."[10] In such an emblematic and symbolic universe, a contemplation of nature could lead to the divine, and Emerson began to distinguish the faculties which might facilitate mystical experience. With Coleridge again, he spoke of the Imagination, the vision which regarded the "world as symbolical & pierces the emblem for the real sense, sees external objects as types."[11] Emerson contrasted this faculty with Fancy which took the world as it was and shaped it into pleasing related groups. Fancy might be the domain of the artist, but Imagination was the work of mystic and seer and would be included in the notion of cultivating the self.

Always, however, the Imagination's contemplation of nature must lead within. The principle of identity meant that Emerson could exhort: "Introvert your eye & your consciousness is a taper in the desart [sic] of Eternity. It is the Channel though now diminished to a thread through which torrents of light roll & flow in the high tides of spontaneity & reveal the landscape of the dusky Universe[.]"[12] In a passage which suggested the warmth of experience, he wrote: "Go inward & I find the ocean; I lose my individuality in its waves. God is Unity, but always works in variety. I go inward until I find Unity universal, that Is before the World was; I come outward to this body a point of variety."[13] Emerson's mystical theory was therefore polytheistic and monistic at once. Each piece of the world, personal or impersonal, could provide the focus for identification; each possessed its God. At the same time, variety and unity were intertwined, and each root or branch led inevitably to the cosmic tree.

The principle of identity suited a mystical theory grounded on a stable universe which moved on a steady, pre-ordained course, as it did in certain traditional forms of mystical teaching. But in Emersonian mystical theory the principle of identity was complemented by the principle of flux. We have already seen that this was so for Emerson's cosmological God in the "NOT ME" of nature and society. But what of the ontological God within each person? Did the God who was the "I" of the self move in a fashion which resembled the more frenetic pattern of "nature" in nineteenth-century America?

Emerson's formulation of an answer began with a discussion of transmigration. For him and his friends, the doctrine expressed the reality that the self which was God possessed corresponding motion in the microcosm, while the nature and norms of this motion were expressed as Emerson articulated his notion of self-culture. In the meantime, he told his journal that the ancient belief in transmigration was not a fable, for a downward ebb was apparent in the very faces of many people. "Look around you at the men & women, & do you not see that they are already only half human; that every animal of the barnyard, the field, & the forest, of the earth, & of the waters that are under the earth, has contrived to get a footing & to leave the print of his features & form in some one or other of these upright heaven-facing walkers?"[14] The semi-humanity of some was explained by the thesis that there were two classes of souls, free and apprentice. Free souls possessed more light and therefore acted morally; apprentice souls were forced by their constitution to radiate less. It was "chemically impossible that they be moral—what talent or good they have."[15]

Emersonian transmigration thus meant elitism. It also meant an understanding of the human body which made of it a prison chamber or at least a bed where the soul-spark lay sleeping. Life was the "sleep of the soul," and the only recourse in this situation was a continual quest for self-knowledge. Purification came through the initiatory technique of self-culture which would lead the soul away from the peripheries and toward the center of the self. Here, from the depths, would come a "certain perception of absolute being . . . which must be the God of God."[16] The human tragedy was the fragmentation which led individuals to the "frontier region of effects," draining their energies in action without soul. Meantime, within each person was "the Soul of the Whole, the Wise Silence, the Universal Beauty to which every part and particle is equally related, the eternal One."[17]

If the understanding seemed Neoplatonic, in good measure it was. Yet contemplation by way of self-culture did not mean transfixed existence. The contemplative moved in a real world and the practical person only in a phenomenal one; that was the difference. The contemplative should and did work. When a contemplative did so, it was life properly so called, while on the contrary, the work of the "practical" person was "boundless pretension."[18] Contemplation overflowed for the "real man" in directed activity, when Intellect was converted into energy and the "Highest" was transformed into both "sage & tiger."[19] If God had been identified with motion, then union with divine energy meant discovery of the secret of perpetual action. The effect of mystical experience was, in Alcott's favorite expression, "energizing." In practice, Emersonian mysticism led to action, and action brought correspondence not only with a divine but also with a human world.

But what sort of action was real? Action easily led into history because it required playing some part in the drama of events. Moreover, history, as it had traditionally been understood in Judaeo-Christianity, meant movement in a linear dimension toward some goal. How could mystical action be reconciled with the essentially public and communal character of the dramatic movement of history?

The answer was that the mysticism of Emerson and his friends could properly be described as gnostic. While Gnosticism, in the narrow sense, refers to certain sects of the second century A.D., the term can also be used in a derivative manner to refer to a religious understanding and experience which shares the views of the second-century sects. These Gnostics believed that there was a divine spark in each human being which had come originally from a heavenly realm and had fallen into the material world of fate, birth, and death. Here the spark existed in a prison from which it must escape to return to the celestial sphere, where its Alter Ego or other Self remained. Yet, paradoxically, the soul imprisoned in matter must seek its Self and All within. Once found there through *gnosis*, this Self would be reintegrated with the eternal Self existing in the divine regions. Not everybody was capable of undergoing this unification: there were classes of souls. Only the elite "knew" and knew that they knew.

However, in order for the elite to reach the identification they longed for, a linear progression toward a goal was necessary. This meant some kind of movement in time, some action; and thus, the Gnostic conception of time and history became significant for Transcendental religion. Both Gnostic time and Transcendental time were inner rather than outer, the time of the self in progressive unfolding, rather that the time of public history in its own dramatic evolution. Important for understanding the Transcendentalists, the time concept of second–century Gnosticism, while opposed to the Judaeo-Christian tradition, was dependent on it. After the concrete presence of a Jewish and Christian linear and eschatological understanding, it was no longer possible to wish history completely away. Jewish and Christian understandings and objections had to be taken into account in the Gnostic's own schema because they were part of the mental world in which he or she lived.

Unlike Judaeo-Christians who, with the Gnostics, were living in an "age of anxiety," the latter did not want to endure history or use it as they awaited the eschaton. But neither could they escape it in the same manner as cultures based more strongly on the worldview of correspondence. Therefore, the Gnostics had to find some other route by which to escape the intolerability of history. They achieved this by an interiorization of the Judaeo-Christian eschatological hope in a theory of self and salvation and by a dualism in which the visible material world was only a mockery of the divine order. Correspondence now had a rift in it which reflected the seriousness of the sacred/profane dichotomy. External history had been de-emphasized by an emphasis on the inner life. Here the Gnostics could "make history" through human projects in which the self journeyed back to the divine. The linear dimension had been kept, but it had been transmuted into autobiography.[20]

Similarly, for Emerson, who fought with tuberculosis, who

suffered the death of a young and loved wife, of two brothers, of his son, who felt that in conscience he could no longer preach from a Unitarian pulpit, correspondence had gone sour, and the struggle with history and tragedy must have seemed insurmountable. For both Emerson and his friends, the insurmountability of history was underlined and reinforced by the age. The new America was caught in a whirlwind of changes which even the proprieties of Boston could not stop. It was a sometimes frightening reality, and if one could make sense of human existence without having to make complete sense of America, that might be a desirable enterprise. Still, just as Gnostics of the second century could not wish away the Judaeo-Christian linear progression to the eschaton, neither could nineteenth-century American gnostics erase the American commitment to motion. So their mysticism turned active, couched in the language of motion and bent on identification with a God who ruled the flux and was the flux. Now, however, the flux was one of inner evolution and development, so that the cult of autobiography, with its fondness for journals and diaries and its love of introspection, became self-culture. While the traditional mystic passed into eternity through the doors of the present, the Emersonian mystic kept stealing glances toward the future. And in his essays, Emerson presented his followers with three keys to the future active self.

The problem with people, said Emerson in "Self-reliance," was that they were drunk or asleep in the world, numbed by the twin hobgoblins of conformity and consistency. Waking up meant turning inward and living from the inside out. Insofar as one touched the soul there would be "power not confident but agent."[21] Such an agent-soul had made friends with its own private devils and refused to lose its freedom by subscribing to popular virtues. "Then again, do not tell me, as a good man did to-day, of my obligation to put all poor men in good situations. Are they *my* poor? I tell thee, thou foolish philanthropist, that I grudge the dollar, the dime, the cent I give to such men as do not belong to me and to whom I do not belong."[22] Genuine action issued from oneself and not from a morality imposed from without. Emerson preferred, he owned, that his life "should be of a lower strain, so it be genuine and equal, than that it should be glittering and unsteady."[23] In Emerson's vision, the shadow side, which some, engaging in external works of charity, might prefer to stuff into the soul's closet, could not be hidden. The dark roots of being must be exposed, and with their authenticity would come the energy which inspired true action.

The person who was really great was as free in society as in solitude, not scattering his or her forces by following customs and usages but originating action which came from within. "Your geniune action will explain itself and will explain your other genuine actions," Emerson urged. "Act singly, and what you have already done singly will justify you now. Greatness appeals to the future."[24] No longer need a person embrace custom and tradition as the worldview of correspondence had enjoined. Instead, Emersonian self-culture grew out of a sense of the destiny which the soul spun for itself by linking its transcendent existence to a historical personality in the world. "A sturdy lad from New Hampshire or Vermont, who in turn tries all the professions, who *teams it, farms it, peddles*, keeps a school, preaches, edits a newspaper, goes to Congress, buys a township, and so forth, in successive years, and always like a cat falls on his feet, is worth a hundred of these city dolls." The first key to the future active self was, therefore, "self-trust." Through it, "new powers" would appear, and each human being could realize that he or she was a biographical "word made flesh."[25]

In "The Over-soul," Emerson hinted at the nature of the second key. If one listened to the revelations of one's own soul, "Time, Space and Nature" would "shrink away."[26] Yet, curiously, the eternal present which he had praised in "Self-reliance" and implied in the notion of an Over-soul melted away into the future. The absorption of the human soul in the Over-soul did not obliterate progress but led to an evolution of a different sort. "After its own law and not by arithmetic is the rate of progess to be computed." The "advances" of the soul did not come "by motion in a straight line, but rather by ascension of state, such as can be represented by metamorphosis,—from the egg to the worm, from the worm to the fly."[27] This was the "law of moral and of mental gain," for "with each divine impulse" the mind would rend "the thin rinds of the visible and finite," and come out "into eternity" to breathe the air.[28]

The highest state meant abandonment to the "Supreme Mind." Once that happened, the soul would "travel a royal road to particular knowledges and powers."[29] The future would be glimpsed in the eye of the present, for there was "adult already in the infant man."[30] By contrast, society's future was false because it was finite. The soul which immersed itself in the infinite present of the Over-soul discovered the real future and ought not to ask what history, which was society's future, would bring. The only way to answer such a question was to "forego all low curiosity, and, accepting the tide of being which floats us into the secret of nature, work and live, work and live, and all unawares the advancing soul has built and forged for itself a new condition, and the question and the answer are one."[31] Union with the Over-soul brought the "infinite enlargement of the heart with a power of growth to a new infinity on every side."[32] The second key to the future active self was mystical union.

In "The Over-soul," Emerson had begun to investigate the kind of motion which could generate the future. He was sure it could not be movement in a "straight line," and with that certainty he rejected the dominant motif of the Judaeo-Christian historical faith as well as its secular equivalent in the new America's goal of mastering history to achieve an earthly paradise. But, if Emerson would not have the Western linear progression, could he and the other Transcendentalists return to the placid circles and harmonious cycles of nature? It was significant that, when he discarded the line, Emerson did not talk about cyclic motion and called instead for "ascension of state" and "metamorphosis." In "Circles," he offered his program for right motion and, like a latter-day Gnostic, he resolved his dilemma by combining line and circle in a new configuration. If it was true that the proper kind of motion was more "natural" and organic than the motion of the Judaeo-Christian tradition and the new America, it was also true that the circles of Emerson were stretching themselves somewhere, and in doing so they received new form. The third key to the future active self was the spiral.

Emerson began by acknowledging that the circle was the

"highest emblem in the cipher of the world"[33] and made it clear that the reason for his opinion was its completeness. Like the traditional mandala, Emerson's circle was perfectly balanced and organized by the principle of compensation so that within its compass "discordant opinions" as well as human vice and virtue achieved reconciliation. However, unlike traditional circles, those of Emerson could always be surrounded by larger circles; they were complete in that they contained the germ or the secret of the whole, but they were incomplete because they could always be extended. "New continents," he said, were "built out of the ruins of an old planet; the new races fed out of the decomposition of the foregoing." "New arts" destroyed old ones, and the "investment of capital in aqueducts" was "made useless by hydraulics; fortifications, by gunpowder; roads and canals, by railways; sails, by steam; steam by electricity."[34] New circles made old ones fall into a pit, and permanence was a "word of degrees." Moons were "no more bounds to spiritual power than bat-balls."[35]

In this context, the nature of God was supremely circular, for he was "the Unattainable, the flying Perfect, around which the hands of man can never meet."[36] All of life participated in the divine circle, yet it did so, in spite of Emerson's disclaimer, in a variation on the line. "Every ultimate fact" was "only the first of a new series."[37] There was a "mysterious ladder" to scale, and the only sin was "limitation."[38] The "coming" was "sacred," and Emerson preached that nature abhorred the old, considering it a disease. "Why should we import rags and relics into the new hour?" he queried. "Fever, intemperance, insanity, stupidity and crime" were all "forms of old age." So were "rest, conservatism, appropriation, inertia."[39] Clearly, Emerson's circle had become a spiral, and this was why, in the opening verse of *Nature*, the "subtle chain of countless rings" would bring the "next unto the farthest."

What Emerson had done was blend the mystical experience which accompanied the worldview of correspondence with the spiritual energy of experiences of conversion and devotion which occurred among those who acknowledged a pronounced sacred/-profane dichotomy. In the experience of conversion, an individual underwent an intense and transforming experience which was characterized above all by its suddenness and spontaneity. Unlike the mystic who might employ long years of technique to reach the center of the soul and realize its identity with the cosmos, the convert was impressed by the profundity of the distance which separated him or her from the holy. There was a hopelessness to any human effort; nothing could be done or suggested or controlled to compel God's presence. Yet the would-be convert never lacked hope. At any moment, God might take the initiative and, like a lightning flash or thunderbolt, rend the spirit of the convert by striking him or her dead to sinful and estranged existence and creating a new being with the power of divine grace. From that time forward, the wretchedness of the old person became only the base line which had been surmounted by a superstructure of grace, and thus separation from the holy, while it could never go away completely, was bridged in the experience of communion. Human faculties throughout the process were ennobled by being used. Instead of going beyond like the unitive mystic, the convert ran the gamut of human passions and experienced God to the fullness which human physical and emotional equipment allowed.

The moment of the saving event became only the first in a lifetime of moments during which the new and supernatural person would toil in faithful service. Meanwhile, God might interfere continually to rescue, sustain, and direct the believer. Power had come initially, not finally as it had for our paradigmatic mystic, so that the convert was pushed forward by the force of God from behind. Instead of expending energy in the quest for a divine encounter as many a mystic did, the convert was an empowered person who lived out his or her story from the time that God had acted. The sinful self was denied, but the "saved" biographical self was cultivated because it was the means by which the convert could do the will of God. Life therefore became linear, for it was a journey which must be made from the moment the convert believed until the time he or she was home with God in heaven. It had become a project which grew out of the moment of conversion and looked toward the final goal of union with God. Emerson had incorporated this sense of the human project in which all the faculties were consciously employed, and Perry Miller was right in discerning a connection between Transcendentalism and the religion of Jonathan Edwards.[40] Self-culture was a new mystical means which, in its exaltation of autobiography, had borrowed much from the experience of the convert. While other forms of mystical technique had tried to dissolve the historical self, Emersonian technique sought to develop it. Emerson's circles did not lie flat, and one did not pass completely beyond the senses in participating in them. Instead, they rose from earth to sky, and so they united correspondence with causality, mysticism with conversion and devotion, unconscious power with conscious will, passivity with activity, femininity with masculinity, and poetry with logic.

The spiral of mystical autobiography, however, did not exist in solitude. Emerson and his friends might try to escape from history, but history was the product of society, and society belonged to the "NOT ME" of philosophical nature. On the other hand, society, for the Transcendentialists meant simply the collective existence of selves. Social beings were so many discrete particles in the stream of human life—a perception which made possible an escape from history in the midst of a history-making people.

For Judaeo-Christian traditionalists and for their brothers and sisters in the new America, on the contrary, history narrated the drama of public events. It was the record of a people as they marched from one point in time to the next, impelled by the sense of a general destiny and protected by a Providence which guided the outcome. As we saw in the first chapter, people made history when they acted in the public arena, in the presence of witnesses, and in a way which produced public consequences. Since the Judaeo-Christian God was preeminently one who acted, a high premium had been placed on history. God had inaugurated the grand march at creation, corrected a profound mistake in orientation by redemption, and now continued to exert his influence as his people progressed toward their final goal at the millennium. When one acted, one imitated the divine Actor, and history became the theater in which the drama of salvation was played out. The way to affirm that something was true was to say that it was historical; that is, it had occurred in space and time in the presence of witnesses. Similarly, one said something was valuable by saying that it "made history," and for Americans of the nineteenth century, making history very quickly became an absolute.

In his essay "History," Emerson, though not a historian, offered a theory of history to extricate himself and his friends from the claims of the history-makers. Like discrete particles, Americans who emerged from diverse ethnic and social groups and moved from place to place formed only small and ad hoc communities. By recognizing this condition and by refusing to cast his lot with society as an organism, Emerson took the first turn which would lead him away from Judaeo-Christian history. The relation of each human piece of the world to the "NOT ME" was by way of correspondence, and "Egypt, Greece, Rome, Gaul, Britain, America" lay "folded already in the first man."[41] History ought to be written and read in the light of correspondence; the mind was one, and nature was its correlative. This meant than the total vista of history was considerably wider than the deeds of a militant humanity. While the morning newspaper could relate some of the action which was historical, it could never be absolutized into the All.[42] Much of the action lay in non-human nature, and Emerson enjoined that "broader and deeper we must write our annals . . . if we would trulier express our central and wide-related nature, instead of this old chronology of selfishness and pride to which we have too long lent our eyes."[43]

The advantage of Emerson's view was that it led out of the public arena and into the realm of private experience. He understood that there were many people who did not "make history" but who nonetheless possessed meaning simply because they were human. Emerson wanted to level history-makers with their non-historical neighbors in such a way that the latter would be seen as not peripheral, but as centers among other centers. "What are Olympiads and Consulates to these neighboring systems of being?" he asked. "Nay, what food or experience or succor have they for the Esquimaux seal-hunter, for the Kanaka in his canoe, for the fisherman, the stevedore, the porter?"[44] Emerson, in short, wanted to stand the history-writing profession on its head so that every history would be "written in a wisdom which divined the range of our affinities and looked at facts as symbols."[45] In Emersonian history, traditional out-groups such as blacks and Indians would receive the same attention as the "righteous empire," not because they made history but because of their common human condition.

More than that, Emersonian history, like Emersonian mysticism, had been collapsed into autobiography. History, Emerson said, struck a chord for each person and reverberated that person's own meaning. "We sympathize in the great moments of history, in the great discoveries, the great resistances, the great prosperities of men;—because there law was enacted, the sea was searched, the land was found, or the blow was struck, *for us*, as we ourselves in that place would have done or applauded."[46] An individual could "live all history in his own person" and therefore should "esteem his own life the text, and books the commentary."[47] All history became subjective, Emerson declared, and there was properly "no history, only biography."[48] "All public facts are to be individualized," he urged, "all private facts are to be generalized. Then at once History becomes fluid and true, and Biography deep and sublime."[49] Emerson could dive for the primeval world within himself as well as "grope for it with researching fingers in catacombs, libraries, and the broken reliefs and torsos of ruined villas."[50]

Like Emersonian mysticism, history led to identification. History, Emerson said, did away with the There and Then and established the Here and Now. Instead of a catalogue of events in developmental form, he saw it as a mythic recreation of the One Event. While Emersonian mysticism took the trappings of the new America with its commitment to motion, Emersonian history tried to do away with time in the ritual re-enactment of the myth of ideal forms. If a human being was the "compend of time," he was also the "correlative of nature." Power consisted of "the multitude of his affinities, in the fact that his life is intertwined with the whole chain of organic and inorganic being."[51]

Finally, Emersonian history was monistic and polytheistic at once. Each natural being and each event contained the all, and each was therefore the source of sacred power. "To the poet, to the philosopher, to the saint, all things are friendly and sacred, all events profitable, all days holy, all men divine." Monism coexisted with the presence of many sacred centers, for "every chemical substance, every plant, every animal in its growth" continued to teach "the unity of cause, the variety of appearance."[52] Emerson, in fact, was a radical sacramentalist who found that there was "nothing but is related to us, nothing that does not interest us,—kingdom, college, tree, horse, or iron shoe,—the roots of all things are in man."[53] Each manifestation of sacred reality was unique and distinct; "the man who has seen the rising moon break out of the clouds at midnight, has been present like an archangel at the creation of light and of the world."[54] Emersonian history would include all people equally since each, whether "idiot" or "Indian" or "child" or "unschooled farmer's boy," was a revelation of sacred reality. In the unending pluralism of America, Emerson found more divinity than most history-makers could dream of.

It was evident that he had emerged from "History" as an anti-historical historian. Yet, despite or perhaps because of his refusal to take history as seriously as the history-makers did, he had offered a formula for making, evaluating, and writing history. If the law for the private individual was self-culture, the corresponding law for the "NOT ME" of nature had to be an analogous cultivation. Developing the self could only proceed in tandem with the development of nature, but since nature included civilization as well as wilderness, a new kind of history must be fostered. Through human action, the processes of both forms of nature could be aided and perhaps even hastened. Humanity through technology could play midwife to the rest of the natural world, but at the same time, humanity must take account of its rhythms, and midwifery must go forward with respect and regard. Correspondence did not abolish making history; it only tried to make it in a different manner.

Furthermore, because nature contained two sides, the evaluation of history did not obliterate the meaning of those who did not participate in the grand public drama. Private people and little people also contained the key to the whole, and the story of each self was as worthy of attention as the tales of the Jacksons, the Biddles, the Garrisons, and the Kneelands. Ordinary folks without the drive to leave their mark in public places celebrated the opacity of nature. They did not spend their time making the clear distinctions of the linear logic which preceded and accompanied the history-makers, but instead they enjoyed the everydayishness of intuition. And intuition, for Emerson, was the highroad to the center of the world. In the writing of history, he had implied that particularity was as important as generality. The One was everywhere, but so were the many, and the historian who neglected the fact lost an occasion to encounter the sacred and discover essential identity with it.

Emerson had come full circle in his prescriptions, since the twin desiderata of self-culture and corresponding history ended in similar assertions. Both self and society led ultimately to autobiography, for self was the clue to the cosmos. Yet, because it was a story, autobiography dealt with the transformations of the self through time, and the Western commitment to history had been reconciled to the worldview of correspondence. Emerson had discovered a mediating position between an orientation based on space and an orientation based on time. There was a corresponding motion in Transcendental religion and the new America, with results which were variations on the theme of linear correspondence.

Beyond this, Emerson the pragmatist had used nature and history to teach him moral lessons, while Emerson the sacramentalist had seen objects in and for themselves. Emerson, it was true, had used the past as the springboard to the future. He wanted both history and its corollary in organic nature to facilitate change and innovation, and in so doing, he had paved the way for the pragmatic philosophy of Charles Peirce, William James, and John Dewey, as some scholars have argued.[55] Indeed, for Emerson, history and nature were objective controls by which a person could study and cultivate the self. It was each human being who was central in the Emersonian scheme of things, as Sherman Paul has pointed out, and it was from the human angle of vision that the various correspondences were perceived.[56] Nature and history were mediating agencies between the human and its divine counterpart, so that the discovery of correspondence was good because it solved the universe and solved the self. Still, Emerson the sacramentalist could not be wished away. The intensity of his search for the *juste mot* strongly suggested that Emerson saw and celebrated each object he encountered. The precision of his verbal imagery often captured a hidden essence by means of which each thing divulged its particularity and uniqueness. Use for Emerson did not destroy wonder, and in many journal passages he thrilled to the power implicit in the object to the point of identification.

Emerson looked through an object, but Emerson also looked *at* it. In an early poem which appeared in the *Western Messenger,* he detailed the twin perception:

> —*As I spoke, beneath my feet*
> *The ground-pine curled its pretty wreath,*
> *Running over the hair-cap burs:*
> *I inhaled the violet's breath;*
> *Around me stood the oaks and firs:*
> *Pine-cones and acorns lay on the ground.*
> *Over me soared the eternal sky*
> *Full of light and of deity;*
> *Again I saw—again I heard,*
> *The rolling river, the morning bird:*
> *Beauty through my senses stole,—*
> *I yielded myself to the perfect Whole.* [57]

Clearly, he was paying attention to particularity. "Each in All" was a sacramental experience in which each piece of the world was unique although it merged ultimately into the "perfect Whole." The Emerson who preached the self-reliance of the solitary individual and refused to become even an idiosyncratic Brook Farmer could hardly, while holding the theory of correspondence, do otherwise than cherish the individual pieces of nature and history.

When the object was personal, it became even easier to see what was at issue. On one occasion, Emerson described his encounter with power in the eyes of another. These eyes were a great river like the Ohio or the Danube: "I beheld him and he turned his eyes on me, his great serious eyes. Then a current of spiritual power ran through me and I looked farther & wider than I was wont, & the visages of all men were altered & the semblance of things."[58] If Emerson was purely pragmatic, then in the experience which he told about, he had merely used his friend. Rather, Emerson used his friend, but Emerson also *saw* his friend in a meeting in which the inner power of the other was manifested in a way which Emerson did not and could not control.

The synthesis which he bequeathed to his fellow-Transcendentalists and other Americans gave clear directions for the evolution of a new America which would not lose its soul. Emerson had tried to put together self and world in such a way that the requirements of all the oppositions could be maintained and yet mediated. For his contemporaries in nineteenth-century America, life was a struggle to tame the domain of the nature that was "NOT ME." This nature was a world in motion, and it called forth an answering activity from the human spirit. Religious meaning and value came from the conscious deeds of men and women, in the dramatic record of their undertakings to conquer whatever obstacles—whether natural or human—they would meet.

Emerson and the other Transcendentalists saw the value of the formula, for they committed themselves to a motion which corresponded in many ways to the motion of the new America. Yet in their common language, they voiced a concern lest the urge to active dominance destroy the opaque and mysterious roots of being, lest the channeled energy of the history-maker travel too far from the nurture of its source. For his own sake, the Transcendentalists seemed to be arguing, the history-maker needed to make friends with the mothering womb of uncultivated nature and her correspondent in the inner self. The Judaeo-Christian sky god needed to celebrate a marriage with the earth in a union which would yield androgyny: religion should include an orientation not only to the transcendent but also to the immanental world. Then outward action would be directed and led by the non-action of inner movement, and the transparent symbols of the linear mind would admit the equal stature of associative thought. The best motion would follow the rhythms of all of nature as well as the historical actions of people. Then *The Dial* could be sacred scripture for other Americans as well as the members of the Transcendental Club.

When Orestes Brownson wrote his careful evaluation of *The Dial* for the *Boston Quarterly Review*, he commented on his friends and their endeavor. "On many sides they expose themselves to ridicule," he wrote, "but at bottom there is a serious, solemn purpose, of which even they are but half conscious."[59] Brownson was more astute than he perhaps realized. Emerson and the other Transcendentalists may not have been aware of every particular which they included under the umbrella of correspondence. Even more, because they had turned so enthusiastically to the associative form of thinking which accompanied correspondence, their religious experience did not spell itself out in the systematic terms with which their more linearly-organized contemporaries and heirs were familiar. Hence, the message has been largely understood as literature, respected from a distance as philosophy, or dismissed as mysticism. Transcendental religion, although it knew intuitively that it kept time with the new America, became largely a private revolution. The Transcendentalists were instructed by the new America, but the new America had still to be instructed by the corresponding motion of Transcendental religion.

Notes

INTRODUCTION

1. See, for example, William R. Hutchison, *The Transcendentalist Ministers: Church Reform in the New England Renaissance* (New Haven: Yale University Press, 1959), and Ronald V. Wells, *Three Christian Transcendentalists: James Marsh, Caleb Sprague Henry, Frederic Henry Hedge* (1943) (New York: Octagon Books, 1972). Two recent studies of individual Transcendentalists from a religious perspective are William A. Clebsch, "The Hospitable Universe of Ralph Waldo Emerson," in *American Religious Thought: A History* (Chicago: University of Chicago Press, 1973), and William J. Wolf, *Thoreau: Mystic, Prophet, Ecologist* (Philadelphia: Pilgrim Press, 1974). For a work on Emerson's religious thought that is somewhat older than the Clebsch essay, see Jonathan Bishop, *Emerson on the Soul* (Cambridge: Harvard University Press, 1964). Even earlier is Stephen E. Whicher's *Freedom and Fate* (Philadelphia: University of Pennsylvania Press, 1953), which treats Emerson's understanding of the relationship between human and divine will. In a recent anthology on Transcendental criticism, Brian M. Barbour has included a section concerning theological perspectives that contains, in addition to a selection from Hutchison's *Transcendentalist Ministers*, an excerpt on "Unitarianism and Transcendentalism" from Harold C. Goddard's (1908) *Studies in New England Transcendentalism*, and Robert C. Albrecht's article, "The Theological Response of the Transcendentalists to the Civil War," originally published in the *New England Quarterly* in 1965. See Brian M. Barbour, ed., *American Transcendentalism: An Anthology of Criticism* (Notre Dame, Ind.: University of Notre Dame Press, 1973). In 1943, Charles H. Foster argued that "Emerson's primary impulse" was "religious rather than literary" ("Emerson as American Scripture," *New England Quarterly* 16, no. 1 [Mar. 1943]: 94 et passim). Other representative articles include Lester Mondale, "The Practical Mysticism of Ralph Waldo Emerson," in Alfred P. Stiernotte, ed., *Mysticism and the Modern Mind* (New York: Liberal Arts Press, 1959), pp. 43–59, and, closer to the present, Robert S. Ward, "Still 'Christians,' Still Infidels," *Southern Humanities Review* 2, no. 3 (Summer 1968): 365–74.

2. For a clear statement, see Joachim Wach, *Sociology of Religion* (1944) (Chicago: University of Chicago Press, 1967), pp. 13–17. Wach follows Rudolf Otto in this understanding (*The Idea of the Holy*, trans. J. W. Harvey [New York: Oxford University Press, 1952]). Jerald C. Brauer, to my knowledge, first suggested the use of history of religions method for the study of American Christianity. See "Changing Perspectives on Religion in America," in *Reinterpretation in American Church History*, vol. 5 of *Essays in Divinity*, ed. Jerald C. Brauer (Chicago: University of Chicago Press, 1968), pp. 1–28, especially 21–24.

3. For a now classical study of Emerson's thought on correspondence from a philosophical as well as literary perspective, see Sherman Paul, *Emerson's Angle of Vision: Man and Nature in American Experience* (1952) (Cambridge: Harvard University Press, 1969). Paul sees Emerson's doctrine of correspondence as the linchpin for interpretation.

4. Two twentieth-century sources have helped me greatly in formulating my side of the dialogue with the Transcendentalists. C. G. Jung first made me aware of the distinction between correspondence and causality in *Synchronicity: An Acausal Connecting Principle*. (See C. G. Jung, *The Collected Works of C. G. Jung*, vol. 8, *The Structure and Dynamics of the Psyche*, 2d ed., trans. R. F. C. Hull [Princeton: Princeton University Press, 1969]: 417–519, and the short appendix, "On Synchronicity," pp. 520–31.) Frederick J. Streng, in his brief and evocative book, *Understanding Religious Man*, initially suggested to me the importance of four different types of religious experience and expression: harmony with cosmic law, mystical insight through spiritual discipline, myth and sacrament, and personal apprehension of a holy presence. Streng's understandings of these four "ways" have been somewhat modified in the course of this study. The use of correspondence and causality as controlling categories is the prime instance of this modification. Another is the relatively greater emphasis which, following the cue of the Transcendentalists, will be placed on the natural world in the explication of correspondence. See Frederick J. Streng, *Understanding Religious Man* (Belmont, Calif.: Dickenson Publishing, 1969) and *Understanding Religious Life*, 2d ed. (Belmont, Calif.: Dickenson Publishing, 1976). See also, F. J. Streng, C. L. Lloyd, Jr., and J. T. Allen, eds., *Ways of Being Religious* (Englewood Cliffs, N.J.: Prentice–Hall, 1973).

5. For a good discussion by a sociologist interested in religion, see Benjamin Zablocki, *The Joyful Community* (Baltimore: Penguin Books, 1971), pp. 149–52. My analysis here follows Zablocki and Herbert Blumer whom he quotes.

6. The anthropologist Victor Turner enunciated his understanding of *communitas* in *The Ritual Process: Structure and Anti-Structure* (Chicago: Aldine Publishing, 1969), especially p. 96. For further discussion by Turner, see

Dramas, Fields, and Metaphors: Symbolic Action in Human Society (Ithaca, N.Y.: Cornell University Press, 1974), especially pp. 231–33, and 272–74.

7. Language has been an important recent focus in religion study. One thinks particularly of the impetus derived from the researches of the French structuralist school and most notably Claude Lévi-Strauss. See *The Savage Mind* (Chicago: University of Chicago Press, Phoenix Books, 1966) and *Totemism* (Boston: Beacon Press, 1963). Turner has taken up the theme of metaphor in *Dramas, Fields, and Metaphors*, pp. 272–98. In the introduction to his *Metahistory*, Hayden White discusses the implications for conceptualization of the four poetic tropes—metaphor, metonymy, synecdoche, and irony. His analysis of the relationship between language and consciousness is germane to this essay. See Hayden White, *Metahistory: The Historical Imagination in Nineteenth-Century Europe* (Baltimore: Johns Hopkins University Press, 1973), pp. 1–38.

8. Unfortunately, no woman was present that first evening, although Margaret Fuller and others became prominent later in the movement.

9. Peter L. Berger and Thomas Luckmann have discussed the sociology of knowledge on the model of this tripartite schema in *The Social Construction of Reality: A Treatise on the Sociology of Knowledge* (Garden City, N.Y.: Doubleday, Anchor Books, 1966). For a good brief summary, see Peter L. Berger, *The Sacred Canopy: Elements of a Sociological Theory of Religion* (Garden City, N.Y.: Doubleday, Anchor Books, 1969). pp. 3–6.

10. Emile Durkheim set forth his seminal thesis in *The Elementary Forms of the Religious Life* (1915) (New York: Free Press, 1965), especially pp. 235–72. For Durkheim, the object of religion is human society, and religious symbols really image society and its laws which assert their priority over individual existence.

11. Here, of course, the name of Sigmund Freud comes immediately to mind. But the twentieth-century schematizations of Freud's former disciple, Carl G. Jung, have developed the theme of the unconscious in directions which have been especially fruitful for the present essay. For a good summary of Jung's work, see his autobiography, *Memories, Dreams, Reflections*, ed. Aniela Jaffé (New York: Random House, Vintage Books, 1963).

CHAPTER I. CHILD OF THE UNIVERSE

1. Ralph Waldo Emerson, *Nature*, in *The Complete Works of Ralph Waldo Emerson*, ed. Edward Waldo Emerson, 12 vols. (Boston: Houghton Mifflin, 1903), 1:71.

2. Ibid., 1:9–10.

3. Ibid., 1:14.

4. Ibid., 1:16.

5. Ibid., 1:25.

6. Ibid., 1:32.

7. Ibid., 1:40–42.

8. Ibid., 1:35.

9. Ibid., 1:66–67. Sherman Paul has discussed the "linear logic" extensively in *Emerson's Angle of Vision: Man and Nature in American Experience* (1952) (Cambridge: Harvard University Press, 1969), pp. 5–26.

10. For an overview of the cosmology of early Egyptians and Babylonians, see Samuel A. B. Mercer, *Early Intellectual Man's Idea of the Cosmos* (London: Headley, ca. 1956).

11. For a short, helpful discussion of *dharma* in Hinduism, see Thomas J. Hopkins, *The Hindu Religious Tradition* (Belmont, Calif.: Dickenson Publishing, 1971), pp. 73–86. A discussion of the correspondence between cosmic myth and individual life-orientation in Hinduism is contained in Ananda K. Coomaraswamy, *Hinduism and Buddhism* (New York: Philosophical Library [1943]), pp. 3–31.

12. Frederick J. Streng, *Understanding Religious Man* (Belmont, Calif.: Dickenson Publishing, 1969), p. 65.

13. Clifford Geertz makes the distinction between "models *of*" and "models *for*" in his now classic article, "Religion as a Cultural System" (1966), reprinted in *The Interpretation of Cultures* (New York: Basic Books, 1973), especially p. 93. The usage here is somewhat modified from Geertz's own understanding.

14. Philo of Alexandria, *De opificio mundi*, 82, 1:67; quoted by Carl G. Jung in *Synchronicity: An Acausal Connecting Principle*, in *The Collected Works of C. G. Jung*, vol. 8, *The Structure and Dynamics of the Psyche*, 2d ed., trans. R. F. C. Hull (Princeton: Princeton University Press, 1969), p. 490.

15. Ibid., pp. 440ff.

16. Franz Cumont, *Oriental Religions in Roman Paganism* (1911; reprint ed., New York: Dover Publications, 1956), p. 165.

17. For a helpful discussion of Chinese religion with some attention to its popular manifestations, see Laurence G. Thompson, *Chinese Religion: An Introduction* (Belmont, Calif.: Dickenson Publishing, 1969). For a philosophical treatment with religious implications, see Fung Yu-lan, *A Short History of Chinese Philosophy*, ed. Derk Bodde (New York: Free Press, 1948). The classic treatment of Chinese religion in terms of correspondence is Marcel Granet's *La Pensée Chinoise* (Paris: La Renaissance du Livre, 1934). See especially "Livre III: Le Système du Monde," pp. 344–418.

18. Yu-lan, *Short History*, p. 45.

19. Arthur Waley, trans., *The Analects of Confucius* (1938), 13.3, 12.11, 12.17 (New York: Random House, Vintage Books, n.d.), pp. 171–72, 166, 167.

20. For a similar modern perception of the connections between socio-political and linguistic health and corruption, see George Orwell, "Politics and the English Language," in Louis Locke et al., eds., *Toward Liberal Education*, vol. 1, *Readings in Liberal Education*, 3d ed. (New York: Rinehart, 1957): 140–50.

21. Lao Tzu, *Tao Te Ching*, in Wing-Tsit Chan et al., eds., *The Great Asian Religions: An Anthology* (New York: Macmillan, 1969), p. 153.

22. *Chuang Tzu*, ibid., p. 159.

23. A useful general introduction to North American Indian religion is Ruth M. Underhill's *Red Man's Religion* (Chicago: University of Chicago Press, 1965).

24. Emerson, *Nature*, pp. 33–34, 68, 69, 70–72.

25. Coomaraswamy, *Hinduism and Buddhism*, p. 6.

26. For a brief discussion, see Underhill, *Red Man's Religion*, pp. 30–39.

27. Mircea Eliade discussed the "terror of history" in its Hegelian valorization in his classic *Cosmos and History: The Myth of the Eternal Return* (1949) (New York: Harper & Row, Harper Torchbooks, 1959). See especially chap. 4, "The Terror of History," pp. 139–62. My analysis of the clash between cosmos and history in the Enlightenment is partially dependent on Eliade.

28. In the discussion of the sacred stories of the Judaeo-Christian tradition, I have been understanding myth as a true story; that is, a narrative symbol which has the power to disclose the meaningful structure of reality—the structure which becomes a collective focus for identification and action. For a good treatment from this perspective, see Mircea Eliade, *Myth and Reality* (New York: Harper & Row, Harper Torchbooks, 1968), pp. 1–20 et passim.

29. Perry Miller has discussed the evolution of the Puritan "mission" along these lines in *The New England Mind: From Colony to Province* (1953) (Boston: Beacon Press, 1961) and *Errand into the Wilderness* (1956) (New York: Harper & Row, Harper Torchbooks, 1964).

30. Emerson, *Nature*, p. 47. See also p. 12.

31. As early as 1941, F. O. Matthiessen noted that Emerson considered the "prevailing thought of his century" to be "its reassertion of the Heraclitean doctrine of the Flowing." See F. O. Matthiessen, *American Renaissance* (1941) (New York: Oxford University Press, 1968), p. 69. A decade later, Vivian C. Hopkins shaped an aesthetic interpretation of

Emerson around the notion of spiritual energy coursing through matter and supplying it with life (*Spires of Form* [Cambridge: Harvard University Press, 1951]). In a short article, Nina Baym discussed the flux in the water imagery of Emerson and Henry David Thoreau ("From Metaphysics to Metaphor: The Image of Water in Emerson and Thoreau," *Studies in Romanticism 5*, no. 4 [Summer 1966]: 231–43). Baym, as this essay argues, saw that for Emerson "God or Spirit is equated with activity." But she explored this identification in terms of Emerson's acquaintance with pre-Socratic and Neoplatonic thought in which it was outlined. This study, however, employs the correspondential perspective of the Transcendentalists as a tactic for scholarship so that it explores the relationships between the religious experience of the Transcendentalists and their contemporary cultural milieu.

32. Emerson, *Nature*, p. 13.

33. Ibid., p. 76

34. Ibid., pp. 4–5.

CHAPTER II. THE NEIGHBORHOOD OF BOSTON

1. Orestes Brownson may or may not have been present at the first meeting of the Transcendental Club. Both Emerson and Alcott, in their respective journals, mentioned his presence at this meeting (Ralph Waldo Emerson, *The Journals and Miscellaneous Notebooks*, ed. William H. Gilman et al., 11 vols. to date [Cambridge: Harvard University Press, Belknap Press, 1960–   ], 5 [20 Sept. 1836]: 194–95 [hereafter cited as *JMN*]; Amos Bronson Alcott, *The Journals*, sel. and ed. Odell Shepard [Boston: Little, Brown, 1938] [19 Sept. 1836], pp. 78–79). Later accounts by Alcott, as well as recollections by others, do not agree. Since the two eyewitness accounts which include Brownson were written within twenty-four hours of the event, it is most likely that he did attend the meeting. However, for the purposes of this exploration of Transcendental consciousness, I have decided not to use Brownson, whose extreme trajectory from left to right drove him quickly outside the Transcendental camp.

2. Lawrence Buell, *Literary Transcendentalism: Style and Vision in the American Renaissance* (Ithaca, N.Y.: Cornell University Press, 1973), pp. 77–101.

3. Josiah Quincy, "Social Life in Boston," in *The Last Hundred Years: Special Topics*, vol. 4 of *The Memorial History of Boston, Including Suffolk County, Massachusetts, 1630–1880*, ed. Justin Winsor (Boston: James R. Osgood, 1881), p. 6.

4. Roland N. Stromberg, "Boston in the 1820's and 1830's," *History Today* 11, no. 9 (Sept. 1961):593.

5. Timothy Dwight, *Travels in New-England and New-York,* 4 vols. (New Haven: S. Converse, 1821), 1:513.

6. Ralph Waldo Emerson, *Journals,* ed. Edward Waldo Emerson and Waldo Emerson Forbes, 10 vols. (Boston: Houghton Mifflin, 1909–14), 8 (Oct. 1852): 339.

7. Conrad Wright, *The Beginnings of Unitarianism in America* (Boston: Starr King Press, 1955), p. 246.

8. William Tudor, *Letters on the Eastern States,* 2d ed. (Boston: Wells & Lilly, 1821), p. 389.

9. Francis J. Grund, *Aristocracy in America from the Sketch-Book of a German Nobleman,* 2 vols. (London: Richard Bentley, 1839), 2:134.

10. Ibid., 2:66.

11. "Unitarian Whiggery," in Daniel Walker Howe, *The Unitarian Conscience: Harvard Moral Philosophy, 1805–1861* (Cambridge: Harvard University Press, 1970), pp. 205–35.

12. Harriet Martineau, *Society in America,* 3 vols. (London: Saunders & Otley, 1837), 3:281–83.

13. Tudor, *Letters on the Eastern States,* p. 99.

14. Wright, *Unitarianism in America,* p. 252.

15. Martineau, *Society in America,* 3:284.

16. Samuel Osgood, *Student Life: Letters and Recollections for a Young Friend* (New York: James Miller, 1861), p. 31.

17. Martineau, *Society in America,* 3:165.

18. Samuel Eliot Morison, *Three Centuries of Harvard, 1636–1936* (Cambridge: Harvard University Press, 1936), p. 260.

19. Emerson, *JMN,* 5 (18 Aug. 1837): 365.

20. Ibid., 7 (14 Sept. 1839): 240.

21. Ralph Waldo Emerson, "New England Reformers," *Essays, Second Series* (1844), in *The Complete Works of Ralph Waldo Emerson,* ed. Edward Waldo Emerson, 12 vols. (Boston: Houghton Mifflin, 1903), 3:258–59.

22. James E. Cabot, *A Memoir of Ralph Waldo Emerson,* 2 vols. (Boston: Houghton Mifflin, 1887), 1:85.

23. Emerson, *JMN,* 8 (15 Oct. 1842): 287–88.

24. Ibid., 8 (Sept, 1841): 87; (14 Oct. 1841): 58.

25. Ibid., 7 (6 Jan. 1839): 163; (16 June 1838): 21.

26. Ibid., 5 (1 Apr. 1838): 471.

27. Ralph Waldo Emerson to Frederic Henry Hedge, 20 Aug. 1839, *The Letters of Ralph Waldo Emerson*, ed. Ralph L. Rusk, 6 vols. (New York: Columbia University Press, 1939), 2:219.

28. Emerson, *JMN*, 8 (26 June 1842): 182; (Mar. 1843): 355; "Religion" (19 Jan. 1837), in *The Early Lectures*, ed. Stephen E. Whicher et al., 3 vols. (Cambridge: Harvard University Press, 1959–72), 2:97.

29. Ralph Waldo Emerson to John Boynton Hill, Boston, 3 Jan. 1823, *Letters of Emerson*, 1:128

30. Emerson, *JMN*, 5 (1 Oct. 1837): 380; (18 Mar. 1838): 464. Conrad Wright discusses this episode in his essay, "Emerson, Barzillai Frost, and the Divinity School Address." See Conrad Wright, *The Liberal Christians: Essays on American Unitarian History* (Boston: Beacon Press, 1970), pp. 41–61.

31. Ibid., 5 (26 May 1838): 502; Ralph Waldo Emerson to Margaret Fuller, Concord (6 Sept. 1839), *Letters of Emerson*, 2:222.

32. Amos Bronson Alcott, *Journals* (1818), quoted by Odell Shepard in *Pedlar's Progress: The Life of Bronson Alcott* (Boston: Little, Brown, 1937), p. 126. Unfortunately, the published journals of Alcott contain only a small portion of the total material which he left.

33. Alcott, *Journals* (18 May 1828), quoted by Franklin B. Sanborn and William T. Harris in *A. Bronson Alcott: His Life and Philosophy*, 2 vols. (Boston: Roberts, 1893), 1:121.

34. Alcott, *Journals* (n.d.), quoted by Shepard in *Pedlar's Progress*, p. 307; Alcott, *Journals* (4 July 1842), p. 162.

35. Alcott, *Journals* (15 Dec. 1835), quoted by Sanborn and Harris in *A. Bronson Alcott*, 1:211.

36. Sanborn and Harris, *A. Bronson Alcott*, 1:191.

37. Shepard, *Pedlar's Progress*, pp. 194–95.

38. Alcott, *Journals* (15 Oct. 1830), p. 25; (8 Nov. 1830), p. 26.

39. Franklin B. Sanborn, *Recollections of Seventy Years*, 2 vols. (Boston: R. G. Badger, 1909), 2:446.

40. Shepard, *Pedlar's Progress*, pp. 336–37.

41. Charles Crowe, *George Ripley: Transcendentalist and Utopian Socialist* (Athens: University of Georgia Press, 1967), pp. 8–9.

42. George Ripley to John Sullivan Dwight, 14 Aug. 1838, quoted by Crowe in *George Ripley: Transcendentalist*, p. 56; George Ripley, *Discourses on the Philosophy of Religion Addressed to Doubters Who Wish to Believe* (Boston: James Munroe, 1836), p. 41; George Ripley, *A Letter Addressed to the Congregational Church in Purchase Street* (privately printed; Boston: 1840), quoted by Octavius B. Frothingham in *George Ripley* (Boston: Houghton Mifflin,

1882), p. 67; George Ripley, *A Farewell Discourse Delivered to the Congregational Church in Purchase Street*, 28 Mar. 1841, quoted by Crowe in *George Ripley: Transcendentalist*, p. 118.

43. Crowe, *George Ripley: Transcendentalist*, p. 113.

44. Ibid., p. 161.

45. James Freeman Clarke, *Autobiography, Diary and Correspondence*, ed. Edward Everett Hale (Boston: Houghton Mifflin, 1899), p. 11.

46. Ibid., pp. 36–41.

47. Francis G. Peabody, *Reminiscences of Present-day Saints* (Boston: Houghton Mifflin, 1927), pp. 53–55.

48. James Freeman Clarke to William Henry Channing, Lexington, 8 Nov. 1833, *Autobiography, Diary and Correspondence*, p. 103.

49. Samuel J. May, "Anti-slavery," in Clarke, *Autobiography, Diary and Correspondence*, pp. 221, 225.

50. Frederic Henry Hedge, *A Sermon on the Character and Ministry of the Late Rev. William Ellery Channing, D.D.* (Bangor, Maine: S. S. Smith, 1842), p. 17. It is noteworthy that the kind of Unitarianism which was embodied by Channing and eulogized by Hedge provided the bridge to Transcendentalism.

51. Frederic Henry Hedge, *An Introductory Lecture Delivered at the Opening of the Bangor Lyceum*, 15 Nov. 1836 (Bangor, Maine: Nourse & Smith, and Duren & Thatcher, 1836), pp. 4, 20; *Conservatism and Reform: An Oration before the Peucinian Society, Bowdoin College*, 5 Sept. 1843 (Boston: C. C. Little & J. Brown, 1843), p. 17; *An Oration Pronounced before the Citizens of Bangor, on the Fourth of July, 1838* (Bangor, Maine: S. S. Smith, 1838), p. 37.

52. Hedge, *Introductory Lecture*, pp. 22–24.

53. Ibid., pp. 18–21.

54. Convers Francis, *Autobiography*, quoted by William Newell in *Memoir of the Rev, Convers Francis*, in *Proceedings of the Massachusetts Historical Society, 1864–1865* (Boston: Wiggin & Lunt, 1866), pp. 238–39.

55. Convers Francis, *Preaching Record*, 1826, quoted by Mosetta I. Vaughan in *Sketch of the Life and Work of Convers Francis, D.D.* (Watertown, Mass.: Historical Society of Watertown, 1944), pp. 10–11.

56. Vaughan, *Life and Work of Francis*, p. 6.

57. Lydia Maria Child to Convers Francis, Boston, 22 Nov. 1833, and Lydia Maria Child to Convers Francis, New Rochelle, 19 Dec. 1835, in Lydia Maria Child, *Letters*, coll. and arr. Harriet Winslow Sewall (1883; reprint ed., New York: Arno Press & New York Times, 1969), pp. 12–13, 18.

58. Theodore Parker to Convers Francis, 3 Feb. 1859, quoted by Newell in *Memoir of Francis*, p. 249.

59. Francis, *Autobiography*, quoted by Newell in *Memoir of Francis*, p. 249.

60. Convers Francis, quoted by John Weiss in *Discourse Occasioned by the Death of Convers Francis, D.D.* (Cambridge, Mass.: John Weiss, 1863), p. 23.

61. Ibid., pp. 28–29.

62. Ibid., p. 34.

63. Here, I follow the sociology of knowledge of Peter Berger. See his summary in *The Sacred Canopy: Elements of a Sociological Theory of Religion* (Garden City, N.Y.: Doubleday, Anchor Books, 1969), pp. 3–6. See also note 9 to the Introduction.

64. Emerson, *JMN*, 11 (Oct. 1848): 19.

CHAPTER III. THE KINETIC REVOLUTION

1. Francis Bowen, "Locke and the Transcendentalists," *Christian Examiner* 33 (1837): 190.

2. Andrews Norton, "The New School in Literature and Religion," *Boston Daily Advertiser*, 27 Aug. 1838.

3. S. X. [Theophilus Parsons], "The New School and Its Opponents," *Boston Daily Advertiser*, 30 Aug. 1838.

4. Andrews Norton, "On the Article in the *Advertiser* of Thursday Concerning the New School," *Boston Daily Advertiser*, 1 Sept. 1838. Mary Edrich argues persuasively that the charges of infidelity leveled against Emerson by Unitarians were "unjustifiably vehement" and that the real point at issue after the Divinity School Address was the character of Emerson's rhetoric. "What should be noted is that the major invectives directed against the address in Emerson's day all stressed the speaker's 'irresponsible' use of language." Edrich's analysis, however, emphasizes the logical ambiguity and personal insult contained in Emerson's language. See Mary W. Edrich, "The Rhetoric of Apostasy," *Texas Studies in Literature and Language* 8, no. 4 (Winter 1967): 547, 550, et passim.

5. Ralph Waldo Emerson, *The Journals and Miscellaneous Notebooks*, ed. William H. Gilman et al., 11 vols. to date (Cambridge: Harvard University Press, Belknap Press, 1960–), 5 (10 Nov. 1836): 246 [hereafter cited as *JMN*].

6. Ralph Waldo Emerson, "The Poet," *Essays, Second Series* (1844), in *The Complete Works of Ralph Waldo Emerson*, ed. Edward Waldo Emerson, 12 vols. (Boston: Houghton Mifflin, 1903), 3:34.

7. Emerson, *JMN*, 5 (19 May 1837): 329.

8. James Freeman Clarke, *The Unitarian Reform*, in *Tracts of the American Unitarian Association*, 1st ser., 12, no. 138 (Boston: James Munroe, 1839): 5.

9. Frederic Henry Hedge, *Conservatism and Reform: An Oration before the Peucinian Society, Bowdoin College*, 5 Sept. 1843 (Boston: C. C. Little & J. Brown, 1843), p. 14.

10. George Ripley, *The Claims of the Age on the Work of the Evangelist* (Boston: Weeks Jordan, 1840), p. 17.

11. Convers Francis, "Discourse 3," *Three Discourses Preached before the Congregational Society in Watertown* (Cambridge, Mass.: Folsom, Wells & Thurston, 1836), p. 45.

12. Ralph Waldo Emerson to John Sterling, Concord, 31 Mar. 1841, *A Correspondence between John Sterling and Ralph Waldo Emerson*, ed. Edward Waldo Emerson (Boston: Houghton Mifflin, 1897), p. 36.

13. Emerson, *JMN*, 5 (9 Aug. 1837): 357; 7 (30 Mar. 1840): 490; and (1 May 1841): 450.

14. Ralph Waldo Emerson to Margaret Fuller, Concord, 12 Oct. 1838, *The Letters of Ralph Waldo Emerson*, ed. Ralph L. Rusk, 6 vols. (New York: Columbia University Press, 1939), 2:168; Emerson, *JMN*, 7 (13 Sept. 1838): 71; Ralph Waldo Emerson to Margaret Fuller, Concord, 19 July 1842, *Letters of Emerson*, 3:75.

15. Ralph Waldo Emerson, "The Over-soul," *Essays, First Series* (1841), in *Complete Works*, 2:268.

16. Emerson, *JMN*, 7 (6 Dec. 1840): 539–40.

17. Ibid., 7 (23 Apr. 1841): 435.

18. Ibid., 5 (17 June 1836): 177; and (26 Mar. 1838): 468.

19. Ibid., 7 (19 June 1838): 25.

20. Ibid., 7 (7 Oct. 1839): 259.

21. Ralph Waldo Emerson to Thomas Carlyle, Concord, 17 Sept. 1836, *The Correspondence of Emerson and Carlyle*, ed. Joseph Slater (New York: Columbia University Press, 1964), p. 150.

22. Emerson, *JMN*, 5 (5 May 1837): 321.

23. Ibid., 7 (14 Nov. 1839): 300.

24. Ralph Waldo Emerson to Margaret Fuller, Concord, 9 Nov. 1841, *Letters of Emerson*, 2:463.

25. Emerson, *JMN*, 8 (ca. 1841–42): 503.

26. Ibid., 5 (1 May 1838): 488.

27. Ibid., 9 (ca. June 1844): 123.

28. Ibid., 7 (28 May 1840): 360.

29. Ibid., 7 (1 May 1841): 449.

30. Ralph Waldo Emerson to Samuel G. Ward, undated (ca. 1840), *Letters from Ralph Waldo Emerson to a Friend, 1838–1853*, ed. Charles Eliot Norton (Boston: Houghton Mifflin, 1899), p. 30.

31. Ralph Waldo Emerson to Margaret Fuller, Concord, 25 Sept. 1840, *Letters of Emerson*, 2:337.

32. Emerson, *JMN*, 7 (9 Mar. 1839): 172.

33. Ralph Waldo Emerson, "The American Scholar" (31 Aug. 1837), in *Complete Works*, 1:85. The address was the Phi Beta Kappa oration at Cambridge.

34. Ibid., pp. 90–111.

35. Ralph Waldo Emerson, "Divinity School Address" (15 July 1838), in *Complete Works* 1:129-50.

36. Ralph Waldo Emerson, "Art" (29 Dec. 1836), in *The Early Lectures*, ed. Stephen E. Whicher et al., 3 vols. (Cambridge: Harvard University Press, 1959–72), 2:42, 50.

37. Ralph Waldo Emerson, "Literature" (5 Jan. 1837), in ibid., 2:66.

38. Ralph Waldo Emerson, "Politics" (12 Jan. 1837), in ibid., 2:76.

39. Ralph Waldo Emerson, "Religion" (19 Jan. 1837), in ibid., 2:96.

40. Ralph Waldo Emerson, "Ethics" (16 Feb. 1837), in ibid., 2:147, 155.

41. Ralph Waldo Emerson, "Indtroductory" (6 Dec. 1837), in ibid., 2:218.

42. Ralph Waldo Emerson, "The Head" (20 Dec. 1837), in ibid., 2:249-50.

43. Ralph Waldo Emerson, "The Heart" (3 Jan. 1838), in ibid., 2:292–93.

44. Ralph Waldo Emerson, "Holiness" (31 Jan. 1838), in ibid., 2:355, 345–46.

45. Ralph Waldo Emerson, "History," *Essays, First Series*, in *Complete Works*, 2:32, 7.

46. Ralph Waldo Emerson, "Self–reliance," in ibid, 2:64–68.

47. Ralph Waldo Emerson, "Compensation," in ibid 2:91–92, 122.

48. Ralph Waldo Emerson, "Love," in ibid, 2:170; Ralph Waldo Emerson, "Friendship," in ibid., 2:193–96.

49. Emerson, "The Over–soul," in ibid., 2:274, 271, 281, 285.

50. Ralph Waldo Emerson, "Circles," in ibid., 2:283ff., 304, 320, 302.

51. Emerson, "The Poet," *Essays, Second Series*, in *Complete Works*, 3:1, 20–21, 19.

52. Michael H. Cowan, *City of the West: Emerson, America, and Urban Metaphor* (New Haven: Yale University Press, 1967), p. 112.

53. Ralph Waldo Emerson, "Experience," *Essays, Second Series*, in *Complete Works*, 3:45, 55, 50, 62, 59.

54. Ralph Waldo Emerson, "Manners," in ibid., 3:127.

55. Ralph Waldo Emerson, "Nature," in ibid., 3:178.

56. Ralph Waldo Emerson, "Politics," in ibid., 3:199.

57. Ralph Waldo Emerson, "Nominalist and Realist," in ibid., 3:239.

58. Amos Bronson Alcott, *The Journals*, sel. and ed. Odell Shepard (Boston: Little, Brown, 1938) (19 Mar, 1839), p. 121.

59. Amos Bronson Alcott, *Conversations with Children on the Gospels*, 2 vols. (Boston: James Munroe, 1836–37), 1:132; 2:15; 1:233, nn. 226, 229.

60. Amos Bronson Alcott to Mrs. James Savage, Temple School, 24 June, *The Letters*, ed. Richard L. Herrnstadt (Ames: Iowa State University Press, 1969), p. 39. The letter was undated, but Herrnstadt has suggested 1838, a date which would coincide with the closing of the Temple School.

61. Amos Bronson Alcott, *The Doctrine and Discipline of Human Culture* (1836; reprint ed. as Amos Bronson Alcott, *Essays on Education* [Gainesville, Fla.: Scholars' Facsimiles & Reprints, 1960]), p. 22

62. Alcott, *Conversations*, 1:135.

63. Ibid., 2:27; 1:137; 2:176; 2:77, 72–73.

64. George Ripley, "James Martineau's *Rationale of Religious Enquiry*," *Christian Examiner* 21 (Nov. 1836):225–27, 246–47, 249, 252, 244.

65. George Ripley, *Boston Daily Advertiser*, 9 Nov. 1836.

66. [George Ripley], *"The Latest Form of Infidelity" Examined: A Letter to Mr. Andrews Norton* (Boston: James Munroe, 1839), pp. 10–11, 116, 158–59.

67. George Ripley, *Defence of "The Latest Form of Infidelity" Examined: A Second Letter to Mr. Andrews Norton* (Boston: James Munroe, 1840), p. 16.

68. George Ripley, *Defence of "The Latest Form of Infidelity" Examined: A Third Letter to Mr. Andrews Norton* (Boston: James Munroe, 1840), pp. 6–7, 146–49.

69. Alcott, *Journals* (18 June 1839), pp. 130–131.

70. Amos Bronson Alcott to Ralph Waldo Emerson, Boston, 9 Oct. 1837, *Letters*, p. 37; Alcott, *Journals* (Week 2, Jan. 1838), p. 99.

71. Alcott, *Journals* (12 Mar. 1836), p. 77; (Week 42, Oct. 1838), p. 106.

72. Ibid. (17 Apr. 1839), p. 124; (Week 16, Apr. 1837), p. 88; (27 Apr. 1839), p. 125; (23 Mar. 1839), p. 120; (22 July 1842), p. 166.

73. George Ripley, *Discourses on the Philosophy of Religion Addressed to Doubters Who Wish to Believe* (Boston: James Munroe, 1836), p. 24.

74. Ibid., pp. 42, 53, 74.

75. Ripley, *Claims of the Age*, p. 7.

76. George Ripley, *A Letter Addressed to the Congregational Church in Purchase Street* (privately printed; Boston: 1840), pp. 7–8, 22–23.

77. Zoltán Haraszti, *The Idyll of Brook Farm: As Revealed by Unpublished Letters in the Boston Public Library* (Boston: Trustees of the Public Library, 1937), p. 5.

78. Amos Bronson Alcott to Mrs. A. B. Alcott, Surrey, 16 July 1842, *The Letters*, p. 85.

79. Amos Bronson Alcott to William Alcott, Alcott House, 30 June 1842, ibid., p. 76.

80. Amos Bronson Alcott to Mrs. A. B. Alcott, Alcott House, 16 Aug. 1842, ibid., p. 90.

81. Amos Bronson Alcott to Junius Alcott, Fruitlands, Harvard, 18 June 1843, ibid., pp. 102–03.

82. Amos Bronson Alcott to Elizabeth Alcott, Fruitlands, Harvard, 24 June 1843, ibid., p. 105.

83. James Freeman Clarke, *The Peculiar Doctrine of Christianity, or Reconciliation by Jesus Christ*, in *Tracts of the American Unitarian Association*, 1st ser., 18, no. 208 (Boston: James Munroe, 1845): 7–24.

84. James Freeman Clarke, *Repentance toward God* (Boston: Office of the Christian World, 1844), pp. 10–19.

85. Clarke, *Unitarian Reform*, pp. 6–15.

86. James Freeman Clarke, *The Well-Instructed Scribe; or, Reform and Conservatism* (Boston: Benjamin H. Greene, 1841), pp. 6–7, 9–10, 12–14.

87. James Freeman Clarke, *A Sermon Preached in Amory Hall, October 9, 1842, Being the Sunday Succeeding the Death of William Ellery Channing* (Boston: Benjamin H. Greene, 1842), pp. 8–20.

88. James Freeman Clarke, "Monthly Record, August, 1836," *Western Messenger* 2, no. 1 (Aug. 1836): 140.

89. James Freeman Clarke, *"The Bible, Its Own Refutation* by Charles G. Olmstead," ibid. 3, no. 1 (Feb. 1837): 455.

90. James Freeman Clarke, "Too Much Charity," ibid. 3, no. 6 (July 1837): 815–16.

91. James Freeman Clarke, "Letter to the Unitarian Clergy, on Preaching the Law and Gospel," ibid. 2, no. 2 (Sept. 1836): 127–28, 134.

92. James Freeman Clarke, "Viaduct over the Little Conemaugh, Pennsylvania," ibid. 2, no. 6 (Jan. 1837): 394.

93. James Freeman Clarke, "The Ohio River," ibid. 3, no. 2 (Mar. 1837): 520.

94. James Freeman Clarke, "The Land of Freedom: A Story for the Fourth of July," ibid. 5, no. 5 (Aug. 1838): 311.

95. James Freeman Clarke, "A Glance into the Future: From the End of the Eighteenth Century" (altered from Jean Paul), ibid. 7, no. 5 (Mar. 1839): 327.

96. Ibid.; Franz Cumont, *The Mysteries of Mithra* (Chicago: Open Court Publishing, 1910), pp. 148, 107.

97. James Freeman Clarke, "Character of James Freeman, D.D.," *Western Messenger* 1, no. 7 (Jan. 1836): 485.

98. Frederic Henry Hedge, "The Transfiguration: A Sermon," ibid. 5, no. 2 (May 1838): 83–85.

99. Frederic Henry Hedge, *Practical Goodness the True Religion* (Bangor, Maine: S. S. Smith, 1840), pp. 14–15, 5.

100. Frederic Henry Hedge, *A Sermon on the Character and Ministry of the Late Rev. William Ellery Channing, D.D.*, 17 Nov. 1842 (Bangor, Maine: S. S. Smith, 1842), pp. 6–13.

101. Hedge, *Conservatism and Reform*, pp. 9–32.

102. Frederic Henry Hedge, *An Introductory Lecture Delivered at the Opening of the Bangor Lyceum*, 15 Nov. 1836 (Bangor, Maine: Nourse & Smith, and Duren & Thatcher, 1836), pp. 4, 10,13, 24–25.

103. Frederic Henry Hedge, *An Oration Pronounced before the Citizens of Bangor, on the Fourth of July, 1838* (Bangor, Maine: S. S. Smith, 1838), pp. 28–31.

104. Ibid., pp. 34–37.

105. Frederic Henry Hedge, *A Discourse on the Death of William Henry Harrison, Ninth President of the United States* (Bangor, Maine: S. S. Smith, 1841), pp. 3–24.

106. Francis, "Discourse 3," *Three Discourses*, p. 49.

107. Ibid., pp. 66–79.

108. Ibid., pp. 68, 70–77, 47.

109. Ibid., pp. 48, 52. The later title for the Club's journal, *The Dial*, seems suggested here.

110. Ibid., pp. 54–67.

111. Convers Francis, *The Death of the Aged* (Boston: James Munroe, 1841), pp. 33–36.

112. Convers Francis, *Christianity as a Purely Internal Principle*, in *Tracts*

of the American Unitarian Association, 1st ser., 9, no. 105 (Boston: Leonard C. Bowles, 1836): 8–20.

113. Convers Francis, *Christ the Way to God* (1842), in *Tracts of the American Unitarian Association*, 1st ser., 16, no. 181 (Boston: James Munroe, 1843): 6–11.

114. Convers Francis, *Life of John Eliot, the Apostle to the Indians*, Library of American Biography (ed. Jared Sparks), 5 (Boston: Hilliard, Gray, 1836): 31.

115. Ibid., 5: 73.

116. Ibid., 5: 190.

117. Ibid., 5: 311.

118. Emerson, "Self-reliance," *Essays, First Series*, pp. 72–73.

CHAPTER IV. THE MOTION OF *THE DIAL*

1. Amos Bronson Alcott, *Journals*, (n.d.), quoted by George W. Cooke in *An Historical and Biographical Introduction to Accompany the Dial*, 2 vols. (Cleveland: Rowfant Club, 1902), 1:58.

2. Ralph Waldo Emerson, "The Editors to the Reader," *The Dial* 1, no. 1 (July 1840): 1.

3. Amos Bronson Alcott to Samuel J. May, Concord, 10 Aug. 1840, *The Letters*, ed. Richard L. Herrnstadt (Ames: Iowa State University Press, 1969), p. 53.

4. James Freeman Clarke to Margaret Fuller, Louisville, 24 May 1840, *The Letters of James Freeman Clarke to Margaret Fuller*, ed. John Wesley Thomas (Hamburg: Cram, de Gruyter, 1957), p. 138.

5. "*The Dial*," *Western Messenger* 8, no. 12 (Apr. 1841): 571.

6. Emerson, "The Editors to the Reader," p. 1.

7. Ibid., p. 4.

8. Ibid., pp. 2–3.

9. Ralph Waldo Emerson to Thomas Carlyle, Concord, 15 Oct. 1842, *The Correspondence of Emerson and Carlyle*, ed. Joseph Slater (New York: Columbia University Press, 1964), p. 332.

10. Mircea Eliade, *Patterns in Comparative Religion*, trans. Rosemary Sheed (New York: Meridian Books, 1963).

11. Erich Neumann has illuminated these distinctions from a psychological perspective by tracing the evolution of consciousness in the race and in the individual through common themes in world mythology. The story of the human race was the tale of the struggle of an emerging ego-con-

sciousness, identified as spirit and masculine, against the nourishing but engulfing maternal womb of the unconscious. A son-lover strove against a Great Mother until, in a more developed stage, he emerged as a hero who was strong enough to fight a dragon and win buried treasure or liberate a captive maiden. The result was a state of wholeness in which the hero (consciousness) incorporated the unconscious mother by making her his peer as the treasure/maiden. See Erich Neumann, *The Origins and History of Consciousness* (New York: Bollingen Foundation, 1954).

12. George Ripley, "Brownson's Writings," *The Dial* 1, no. 1:23.

13. Ralph Waldo Emerson, "Thoughts on Art," ibid. 1, no. 3 (Jan. 1841): 367.

14. Amos Bronson Alcott, "Orphic Sayings," ibid. 1, no. 1:94; and *Spiritual Culture*, as quoted by Charles Lane in "A. Bronson Alcott's Works," ibid. 3, no. 4 (Apr. 1843): 438.

15. Alcott, "Orphic Sayings," p. 94.

16. James Freeman Clarke, "First Crossing the Alleghanies," *The Dial* 1, no. 2 (Oct. 1840):160.

17. Alcott, "Orphic Sayings," p. 93.

18. Frederic Henry Hedge, "The Art of Life,—The Scholar's Calling," *The Dial* 1, no. 2:181.

19. Ralph Waldo Emerson, "Fourierism and the Socialists," ibid. 3, no. 1 (July 1842): 88.

20. Ralph Waldo Emerson, "Lectures on the Times: III, The Transcendentalist," ibid. 3, no. 3 (Jan. 1843): 302.

21. Alcott, "Orphic Sayings," pp. 90–91.

22. Ralph Waldo Emerson, "Thoughts on Modern Literature," *The Dial* 1, no. 2:156.

23. Ralph Waldo Emerson, "Tantalus," ibid. 4, no. 3 (Jan. 1844): 357.

24. Alcott, "Orphic Sayings," p. 94.

25. Ralph Waldo Emerson, "Lectures on the Times," *The Dial* 3, no. 1:3.

26. Emerson, "Art," p. 367.

27. Clarke, "First Crossing the Alleghanies," p. 160.

28. Ralph Waldo Emerson, "The Snow-storm," *The Dial* 1, no. 3:339.

29. Emerson, "Modern Literature," p. 147.

30. Ralph Waldo Emerson, "The Sphinx," *The Dial* 1, no. 3:348–51.

31. Ralph Waldo Emerson, "Saadi," ibid. 3, no. 2 (Oct. 1842): 268.

32. Ralph Waldo Emerson, "Woodnotes—No. II," ibid. 2, no. 2 (Oct. 1841): 210. Carl F. Strauch reads "Woodnotes" and a number of Emerson's

other poems as affirmations of the ancient Greek doctrine of sympathy—
one expression of what I term correspondence in this study. See Carl F.
Strauch, "Emerson and the Doctrine of Sympathy," *Studies in Romanticism* 6,
no. 3 (Spring 1967): 152–74.

33. Amos Bronson Alcott, "Orphic Sayings," ibid. 1, no. 3:357.

34. Emerson, "Saadi," p. 267.

35. Amos Bronson Alcott, "Days from a Diary," *The Dial* 2, no. 4
(Apr. 1842): 416.

36. Frederic Henry Hedge, "Questionings," ibid. 1, no. 3:290; James
Freeman Clarke, "Hymn and Prayer," ibid., p. 292.

37. Alcott, "Orphic Sayings," ibid. 1, no. 1:97; Emerson, "Lectures on
the Times: III," p. 312.

38. Alcott, "Orphic Sayings," *The Dial* 1, no. 1:89.

39. Emerson, "Saadi," p. 268.

40. Emerson, "Woodnotes—No. II," pp. 209–10.

41. Ralph Waldo Emerson, "To Eva at the South," *The Dial* 3, no.
3:327–28.

42. Alcott, "Orphic Sayings," ibid. 1, no. 1:87–88.

43. Ralph Waldo Emerson, "The Comic," ibid. 4, no. 2 (Oct.
1843): 250.

44. Ralph Waldo Emerson, "Man the Reformer," ibid. 1, no. 4 (Apr.
1841): 531.

45. Ibid. The metaphor, of course, recalls the Platonic dialogue, *Phae-
drus.*

46. George Ripley, "Letter to a Theological Student," *The Dial* 1, no.
2:185.

47. Alcott, "Days from a Diary," p. 418.

48. Emerson, "Lectures on the Times: III," p. 312.

49. Emerson, "Woodnotes—No. II," p. 208.

50. Ralph Waldo Emerson, "The Young American," *The Dial* 4, no. 4
(Apr. 1844): 488.

51. Ralph Waldo Emerson, "The Tragic," ibid., p. 516.

52. Emerson, "Tantalus," p. 358.

53. Emerson, "Lectures on the Times: III," p. 312.

54. Emerson, "Art," pp. 369–70.

55. Ralph Waldo Emerson, "Literary Intelligence," *The Dial* 3, no.
3:387.

56. Emerson, "Modern Literature," p. 149.

57. Alcott, "Orphic Sayings," *The Dial* 1, no. 3:354.

58. Emerson, "Man the Reformer," p. 534.

59. Alcott, "Orphic Sayings," *The Dial* 1, no. 1:86; 1, no. 3:352, 358–59.

60. Ibid. 1, no. 1:85.

61. George Ripley, "Book Review of *The Works of William E. Channing*," *The Dial* 1, no. 2:247.

62. Emerson, "Art," p. 367.

63. Emerson, "Woodnotes—No. II," p. 213.

64. Ralph Waldo Emerson, "The Senses and the Soul," *The Dial* 2, no. 3 (Jan. 1841): 374.

65. James Freeman Clarke, "To Nydia," ibid. 1, no. 3:313.

66. Alcott, "Days from a Diary," p. 415; Emerson, "The Senses and the Soul," p. 375.

67. Alcott, "Orphic Sayings," *The Dial* 1, no. 1:90.

68. James Freeman Clarke, "Nature and Art, or the Three Landscapes," ibid. 1, no. 2:173.

69. Ralph Waldo Emerson, "*America—an Ode; and Other Poems* by N. W. Coffin," ibid. 4, no. 1 (July 1843): 134.

70. Ralph Waldo Emerson, "Woodnotes," ibid. 1, no. 2:245.

71. Ripley, " Letter to a Student," p. 183.

72. George Ripley, "*A Letter to Those Who Think* by E. Palmer," *The Dial* 1, no. 2:256.

73. Emerson, "The Young American," p. 503; "The Senses and the Soul," p. 374; "Lectures on the Times," pp. 16, 8.

74. Ralph Waldo Emerson, "Gifts," *The Dial* 4, no. 1:94. The essay also appeared as part of *Essays, Second Series* (1844).

75. Alcott, "Days from a Diary," p. 416.

76. Emerson, "Woodnotes," p. 244; "Modern Literature," p. 138.

77. Ralph Waldo Emerson, "Jones Very's *Essays and Poems*," *The Dial* 2, no. 1 (July 1841): 130.

78. Emerson, "Tantalus," p. 363.

79. Clarke, "Hymn and Prayer," p. 292.

80. Emerson, "Tantalus," p. 362.

81. Alcott, "Orphic Sayings," *The Dial* 1, no. 1:87–88.

82. Ralph Waldo Emerson, "Water" (17 Jan. 1834), in *The Early Lectures*, ed. Stephen E. Whicher et al., 3 vols. (Cambridge: Harvard University Press, 1959–72), 1:52.

83. Clarke, "First Crossing the Alleghanies," p. 159.

84. Ibid.

85. For a discussion of religious similarities from the perspective of C. G. Jung, see Carl G. Jung, *Memories, Dreams, Reflections,* ed. Aniela Jaffé (New York: Random House, Vintage Books, 1963), p. 335 et passim.

86. Emerson, "Woodnotes," p. 243; "Man the Reformer," p. 538.

87. Alcott, "Orphic Sayings," *The Dial* 1, no. 1:95.

88. Clarke, "First Crossing the Alleghanies," p. 159.

89. Emerson, "The Sphinx," p. 349.

90. Emerson, "The Senses and the Soul," pp. 374ff.; "Modern Literature," p. 155; "The Amulet," *The Dial* 3, no. 1: 73–74.

91. Clarke, "To Nydia," p. 312; "Poems on Art: The Real and the Ideal—On the Marble Bust of Schiller," *The Dial* 1, no. 4: 468–69.

92. Frederic Henry Hedge, "From Uhland: The Castle by the Sea," ibid. 3, no. 1: 74.

93. James Freeman Clarke, "Dream," ibid. 1, no. 4: 445.

94. Ralph Waldo Emerson, "Lectures on the Times: II, The Conservative," ibid. 3, no. 2: 183.

95. Alcott, "Orphic Sayings," ibid. 1, no. 1: 85.

96. Emerson, "The Editors to the Reader," p. 3.

97. Ralph Waldo Emerson, "To Rhea," *The Dial* 4, no. 1: 104.

98. Emerson, "Woodnotes," p. 242.

99. Emerson, "Woodnotes—No. II," p. 213.

100. Alcott, *Spiritual Culture,* as quoted by Lane in "Alcott's Works," p. 440.

101. Emerson, "The Tragic," p. 519.

102. Alcott, "Orphic Sayings," *The Dial* 1, no. 1: 91.

103. Clarke, "Hymn and Prayer," p. 292.

104. Emerson, "Lectures on the Times," p. 12.

105. Ibid., p. 17.

106. Emerson, "Lectures on the Times," p. 17; "Fate," *The Dial* 2, no. 2: 206.

107. Emerson, "Fate," p. 206.

108. Hedge, "The Art of Life," p. 177.

109. Alcott, "Orphic Sayings," *The Dial* 1, no. 3: 359–60; "Days from a Diary," pp. 434–35.

110. Ripley, "Letter to a Student," p. 183.

111. Alcott, "Orphic Sayings," *The Dial* 1, no. 3: 351.

112. Alcott, "Days from a Diary," p. 414.

113. Emerson, "The Young American," p. 494.

CHAPTER V. A CORRESPONDING REVOLUTION IN THINGS

1. Victor S. Clark, *History of Manufactures in the United States*, 3 vols. (1929; reprint ed., New York: Peter Smith, 1949), 1:529.

2. Ibid., 1: 431.

3. Ibid., 1: 578.

4. Baron de Gerstner, quoted by Daniel J. Boorstin in *The Americans: The National Experience* (New York: Vintage Books, 1965), pp. 98–99.

5. Charles Dickens, *American Notes* (London: Oxford University Press, 1957), pp. 64–65. (Originally published as *American Notes for General Circulation* [London: Chapman & Hall, 1842].)

6. Frederick Jackson Turner, *The United States 1830–1850: The Nation and Its Sections* (New York: Henry Holt, 1935), p. 350.

7. Henry F. Janes, "Early Reminiscences of Janesville," in *Collections of the State Historical Society of Wisconsin*, 6, ed. Lyman C. Draper (1872; reprint ed., Madison: State Historical Society of Wisconsin, 1908): 434.

8. George Rogers Taylor, *The Transportation Revolution: 1815–1860* (1951) (New York: Harper & Row, Harper Torchbooks, 1968), pp. 6, 388.

9. George Rogers Taylor, "American Urban Growth Preceding the Railway Age," *Journal of Economic History* 27, no. 3 (Sept. 1967): 311.

10. *Report of the Committee of Internal Health on the Asiatic Cholera* (Boston: J. H. Eastburn, 1849), pp. 14–15.

11. Arthur M. Schlesinger, Jr., *The Age of Jackson* (Boston: Little, Brown, 1945), p. 43.

12. Richard P. McCormick, *The Second American Party System: Party Formation in the Jacksonian Era* (Chapel Hill: University of North Carolina Press, 1966), p. 343.

13. Michel Chevalier, *Society, Manners, and Politics in the United States* (3d ed., 1838), ed. John W. Ward (1961; reprint ed., Gloucester, Mass.: Peter Smith, 1967), pp. 298–99.

14. Ibid., p. 299. The phrase, "heyday of the entrepreneur" is a *juste mot* borrowed from Glyndon G. Van Deusen, *The Jacksonian Era: 1828–1848* (New York: Harper & Row, 1959), p. 13.

15. Chevalier, *Society, Manners, and Politics*, p. 299.

16. Convers Francis, *Autobiography*, quoted by William Newell in

Memoir of the Rev. Convers Francis, in *Proceedings of the Massachusetts Historical Society, 1864–1865* (Boston: Wiggin & Lunt, 1866), p. 235.

17. James Freeman Clarke to Margaret Fuller, Nov. 1830, *The Letters of James Freeman Clarke to Margaret Fuller,* ed. John Wesley Thomas (Hamburg: Cram, de Gruyter, 1957), p. 19.

18. Ralph Waldo Emerson to William Emerson, Cambridge, 20 and 21 July 1818, *The Letters of Ralph Waldo Emerson,* ed. Ralph L. Rusk, 6 vols. (New York: Columbia University Press, 1939), 1:67; Ralph Waldo Emerson, *The Journals and Miscellaneous Notebooks,* ed. William H. Gilman et al., 11 vols. to date (Cambridge: Harvard University Press, Belknap Press, 1960–   ), 2 (28 Aug. 1823): 184 [hereafter cited as *JMN*].

19. Emerson, *JMN,* 3 (20 Aug. 1831): 281.

20. Ibid., 4 (7 July 1834): 389.

21. Ibid., 5 (21 Apr. 1837): 301. In his biography of Emerson, Ralph L. Rusk described him at this time as "gay as a canary bird" (*The Life of Ralph Waldo Emerson* [New York: Charles Scribner, 1949], pp. 257–58).

22. Emerson, *JMN,* 7 (7 Apr. 1840): 342.

23. Ralph Waldo Emerson, "Trades and Professions" (2 Feb. 1837), as summarized in James E. Cabot, *A Memoir of Ralph Waldo Emerson,* 2 vols. (Boston: Houghton Mifflin, 1887), 2:730.

24. Ralph Waldo Emerson, "Doctrine of the Hands" (13 Dec. 1837), in *The Early Lectures,* ed. Stephen E. Whicher et al., 3 vols. (Cambridge: Harvard University Press, 1959–72), 2:234–35.

25. Amos Bronson Alcott, quoted by Franklin B. Sanborn and William T. Harris in *A. Bronson Alcott: His Life and Philosophy,* 2 vols. (Boston: Roberts, 1893), 1:23.

26. Lydia Maria Child to Convers Francis, Northampton, 30 Oct. 1840, in Lydia Maria Child, *Letters,* coll. and arr. Harriet Winslow Sewall (1883; reprint ed., New York: Arno Press & New York Times, 1969), p. 39.

27. See the discussion of Hedge's addresses in the second and third chapters.

28. Emerson, *JMN,* 4 (30 Aug. 1834): 316; 5 (22 Mar. 1836): 145.

29. Ralph Waldo Emerson to Thomas Carlyle, Concord, 29 Apr. 1843, *The Correspondence of Emerson and Carlyle,* ed. Joseph Slater (New York: Columbia University Press, 1964), p. 341.

30. Emerson, *JMN,* 4 (3 Sept. 1833): 82.

31. Ralph Waldo Emerson to William Emerson, Concord, 24 Jan. 1842, *Letters of Emerson,* 3:4. Emerson finally did subscribe to the local railroad stock and had paid the first installment when the trains began running between Concord and Boston in 1844.

32. Ralph Waldo Emerson to William Emerson, Concord, 24 Apr. 1843, *Letters of Emerson*, 3:168.

33. Emerson, *JMN*, 4 (15 Apr. 1834): 277.

34. Ibid., 4 (10 June 1834): 296.

35. Ibid., 8 (7 Jan. 1843): 330.

36. Ibid., 7 (ca. Dec. 1842): 482.

37. Ibid., 8 (May 1843): 397.

38. James Freeman Clarke to Margaret Fuller, Ohio River, 31 July 1833, *Autobiography, Diary and Correspondence*, ed. Edward Everett Hale (Boston: Houghton Mifflin, 1899), p. 100.

39. James Freeman Clarke to Margaret Fuller, 19 Dec. 1833, *Letters of Clarke*, p. 68.

40. Clarke, *Autobiography, Diary and Correspondence*, p. 59.

41. James Freeman Clarke, "Monthly Record: For December," *Western Messenger* 4, no. 5 (Jan. 1838): 360.

42. James Freeman Clarke, "A Trip to Owensboro," ibid. 5, no. 4 (July 1838): 234–36.

43. Introductory Statement, Brook Farm Constitution (1844), quoted by Octavius B. Frothingham in *George Ripley* (Boston: Houghton Mifflin, 1882), p. 169.

44. Amos Bronson Alcott, quoted by Odell Shepard in *Pedlar's Progress: The Life of Bronson Alcott* (Boston: Little, Brown, 1937), p. 240.

45. Amos Bronson Alcott to Chatfield Alcott, Fruitlands, Harvard, 4 Aug. 1843, *The Letters*, ed. Richard L. Herrnstadt (Ames: Iowa State University Press, 1969), p. 108.

46. Ralph Waldo Emerson to Edward Bliss Emerson, Boston, 17 Nov. 1816, *Letters of Emerson*, 1:27.

47. Ralph Waldo Emerson, "The Present Age" (23 Feb. 1837), in *Early Lectures*, 2:160; Emerson, "Introductory" (6 Dec. 1837), ibid., 2:225.

48. Emerson, "Doctrine of the Hands," p. 243.

49. Emerson, "The Young American," *The Dial* 4, no. 4 (Apr. 1844): 496.

50. Emerson, *JMN*, 5 (22 Apr. 1837): 304.

51. George Ripley, *Temptations of the Times* (Boston: Hilliard, Gray, 1837), pp. 7–14.

52. James Freeman Clarke, "Correspondence," *Western Messenger* 1, no. 8 (Feb. 1836): 587.

53. James Freeman Clarke, "A Visit to Mobile," ibid. 1, no. 10 (May 1836): 703–04.

54. Amos Bronson Alcott, "Orphic Sayings," *Boston Quarterly Review* 4, no. 4 (Oct. 1841): 494.

55. Ralph Waldo Emerson, "Find Your Calling" (5 Feb. 1832), in *Young Emerson Speaks*, ed. Arthur McGiffert (Boston: Houghton Mifflin, 1938), p. 163.

56. Ralph Waldo Emerson to Thomas Carlyle, New York, 18 Mar. 1840, *The Correspondence of Emerson and Carlyle*, p. 260.

57. Ralph Waldo Emerson, "Charity" (14 June 1829), in *Young Emerson Speaks*, p. 242.

58. Amos Bronson Alcott, *The Journals*, sel. and ed. Odell Shepard (Boston: Little, Brown, 1938) (26 Oct. 1828), p. 15; (June 1832), p. 31.

59. Ibid. (13 Mar. 1829), p. 117.

60. Ibid. (17 June 1842), p. 161.

61. Amos Bronson Alcott, "Sayings," *The Present* 1, nos. 5 and 6 (15 Dec. 1843): 171.

62. George Ripley to the Friends of Association, Clinton Hall, New York, 4 Apr. 1844, in "Speeches of Messrs. Dana and Ripley at the Festival," *The Phalanx* 1, no. 8 (20 Apr. 1844): 102.

63. James Freeman Clarke to Margaret Fuller, Louisville, 24 Feb. 1834, *Letters of Clarke*, p. 73.

64. Emerson, *JMN*, 8 (31 Aug. 1841): 38.

65. Ibid., 9 (ca. 25 Aug. 1843): 13.

66. Ibid., 9 (ca. 13 Sept. 1843): 23; Emerson, "The Young American," p. 486.

67. Emerson, *JMN*, 2 (8 Apr. 1823): 115.

68. Ralph Waldo Emerson to Ezra Ripley, Boston, 1 Apr. 1832, *Letters of Emerson* 1:350.

69. Emerson, *JMN*, 7 (22 Apr. 1841): 433.

70. Ralph Waldo Emerson, "The Head" (20 Dec. 1841), in *Early Lectures*, 2:248.

71. Clarke, *Autobiography, Diary and Correspondence*, p. 50.

72. Ibid., p. 79.

73. Emerson, *JMN*, 7 (17 Oct. 1840): 408.

74. Moncure Daniel Conway, *Emerson at Home and Abroad* (Boston: James R. Osgood, 1881), p. 299.

75. Ralph Waldo Emerson, "Heroism" (24 Jan. 1838), in *Early Lectures*, 2:338.

76. Cabot, *Memoir of Emerson*, 2:425. The lecture, according to Cabot, was missing.

77. Emerson, *JMN*, 5 (19 Apr. 1838): 475.

78. Emerson, *JMN*, 6 (1827): 56; 5 (14 Mar. 1837): 287; (17 Nov. 1837): 440.

79. Ralph Waldo Emerson to Margaret Fuller, Concord, 3 Sept. 1839, *Letters of Emerson*, 2:220; Emerson, *JMN*, 8 (Sept. 1842): 273.

80. Emerson, *JMN*, 3 (26 Jan. 1832): 262; 4 (14 Dec. 1834): 360.

81. Ralph Waldo Emerson, "Manners," *Essays, Second Series* (1844), in *The Complete Works of Ralph Waldo Emerson*, ed. Edward Waldo Emerson, 12 vols. (Boston: Houghton Mifflin, 1903), 3:150.

82. Ralph Waldo Emerson, "The Chardon Street Convention," in *Complete Works*, 10:374–75.

83. Francis, as a member of the Divinity School faculty of Harvard University, was an outspoken abolitionist. His diary of 1844 disclosed an extended discussion with Divinity School students concerning a letter from the Unitarian ministers of England to those in America on the subject of slavery. "I was glad to find that almost all the School thought and felt strongly as antislavery men. Fenner said that Garrison, Wendell Phillips, Edmund Quincy, etc., were to these times what the prophets of old were to theirs. I said all I could to encourage them in their resistance to this sin of our land, and told them I hoped every member of the School would go forth into the ministry prepared to set his face as a flint against this terrible iniquity" ("The Letter of the English Unitarian Ministers on Slavery," *Christian Register*, 20 Apr. 1844).

84. Ralph Waldo Emerson, "*The Worship of the Soul* by Samuel D. Robbins," *The Dial* 1, no. 3 (Jan. 1841): 403.

CHAPTER VI. DESIDERATA

1. Ralph Waldo Emerson, *Nature*, in *The Complete Works of Ralph Waldo Emerson*, ed. Edward Waldo Emerson, 12 vols. (Boston: Houghton Mifflin, 1903), 1:1. The second edition appeared in 1849.

2. Ralph Waldo Emerson, *The Journals and Miscellaneous Notebooks*, ed. William H. Gilman et al., 11 vols. to date (Cambridge: Harvard University Press, Belknap Press, 1960–), 6 (ca. 1834–35): 222 [hereafter cited as *JMN*].

3. Ibid., 5 (28 Oct. 1835): 103.

4. Ibid., 3 (10 Dec. 1830): 213.

5. Ibid., 5 (June 1835): 270.

6. Ibid., 5 (ca. 1835–38): 180.

7. Ralph Waldo Emerson, *Journals*, ed. Edward Waldo Emerson and

Waldo Emerson Forbes, 10 vols. (Boston: Houghton Mifflin, 1909–14), 9 (29 Feb. 1856): 14.

8. Emerson, *JMN*, 10 (Sept. 1848): 355.

9. Emerson, *Journals*, 8 (1853): 421.

10. Emerson, *JMN*, 9 (Sept. 1845): 278.

11. Ibid., 5 (1 Aug. 1835): 75.

12. Ibid., 9 (30 Jan. 1844): 66.

13. Ibid., 5 (17 June 1836): 177.

14. Ibid., 7 (26 July 1840): 385.

15. Emerson, *Journals*, 8 (18 July 1852): 311.

16. Emerson, *JMN*, 5 (29 Apr. 1837): 307.

17. Ibid., 7 (12 Oct. 1838): 105–06.

18. Ibid., 4 (27 Oct. 1834): 327.

19. Ibid., 9 (ca. 30 Jan. 1844): 70.

20. For a more detailed discussion of the Gnostic conception of time and history, see Catherine L. Albanese, "Inwardness: A Study of Some Gnostic Themes and Their Relation to Early Christianity with Specific Reference to the Gospel According to Thomas," *Recherches de Théologie Ancienne et Médiévale* 18 (1976): 64–88.

21. Ralph Waldo Emerson, "Self-reliance," *Essays, First Series* (1841), in *Complete Works*, 2:69.

22. Ibid., 2:52.

23. Ibid., 2:53.

24. Ibid., 2:59.

25. Ibid., 2:76.

26. Ralph Waldo Emerson, "The Over-soul," *Essays, First Series*, in *Complete Works*, 2:273.

27. Ibid., 2:274.

28. Ibid., 2:275.

29. Ibid., 2:276.

30. Ibid., 2:279.

31. Ibid., 2:284–85.

32. Ibid., 2:292–93.

33. Ralph Waldo Emerson, "Circles," *Essays, First Series*, in *Complete Works*, 2:301.

34. Ibid., 2:302.

35. Ibid., 2:302–03.

36. Ibid., 2:301.

37. Ibid., 2:304.

38. Ibid., 2:305, 308.

39. Ibid., 2:319.

40. Perry Miller, "From Edwards to Emerson," in *Errand into the Wilderness* (1956) (New York: Harper & Row, Harper Torchbooks, 1964), pp. 184–203. The typology of conversion/devotion outlined here suggests an alternate interpretation to that of Miller, who described the continuity in terms of a common mysticism. But Edwards, a complex figure, was drawn toward correspondence too.

41. Ralph Waldo Emerson, "History," *Essays, First Series*, in *Complete Works*, 2:4. A useful recent treatment of Emerson's understanding of history is Gustaaf Van Cromphout, "Emerson and the Dialectics of History," *PMLA* 91, no. 1 (Jan. 1976): 54–65. The classic study is Philip L. Nicoloff, *Emerson on Race and History* (New York: Columbia University Press, 1961).

42. Mircea Eliade has warned modern man against "following Hegel's example" and "'communing with the Universal Spirit' while reading his newspaper every morning" (*Myth and Reality* [New York: Harper & Row, Harper Torchbooks, 1968], p. 137).

43. Emerson, "History," 2:40.

44. Ibid.

45. Ibid.

46. Ibid., 2:6–7.

47. Ibid., 2:8.

48. Ibid., 2:10.

49. Ibid., 2:21.

50. Ibid., 2:23.

51. Ibid., 2:35–36.

52. Ibid., 2:12.

53. Ibid., 2:17.

54. Ibid., 2:18.

55. For a good example, see Frederic Ives Carpenter, *Emerson Handbook* (New York: Hendricks House, 1953), pp. 164–78.

56. Sherman Paul, *Emerson's Angle of Vision: Man and Nature in American Experience* (1952) (Cambridge: Harvard University Press, 1969), pp. 71–102. Paul's chapter, "The Linear Logic" (pp. 5–26), provides an excellent discussion of Emerson's suspicion of rationalism.

57. Ralph Waldo Emerson, "Each in All," *Western Messenger* 6, no. 4 (Feb. 1839): 230.

58. Emerson, *JMN*, 7 (24 Apr. 1841): 439.

59. Orestes A. Brownson, "Literary Notices: *The Dial*," *Boston Quarterly Review* 4, no. 1 (Jan. 1841): 132.

Index